I0796949

A WITCH'S YEAR

Making Practical Magic
Through the Changing Seasons

A WITCH'S YEAR

Making Practical Magic Through the Changing Seasons

LEVANNAH MORGAN

With illustrations by
Nooka Shepherd

ROBERT HALE

To my brother Geoff

Contents

Foreword

Back in time, nearer the start of the twentieth-century revival of interest in witchcraft, there was a creative, non-dogmatic approach to magic. More recently, there have been some to whom a fixed and definitive system based on, so far as anyone knows, the ways that witchcraft was practised historically, has had greater appeal. The approach in *A Witch's Year* is open-ended and invites innovation and endless creativity, but it is firmly based in magical traditions and folklore – giving us, as it were, the best of both worlds. It is a sourcebook of ideas for things a witch can make or do for magical purposes. All are grounded in animistic beliefs, for witchcraft deals with the world of spirits – such as those of herbs, trees, stones, creatures, places, ancestors, faeriekind and the deities.

Month by month, Levannah Morgan guides us in magical practices such as the casting of spells with herbal oils, magical gardens, sewing or knitting, spirit journeys, poppets, herb sachets and much more besides. And it is the book's main theme that the things we make or do for magic create a channel for our spells to have a good physical result in the world we live in. Our magical activities unite the spirit dimension with our own mundane world. These things are keys to a deep sense of nature-based spirituality as well as to magical success, providing they are based in seasonal magical lore. With Levannah Morgan guiding us, we are in safe hands. We are carefully instructed in the magical powers and processes of every season while also being set free to explore. Even as a witch with more than forty years experience, I was constantly intrigued. Over and again, I stopped reading and thought, 'Oh, I'd like to try that! And that!' This is not witchcraft by rote. Instead, within all the practical magical suggestions, there is a silence which allows something beyond words to simply be.

Rae Beth
July 2024

Introduction

Unfolding and Becoming with the Seasons

A Witch's Year is a year-round guide to the practice of witchcraft that will show you how to create your own magic based on the ever-changing cycle of the seasons. It is a compendium of magic, lore, rituals, observances, spells, projects and all manner of things, that aims to show that there is a lot more to witchcraft in the twenty-first century than simply observing a brief series of seasonal festivals. Witchcraft can be a day-by-day, week-by-week and month-by-month magical and spiritual practice that will enrich your life, inspire and delight you, and bring you into a deeper relationship with all the beings who share this world with us, with the spirit world and with the gods.

I am a witch and a magical practitioner; working with the spirit world is at the heart of what I do, and I make magic with my familiar spirits and with the spirits of the land. Like many contemporary witches, I am also a Pagan and perform rituals dedicated to Pagan goddesses and gods, both old and new. You will find in this book a combination of practical magic, ways to connect with the spirits, and rituals that honour the gods and celebrate seasonal festivals or Sabbats. It contains practical projects; things to make and places to visit. First and foremost, the witchcraft I practise is experiential; it does not always happen in words, and sometimes the deepest magic comes from uniting mind and body in doing something that may appear simple but can have profound results: tying feathers into a length of yarn or weaving a sun wheel; sitting quietly under a hawthorn tree or looking into a still pool.

Witchcraft for me is a constant process of unfolding and becoming; with every passing season, I learn more about the great time cycles that animate our lives, about the goddesses and gods, the world of spirit, and also how to live here in this world now. Witchcraft has, over many years, profoundly changed the way I experience time and the seasons. It has meant putting the journey of our earth around the sun and its monthly dance with our moon at the heart of my experience of life, rather than simply bowing to the demands and pressures of 'human' time, which are so often at odds with how we yearn to be, and with the needs and rhythms of the rest of life on the earth. Living day to day by the lunar and solar rhythms, and experiencing the constantly changing seasons as fully as possible, has a very beneficial effect. Noticing the crescent moon just after sunset for the first time at the start of a month, or seeing and hearing a flock of migrating swans passing over a city, or standing in a bluebell wood in Maytime, or experiencing the power of the highest tide of the year; all of these can remind us of who we really are and where we live.

Making the lunar and solar time cycles central to your life will change the way you experience time and the passing of the seasons. The moon is at the heart of witchcraft. For witches, the moon is a goddess whose rhythms influence the tides of our bodies and minds, just as they control the tides and the growth of plants. Witchcraft is mostly practised at night, and as the moon waxes and wanes, she shapes our magic and guides our rituals and our dreams and visions. To be a witch means to put the lunar rhythm at the centre of your life and experience it to the full. The moon was our earliest measure of time. We divide our calendars into months; (these were originally lunar months) and months are divided into weeks (originally the period from one lunar quarter to the next). Use a lunar calendar to make the moon central to your Witch's Year and structure your time. Learn to recognise how the moon's phases affect your emotions as well as your bodily feelings. The moon will be fundamental to all your witchcraft; the lunar calendar will be your first consideration when planning rituals or practical magic.

The other great rhythm is that of the solar year; the passing of the seasons from Solstice to Equinox to Solstice again as the earth orbits the sun. Pagan witches structure their seasonal festivals by this great circular rhythm and refer to it as the Wheel of the Year. The sun, the bringer of light, warmth and life, is also personified and honoured as a deity, usually a god. It is the interplay between moon and sun, the way they dance together through our seasons, that creates the Witch's Year. The constant, ceaseless, tidal lunar rhythm is the essential background to the events and festivals that mark the solar year. The year too has its magical great tide, as the sun passes through the signs of the zodiac, each of which relates to one of the four elements: air, fire, water and earth. The great tide begins anew every Spring Equinox, when the sun enters Aries, the cardinal sign of fire. As we move through the Witch's Year you will learn to recognise how this great tide works through your magical life.

A SOURCEBOOK OF IDEAS

In this book you will find the stories of goddesses and gods of sun, moon, earth, sky, the land and growing things, some of them ancient and some of them woven by witches and

The Great Tide

Tide of Fire (flowing/rising): Spring Equinox (Aries) – Summer Solstice
Tide of Water (ebbing/falling): Summer Solstice (Cancer) – Autumn Equinox
Tide of Air (flowing): Autumn Equinox (Libra) – Winter Solstice
Tide of Earth (ebbing): Winter Solstice (Capricorn) – Spring Equinox

Pagans now, and suggestions as to how you can honour these deities around the year. It is not a book of rituals that you are expected to follow word for word; rather, it is a sourcebook of ideas that I hope will inspire you to use your creativity and devise your own seasonal rituals, practical magic and inner journeys that will work for you and enrich your practice. There is also information about special places that you may wish to visit at various times of the year, and folk customs that mark the turning of the seasons. It is wonderful to see that precious old places are being honoured and cared for again, and that folk customs, far from dying out, are becoming increasingly valued as community celebrations that place us in a closer relationship with the world around us and that, for witches, can contain much spiritual meaning.

My witchcraft is an eclectic practice and *A Witch's Year* reflects that. I was fortunate to learn my craft from several wise and wonderful teachers who all impressed upon me that passing on the knowledge that they so generously shared with me would be part of my duty, and I hope this book does justice to them and to the insights and knowledge they entrusted to me. Down the years I have learnt much through experience; through working magic in different times and places, sometimes alone, but often with other witches and magical practitioners. New discoveries have been made, spells worked, and rituals created. Often the moon, the sun, the sea and the land have been my teachers. All these different elements have been blended in the cauldron into my own witch's brew.

Witchcraft has an animist worldview; all of this world has its own life, and everything has its own indwelling spirit that must be respected, including things that most people might consider to be inanimate. Being a witch means working with all the other beings who share the earth with us, so you will learn from *A Witch's Year* about the magical relationships the witch can establish with animals and birds, with plants and trees, with rivers and rocks and with the land itself. In the witch's worldview, humans are not superior to these beings; they are not there for our use, or to be exploited for our gain. We must learn to respect them, gain their trust and work with them; this is vital at a time when human activity is threatening the future of all life on earth. At the heart of my witchcraft is the honouring of goddesses of earth, moon and tides, and the gods of all growing things, so witchcraft to me means doing all that I can to live responsibly and sustainably, but also working, albeit in my own small way, to repair the damage humans are doing.

This is a practical book, which contains many things that you can try for yourself day by day as the year spirals round. These include not only magical observances and spells, but also craft projects and things to make and do. Making something can be just as much an act of magic as performing a ritual or casting a spell if it is done with magical intent, because the best magic is made with the body and the senses as well as the mind. I hope that you will try them. My approach to witchcraft is not only practical, but also very frugal. It is based on working with simple things that you will find in the home, garden or on a country or seaside ramble, and on recycling and repurposing. It requires you to spend time, but not a lot of money. Things that you make for yourself will have a power and beauty that is very special, so please do try these ideas for yourself.

I grew up by the sea in Ynys Môn, a very rural part of North Wales, and have lived for most of my adult life in Devon in the south-west of England. *A Witch's Year* is rooted in my own experience of these places, and of living in a northern latitude where day length varies greatly around the year, where it sometimes rains a lot and where the sea coasts are subject to very high and low tides. The book's guiding principle, that you can create your own witchcraft and magic through a myriad of small observances and practices, and make your own discoveries, can be adapted and applied wherever you live in the world. Work with the seasons as you experience them and seek out and celebrate customs and traditions that are local to you. If you can't find any, make your own. I live in a rural place, but you can just as easily practise your witchcraft in an urban location, and some of the best magic I have encountered has taken place in cities. Witchcraft happens wherever witches are. The book is also pragmatic and recognises that the way we live is constantly changing and evolving. The grain harvest no longer begins in August, and climate change means that hawthorns now flower in April. My month-by-month practice of observances and customs reflects the world now, and practical, lived experience, rather than as it was in past ages. Be creative, and use this book as a guide to make your own seasonal observances and traditions that are meaningful to you and the world around you.

HOW TO USE THIS BOOK

A Witch's Year is for anyone interested in witchcraft, and whether you are an experienced practitioner or an absolute beginner, I hope you will find things in it that will inspire you to create and make and try things out for yourself. I hope you will use it a bit like a recipe book at different times of the year, and the ideas in it as starting points for your own rituals and spells and projects.

The book is organised into monthly chapters for ease of use. The month, the time our moon takes to journey once around the earth, is one of the most basic and universal measurements of time. Humans have been dividing the solar year into 12 approximate divisions for the last 5,000 years, even though making the solar and lunar years fit together exactly has never quite worked, so I am simply continuing the tradition. In each chapter you will find magical observances, spells, stories, customs and practical projects. Each chapter concludes with a brief meditation for those who wish to travel deeper into the mysteries of the year.

Keeping a Record

I recommend keeping a journal or notebook in which you can record details of any of the work you do, projects you create, and discoveries that you make. Especially if you are new to witchcraft, you will find that this record will become an essential part of your craft. A physical record of magical practice works much better than an online one. Use whatever methods you feel comfortable with: notes; drawings; cut-and-paste; details of what works well and what does not; recipes; spells; and anything else that helps you. Be creative and don't worry about making a mess. I use a large artist's sketchbook with thick paper and hard covers that will withstand spills and incense burns, and has scraps of paper and bits of plant material and much besides stuck into its pages. It isn't meant to be pretty but it is immensely useful. Use whatever works best for you.

Practices

A Witch's Year provides details of magical practices that form a repertoire of the basic techniques of witchcraft. They include casting a circle (creating sacred space), consecrating tools, making a personal altar, attracting a familiar spirit and much more. These practices are introduced early in the year so that you can familiarise yourself with them and then use them throughout the year.

Sabbat Rituals

The Sabbats are the nine seasonal rituals of witchcraft. All the rituals are suitable for both solo and group practice. I provide outlines and suggest the form that these rituals can take, but mostly avoid giving specific words for participants to speak. If you only repeat words you have been given, you may not fully experience the meaning and power of the ritual. It is far better that you create a form of words for yourself, and say what is in your heart. Research the goddesses and gods; read their myths and study their images and stories. Use my suggestions as templates, but be inspired to invent your own invocations and rituals. This way your witchcraft will grow into your own individual creative and experiential practice.

Projects

All the practical projects have been tried and thoroughly tested by me and by other witches, and do not require you to have any specialist craft skills – just enthusiasm and a little determination. They are intended for adults, not children, unless stated. Please take reasonable precautions and be sensible when cooking, using heat, naked flames or sharp objects. Ingredients and equipment are listed and directions given.

Spells

In practical magic the body and the mind work together and the spells are a combination of physical and mental activity. As with the projects, any ingredients and equipment that you will need are listed and directions given. It is also important that the spells are worked at the specified times.

Meditations

Each chapter of *A Witch's Year* ends with a short meditation designed to provide a direct imaginal experience of the themes and projects for that month. Each meditation is a creative visualisation that takes the form of a visual journey that you should follow in your mind's eye with your eyes closed. Memorise the outline of the meditation, or record it and play it back to yourself, or have someone read it to you. Visualisation is a core part of most forms of witchcraft so this may already come easily to you. If you are new to visualisation, you may need to try it several times before it works. You will find it is a very rewarding practice and that you will soon be able to create your own visualisations and inner journeys. In order to visualise successfully, you will need to create the right environment. Find somewhere quiet where you will not be disturbed or distracted by external stimuli, and avoid bright light. Sit upright; this is a good posture in which to relax. If you lie down, you may find that you drift off to sleep. Before you begin, you need to relax. If you have studied yoga or mindfulness or a similar technique, you may already have a method for doing this. If not, close your eyes and breathe slowly and deeply. Breathe in and then out to a slow count of five. As you do this, consciously relax your body beginning with your feet and then allowing the relaxation to travel upwards until your entire body is relaxed. Empty your mind of all distracting superficial thoughts and everyday mental clutter. When I find this difficult, I visualise putting all the distracting thoughts into a big box and locking them away. Once you have done this, begin your meditation. Don't stress, and don't worry if you need to try it several times before it works; this is perfectly normal.

When you have finished your meditation, always eat and drink something to 'earth' yourself; that is, to return yourself fully to your body and the everyday world. Make notes, draw or record anything important that you wish to remember.

ETIQUETTE FOR WITCHES

Witches understand the importance of behaving honourably and respectfully towards the earth and all other beings when practising their craft. When looking for pebbles on the beach, sea shells, wood in the forest and other natural materials, please remember that this is bounty that our mother earth has bestowed on you. Act responsibly and don't be greedy; take only what you need and give thanks for it. Animals and birds depend on wild fruit and berries for their food, so leave plenty for them. Return the earth's generosity by caring for the environment around you. Always be aware of fragile habitats and tread lightly on the earth.

Outdoor Rituals

Try to leave as few traces of your presence when you work in wild places as possible. Whatever you bring with you should be taken away when you leave. Be aware that lighting fires can do serious damage in many places (*see* below); if in doubt, don't do it. There is usually no need for elaborate equipment or paraphernalia when working outdoors, and the less encumbered you are, the more you will gain from and enjoy the experience.

Visiting Special Places and Folk Customs

Don't leave litter at special places such as holy wells and 'sacred sites'. Well-meant offerings that do not decay, such as artificial fabrics or plastic tied around trees, and tealights and candles, can damage the environment and hurt or kill animals if ingested. 'Leave only your footprints' is wise advice. The desire to leave a gift for places and their spirits that give us so much is a natural and heartfelt one, but the best offering in a special place is a respectful magical good wish. Honour the place with your magical will. If you must leave a physical offering, choose something organic that will decay and do no harm.

At folk customs, be aware that you are a visitor. Always behave respectfully and be sensitive to the wishes of local communities. Some places will welcome your active participation; at others you may be expected to observe. Be sensitive about taking photographs and filming; if it is not welcome, don't do it.

WORKING SAFELY

When visiting remote areas such as moorland or the coast, take a proper map. Mobile phone signals are not always good in remote places so don't rely on them. Be aware of weather forecasts and take suitable clothing if bad weather is expected, and good, practical footwear if you intend to walk long distances or over rough terrain. Be aware of tide times; beaches where I live have a nasty habit of disappearing entirely at high tides, which can be disastrous if you are not prepared for it. If you are going to remote places alone, always tell someone in advance where you are going and what time you expect to be back.

Please exercise extreme care when lighting open fires in wild places. Wildfires cause horrific harm to wildlife and fragile habitats. They are easily started and difficult to stop, and there is no acceptable level of risk. Never use 'disposable' barbecues; the metal casings overheat quickly and they are a frequent cause of wildfires. My own practice is to light open fires in my own garden or on private land, where I have the owner's permission and there are fire prevention measures in place.

Follow good practice; honour and respect the spirits of the land, practise your craft, celebrate your rituals and enjoy the glories of the earth.

I hope that this book will help make witchcraft a lived, experiential reality for you that will unfold like the year, day by day, week by week and month by month, as the moon and sun dance and the seasons change.

Levannah Morgan

JANUARY

January

Renewal and Reminiscence

New Beginnings

It is Old Twelfth Night, 17 January. The calendar may have been updated in the eighteenth century, but in West Somerset they like to keep their feasts on the old dates. It is clear and very cold; too cold for snow, someone says, and early evening. The chilly air nips at hands and noses. As darkness falls, Orion rises above the Quantock Hills into an intensely cold January blue sky that shades into inky blackness in the north. At Carhampton there are no signposts or notices; everyone knows where to go. The orchard is next to the road, and fires are already burning in braziers beneath a group of ancient, gnarled apple trees. I worry that, as outsiders, we will not be welcome, but an elderly lady greets us with a glass of hot cider and says, 'The more, the merrier.'

They have always wassailed their apple trees, since who knows when. Now wassailing has been revived in many places, but by the 1970s it had more or less died out, and Carhampton's ceremony was one of very few that had survived. The village kept its old tradition alive and saved it from various threats, including the sale of its old orchards for building land. This has become the pattern for new ceremonies held wherever apple trees grow, and variants of its lovely Wassail Song can be heard around the country when trees are blessed in January.

The company assembles: the Master of Ceremonies wearing a black top hat, a band of musicians, women with pots and pans, and several men armed with large shotguns. The wassail song is sung ('Old apple tree, we wassail thee'), and we all urge the apple trees to grow well and bear a big crop of apples in the coming year ('Hatfuls, capfuls, three-bushel bagfuls, and little heaps under the stairs!') and loud cheers break out. Pieces of toast are soaked in hot cider and placed in the branches of the trees. Children stand on elders' shoulders and reach up into the trees with toasts. The lady who welcomed me says that this is to entice robins to eat the toast and rid the trees of bugs. Last year, she says, there were two robins in the trees the morning after the wassail, pecking at

January Associations

Festivals: New Year (1st), Twelfth Night (6th), Wassailing (various)

Figures: Janus, Mari Llwyd

More than Human: The night sky, robin

Totems and Symbols: Wheel of the Year, circle

the toast, which was a very good omen for the resulting bumper crop. Then people start banging pots and pans and the men with guns fire a deafening volley of shots into the trees; enough to frighten away anything, insect or spirit, that might try to harm the apple crop. There is rejoicing all round. Once the apple trees have been wassailed, all is right with the world, and a new year begins.

In January we let the New Year in and banish the spirits of the old year. We bless the trees and prepare for the year ahead. We meet the moon, gaze at the stars, create an altar and learn to cast the witch's circle; the space between the worlds. At the first witches' Sabbat, the young sun god dances the circle of the zodiac.

A few days after the winter Solstice, the New Year arrives. The solar standstill with its sense of timeless peace ends. The earth moves on, the days grow imperceptibly longer, and January begins in earnest. People all over the world mark the moment when the New Year starts with fireworks, singing and parties, and celebrating this moment fulfils a deep need. Witches find a wealth of significance in some of our New Year customs, but behind some of the celebrations is a deeper meaning. The New Year is a major moment of change which must be not just acknowledged but also honoured. Yule, the Midwinter Solstice, is a time of intense spiritual beauty for witches, but now it is over and it is time to move on. The sunlight has begun to return and growth is beginning, but none of this can really be seen or felt yet; everything is uncertain and no one knows what the New Year will bring. It is necessary to let go of the sleepy, safe warmth of Midwinter, let the old fade away and allow the new in, whatever it may bring.

TRADITIONAL CUSTOMS

The traditional New Year folk customs are joyous, but they also reflect a scary sense of uncertainty, and force us to let go of the old. First footing is a custom that is celebrated across Scotland and the North of England. The first person to enter a house at New Year should traditionally be a man with dark hair, and they should carry coal, bread, salt, and a little money, which must be given to the lady of the house (these days you can obviously adapt these gender-specific roles to suit your own requirements). Their dark hair represents the darkness of winter, and the gifts they bring symbolise our basic needs: warmth, food, savour and prosperity. When the first footer knocks on the door, the inhabitants of the house are scared and resist, until after a while they are have to let the New Year in. The first footer is then welcomed with a dram of whisky or some other celebratory drink and the year can begin anew.

In Wales Mari Llwyd (Grey Mary) is abroad on New Year's Eve. This forbidding figure has a horse's skull, articulated so that its jaws work and its teeth clack noisily. Her human body is draped in white sheeting and adorned with red and green ribbons. Mari is accompanied by a band of musicians and revellers singing the Mari Llwyd song. She visits each house. The inhabitants make a great show of being frightened of her and try not to let her in. A competition of riddles ensues: the Mari Llwyd and her band sing and ask riddling questions which those inside the house must answer. The riddles become progressively more difficult, until there is one that the household cannot answer, and with much noise and kerfuffle, Mari Llwyd is admitted and capers around the house. Her revellers are given drinks. The skeletal, starving cold of Midwinter and the old year have been acknowledged, and the new has been admitted, but not without a struggle. Fifty years ago, Mari Llwyd was becoming a thing of the past, confined to a few villages in West Wales. A sad Mari Llwyd figure, bereft of life, lay carefully preserved in a glass case in the Welsh National Folk Museum. Happily, things have changed; now she is marvellously resurgent, and appears throughout the land on New Year's Eve, especially in Chepstow close to the Severn and the border with England, where dancing with Mari Llwyd at New Year is a glorious experience.

Later in January, around the time of Old Twelfth Night, apple trees are wassailed. The word 'wassail', comes from the old Saxon *was hael* (good health). This once-threatened custom is being reinstated everywhere; not just in the West Country, where apples and cider are an essential part of life, and is even spreading across the Atlantic. Wherever apples grow, you will find enthusiastic wassailers singing, banging pots and pans and firing guns, and generally having a riotously good time as they bless their apple trees. It is usually the oldest, gnarliest tree that is wassailed. Often this tree will be called the Old Man or Old Lady and will be the embodiment of the living spirit of the orchard.

The growth of interest in witchcraft and Paganism has played an important role in the resurgence of folk customs and traditions, because so many of them are full of spiritual and magical resonances that chime with witch beliefs and practices. Folklorists argue over how and when these customs originated, but the supposition that began in Victorian times, that they are survivals of an intact, pre-Christian Paganism, is almost certainly incorrect. Their age, or lack of it, does not matter to me at all; it is their meaning, their magic and their sense of timelessness that are important. They grow and change; take on new shades of meaning, welcome new participants and audiences, and are full of life and joy. What better way for a witch to begin their year than to partake of first footing, riddle with Mari Llwyd or wassail apple trees? If you cannot find a celebration to join in with, why not start your own?

LOOKING BACK AND FORWARD

January is for most people a rather unloved month. It is cold and dark and the celebrations and excesses of Yule are over, but I am very fond of it. January is the beginning; time to look forward to the year ahead, to plan for the seasons to come, and to begin the adventure through the Witch's Year. As the year starts, I consult the lunar calendar see how the moon's phases will coincide with the Sabbats and seasonal festivals. A Sabbat that coincides with a full moon will have a very different dynamic to one that falls at a lunar quarter or a new moon. If an Equinox coincides with a new or full moon, there will be very high tides that will make a ritual at the coast a special experience. In January, the great tide of the year is in the element of earth. The earth tide nurtures the seeds of all that is to come in the growing year, but it is also an ebb tide; a tide of letting go, and time to review and get rid of whatever is no longer needed. The process can be dedicated to the Roman god Janus who gave his name to January. He had two faces; one that looked back to the year just gone, and one that looked forward to the year to come.

Yuletide decorations must be removed by Twelfth Night (6 January) or hobgoblins (pesky, mischievous spirits) will infest your home and wreak all sorts of havoc. As a prelude to Twelfth Night (*see* below), I burn the Yule evergreens that decorated my hearth. Everything that is used in the practice of magic is inspected and cleaned and if magical supplies such as herbs have deteriorated they are composted or burned. Things cluttering up my living space or my psyche that I no longer want or need (books, clothes, magical paraphernalia and other possessions) are either passed on to someone who can make use of them or are recycled. This feeling of starting the year afresh is a strong impulse that can be a powerful aid to the making of magic, so do not be afraid to use it. Although much of the plant and animal world is still sleeping, you will create a focused and positive sense that everything is ready and waiting.

Practice: Meeting the Moon

At the beginning of every year, at the January full moon, I conduct a simple but profound act of dedication to the moon goddess. If you are new to witchcraft, doing this for the first time can be a powerful act of self-initiation to the mysteries of the moon goddess. If you are an experienced witch, I recommend doing it every year as an act of re-dedication. It will link you to the moon in a very physical, instinctive way.

Conduct the rite in a place where you can see the moon easily. It requires no specific equipment. You should be in a quiet and relaxed but focused frame of mind. Begin by thinking of the moon goddess. If you know her by a particular name (Isis, Diana, Hera or Ceridwen, for example), silently speak that name. Then let the moon's light shine on your body, from your head down to your feet. Do it slowly and deliberately, experiencing it to the full, allowing the silver light to flow over your body and fill your mind. Dedicate yourself and your witchcraft to the moon goddess and thank her.

As with any intense ritual, it is advisable to drink or eat something small afterwards (water and a little bread will do) to return yourself to the plane of earth from the inner world. This rite can be repeated at any full moon during the year, but doing it at the first full moon of the year creates a strong bond with the goddess of the moon that will influence your entire journey through the Witch's Year.

The moon goddess rules the night time realm of dreams. Learn to pay close attention to your dreams; dream oracles have always been an important element of magical practice and they are central to witchcraft. Learn to recognise significant dreams; the dream itself will tell you that it is important and must be acknowledged, and will reveal its meaning to you in its own way. If you begin recording your dreams at the start of your Witch's Year, you may begin to see patterns linking your dreams to the cycles of the sun and the moon as the year progresses. You may experience very different dreams in the dark and light periods of the year, and discover that it is at the Equinoxes, when we move from dark into light or light into dark, that you notice these changes most. You may find that your dreams vary at different phases of the lunar cycle and experience a peak of vivid dreaming around the full moon. Women may experience a phase of intense dreaming just before their menstrual period. All these patterns can become part of your understanding and practice of witchcraft, so do as much as you can to notice and celebrate them.

A WITCH'S ALTAR

As most witchcraft takes place in the home, a household altar is an important part of the witch's practice where the gods and spirits can be honoured, and magic worked. Witchcraft is not alone in this; many religions and spiritual traditions including Hinduism, Buddhism, Roman Catholicism and many animist traditions will include a sacred space or shrine within the home.

The witch's altar is traditionally placed in the north, the direction attributed to the element of earth; but most importantly, it needs to be in a quiet place where you can sit and be with the goddess and god. It should not be in a doorway or other busy place that will constantly be disturbed or where it can be overlooked from the outside. You should make your altar in a place that instinctively feels right to you. An altar can be a table or a shelf or even a cupboard that can be shielded from prying eyes if you wish. It may be a large, elaborate affair, or a small, unassuming presence. In all instances, it will be imbued with the witch's magical personality. January is an ideal time to create your altar, or, as the earth tide ebbs away, to clean and renew an existing altar and make any changes that are needed.

An altar is the living, beating heart of the magical home that is visited by deities and spirits and should always be kept clean and tidy as a mark of respect to them.

Making your altar is a creative process. It will usually contain an image of the witch's goddess and god. Some witches acquire statues or figurines made by Pagan artists, or museum reproductions of ancient Pagan images. Others create something themselves, or copy an image, or use a found natural object, such as a stone that suggests the goddess in some way, or a shed deer horn for the god. There are no rules about this; do what is meaningful to you. I would encourage you to be creative rather than spending money you don't have. When the gods and spirits know you are looking, the right things will turn up, often in unexpected places, and a car boot sale or junk shop, or a beach or countryside walk on a January afternoon may yield all sorts of treasures. An altar cloth can easily be made from a fabric remnant and if you can sew or embroider you may wish to spend some time making something special.

The four elements can be represented on the witch's altar. A beautiful feather, found on a woodland walk, might symbolise air, a special stone from the beach or a piece of wood, sculpted by wind and water, could represent earth. Fire could be something made of iron or a design burnt into wood, and a seashell could symbolise water. The choice is endless, but trust that things will appear at the right time. Personal items that hold family memories sometimes find a special place on the altar. On my own altar are a jar of shells that my brother and I collected when we were children, a lock of hair from a beloved cat, a wooden owl's head that my father made in a woodwork class at school, and a locket containing a picture of my grandfather that my grandmother wore when he went away to the First World War. There are also reminders of special rituals: a round pebble from a beach ritual and a pine cone from a Dartmoor forest, and a rather kitsch tiny brass cauldron from a souvenir shop. Begin work on your altar in January and announce your intention to the deities and spirits, but let it come together over time.

You can change the items on your altar to reflect the changing seasons, adding flowers in spring and summer and fruits in autumn, but remember to remove these when they are past their best. There should be a place for candles and incense. Candles are lit on the altar to mark the seasonal festivals and at monthly lunar rites. The incense used in witchcraft is usually loose incense, often made or blended from plant materials by the witch themself, and burnt on a charcoal block. We will learn how to make incense in August.

Spells that you make will be placed on your altar to charge them magically and increase their power before you send them on their way. Whenever I make a spell, it will spend some time, often a lunar month, on my altar while my familiar spirits get to work on it. Even after many years of practice, my altar continually teaches me new things about my craft. As I make it ready for the year ahead, I look forward to seeing how it will grow and change.

Burning Loose Blended Incense

Take care with incense; burning charcoal gets very hot and it is important to burn it safely. Use a heat-proof incense burner or censer. Many attractive and expensive ones are available, but not essential. I like to use a ceramic bowl filled with sand from a beach where I work magic. Charcoal blocks can be obtained from magical or church suppliers. Keep them in an airtight container as if they get damp they will be difficult to light and can fall apart. Use tongs to hold the charcoal block (barbecue tongs work well) while you light it. The block will spark into flame, then become red and glowing. Place it in the burner and add your incense. The incense should produce gentle smoke rather than flames.

THE WITCH'S TOOLS

The tools that play a central part in witchcraft rituals vary from tradition to tradition, but usually include the following:

- *The Wand* represents the element of fire in some traditions and air in others. You will learn how to make your wand in March.
- *The Cup or Chalice* represents the element of water.
- *The Pentacle* is a platter or dish that represents the element of earth. It can be made from wood, metal or ceramics.
- *The ritual knife or athame* (used mainly by Wiccans) represents the element of air but in some traditions is attributed to fire.
- *The witch's mirror* is a very personal tool used to commune with the moon and sun, and to look into the inner realms. You will learn how to create a witch's mirror in February.

Working tools have indwelling spirits of their own and must be honoured and respected. They are kept safe in their own 'houses' when not in use and are never shown to non-witches. My coven also has a lovely ritual sword, given to us long ago by an older coven, that has been used in witchcraft rituals for over 70 years.

An incense burner and two small vessels to contain salt and water will also be used in rituals. Most witchcraft rituals require you to light a fire. Indoors, an open hearth or woodburning stove are ideal, and a fire basket or bowl is really useful for outdoor rituals.

When I first joined a coven, I was taught that tools should either be made, or would come to the witch in their own time, and I still try to abide by this way of working. In those days, it was not possible to buy ready-made witch's tools. This is a matter of personal choice, but something you have made yourself, even if, like most of us, you are not a skilled craftsperson, will have a magical power and connection with you that something purchased can never have. Witchcraft is for everyone, irrespective of their wealth or lack of it, so I also like to be frugal and if something cannot be made, I forage, recycle and reuse whenever I can, so that I do not squander mother earth's resources. My magical tools have been made, acquired in junk shops, foraged, bartered or gifted. In January the tools are inspected and cleaned, ready for the year ahead.

RITUAL CLOTHING

Ritual clothing is useful; it is only used in magical practice and signifies that the witch has stepped away from the everyday world into a different place where the gods are honoured and magic is worked. It is not intended to attract attention or distract from the ritual, so witches tend to wear simple, inconspicuous robes, usually of black, green or earth colours. A basic robe is easy to make, or an existing garment can be re-purposed. The robe that I wear in magical ritual (a very simple black cotton home-made thing) is washed in January and a little vervain added to the water for blessing. A torn or damaged robe should be darned and mended; visible mending can become a rather beautiful and important part of the story of a ritual garment.

A cord may also be worn around the waist, and can be used in spell casting. Different branches of the craft attribute significance to the colour of the cord.

Practice: Casting the Circle

The circle is the witch's sacred space; it makes the working place sacred for the worship of the gods and the working of magic, and it can be created anywhere at any time when the witch has need of it. Casting the circle, that is, making the space sacred, is the first step in all witchcraft rituals from solo rites to large scale group celebrations. I have cast a circle around a field containing four hundred bikers to celebrate a wedding at a motorcycle rally, and created one around a hospital bed when it was needed. The circle is usually cast sunwise (clockwise), but sometime a widdershins (anti-clockwise) direction may be used.

Contrary to popular belief, a widdershins circle is not necessarily associated with malefic magic. It has various uses. A circle may be cast widdershins in lunar rituals, because the anti-clockwise motion mirrors the appearance of the motion of the moon around the earth. In some forms of witchcraft the circle is cast sunwise then closed widdershins to signify the reverse of the opening process.

It is important to understand not just how to cast a circle, but also the many layers of meaning that go into its making. The circle is an image of the witch's wholistic universe. It encompasses time (the lunar, solar and stellar time cycles) and space, goddess and god, the world of spirit and the witch within them. The four compass directions (north, east, south and west) are placed around the circle, as are the four elements, the Solstices and Equinoxes, and the hours of the day, and the witch stands at its centre. When a witch enters the circle, they step out of the everyday world; it is outside normal time and space and witches refer to it as 'the place between the worlds'. It is a safe place where the witch works with the deities and spirits. Every aspect of the circle (the elements, directions, colours, for example) is part of a chain of magical symbolism, known as correspondences, and all the different aspects of the symbolism are activated in one unified whole when the witch casts the circle.

Some traditions specify a correct size for the circle but I work with whatever is practical. There are many circle-casting rituals available that reflect different magical practices and traditions. This is a simple one that anyone should be able to use, working alone or with others, in the home or outdoors. I have departed from my usual practice of not providing a specific ritual wording; if you are new to circle casting, use my words as a guide to meaning, but feel free to invent your own.

You will need

- A wand or athame if you have one. If you do not have these things yet, use the index finger of the hand you write with
- Two small vessels, one containing salt and one containing water. Use sea or rock salt without chemical additives, and water from a holy well or spring (*see* February and July)
- Four candles in holders for the four directions or quarters. The elemental colours for these are: yellow or gold in the east (air); red in the south (fire); blue in the west (water) and green in the north (earth)
- Matches to light candles
- Candle snuffer to put out the candles. Do not blow candles out; this is using one element (air) against another (fire) and is bad practice.
- Optional: a broomstick (*see* April)
- Incense, charcoal and incense burner

Preparation

Ascertain where north is (use a compass if necessary), and place the candles at the four quarters.

You should be in a calm, focused state of mind. Banish all distracting thoughts. If you are working with others, everyone should be at peace with one another; bad feelings and enmity must not be brought into the circle.

Method

Cleanse the space. If you have a broom, sweep around the edge of the circle, mentally banishing all psychic dirt, unwanted energies and negativity. Otherwise do this by pacing purposefully around the edge of the circle.

Light the incense. Then, beginning in the East, light the candles at each of the quarters.

Purify the space. Pour the salt into the water, asking the goddess to bless it as you do so. Beginning in the east, sprinkle drops of water around the edge of the circle. Place a drop of water on your forehead and do the same for all others present.

Cast the circle. Beginning between the north and east, hold up the wand or ritual knife, or the forefinger of the hand you write with. Visualise a line of light or energy emanating from your hand. Pace slowly and deliberately around the circle, all the while visualising the line of energy or light, until you arrive back at your starting point and have created an entire circle of energy or light. Say as you go:

> *I conjure thee O circle of power, that thou be a meeting place of love, joy and truth.*
> *Be thou a rampart between the mortal world and the realms of the mighty ones.*
> *Be thou a protection that shall preserve and contain the power that I shall raise within thee,*
> *Wherefore do I bless and consecrate thee in the names of the Old Ones*and the spirits of this place.*

*Goddess and god names may be used here. I do not make a habit of using archaic language, but these words have been used in many times and many places and they work well.

Ask the elemental powers of the four quarters to bless the circle. Stand in the east and say:

> *O ye mighty ones of the east, guardians of air,*
> *I do summon, stir and call ye up to guard this circle and witness the rite,*
> *And I do bid ye hail and welcome.*

As you do this, visualise the element of air in whatever way seems right. These words are repeated at the other quarters, saying:

> South: *Oh ye mighty ones of the south, guardians of fire,*
> *I do summon, stir and call ye up to guard this circle and witness the rite,*
> *And I do bid ye hail and welcome.*
> West: *Oh ye mighty ones of the west, guardians of water,*

I do summon, stir and call ye up to guard this circle and witness the rite,
And I do bid ye hail and welcome.
North: *Oh ye mighty ones of the north, guardians of earth,*
I do summon, stir and call ye up to guard this circle and witness the rite,
And I do bid ye hail and welcome.

The circle is now complete; it is outside time and space and whatever ritual and magical work is desired may take place.

Once the work has been completed, it is very important that the circle is closed down. It should never be left in place. Any deities or spirits that have been present are respectfully thanked. Then the circle is closed.

Beginning in the east, say:

O ye mighty ones of the east, guardians of air,
I thank you for attending the circle and witnessing the rite
And ere ye depart to your fair and lovely realms,
I do bid you hail and farewell.

The formula is repeated with the other elements and directions. As you pace around the circle visualise the line of energy or light that you cast falling gently into the ground and fading away. This returns the circle to everyday time and space. Snuff the candles out, beginning in the east. The circle is now closed.

Try to memorise the words of the circle casting, so that you concentrate on the meaning. You can create your own form of words if you wish.

Correspondences

East: Air, yellow or gold, dawn, Spring Equinox, moon's first quarter
South: Fire, red, noon, Midsummer, full moon
West: Water, blue, sunset, Autumn Equinox, moon's last quarter
North: Earth, green, midnight, Midwinter, dark/new moon

Practice: The First Sabbat – Twelfth Night

The first Sabbat of the year is celebrated on Twelfth Night, 6 January. Contemporary popular Paganism has eight seasonal festivals celebrated at the Solstices and Equinoxes and the midpoints between them, but some of the older, more occult traditions of the craft celebrate a ritual year of nine Sabbats. At Twelfth Night, the young god of the witches, the Unconquered Sun who was born anew at Yule, is honoured and welcomed. He is presented with his magical tools and weapons and dances the circle of the zodiac, signifying his journey around the Witch's Year.

Preparation

The young sun god has many names and guises: in ancient Egypt he was Horus, in Greece and Rome Apollo, for the Britons of Roman times Belinus, in Wales Lleu, and in Ireland Lugh. We will learn more of his story as we journey through the year. His mother, the witches' goddess, can be honoured at Twelfth Night as Holda or Holle, Arianrhod or Ceridwen, but is often just called the Mother. Read the myths for yourself, find names and stories that resonate with you and use them in your ritual.

This ritual can be performed at your altar. You will need your witch's tools. If you do not yet have these, find one special object such as a stone or feather to present to the god. You will need your incense burner, incense of your choice, your salt and water vessels, a single altar candle, and a little dried mugwort. If you do not have mugwort, use dried rose petals.

The ritual is a small one that does not call for a ritual feast. Instead, cakes and wine are presented to the gods. If you wish, make some simple biscuits and include some oats and a little honey in the recipe, or use oatcakes and red wine or apple juice.

The ritual

The circle is cast (see Practice on pages 22–25). Light the incense and the altar candle. Then call upon the mother goddess in her winter guise and ask her to be present. Call upon the young sun god and ask him to be present.

Next purify and bless the ritual tools. Each tool is first passed three times through incense smoke, and the element of air is asked to give its blessing. Then it is passed through a candle flame and fire is asked to give its blessing. Each tool is sprinkled three times with salt water and water is asked to give its blessing. Lastly each tool is rubbed three times with mugwort, and earth is asked to give its blessing.

The tools are then presented to the god at the altar.

There follows a meditation in which the god is visualised dancing across the night sky, on a circular path through all the constellations of the zodiac.

The rite concludes with a dance around the circle, in honour of the god. Ask the goddess and god to bless the cakes and wine, then eat and drink in their honour. Thank the goddess and god and bid them farewell. Put out the altar candle and close your circle.

Go outside after the ritual and look up at the constellations (if the sky is clear) as your witchcraft is both a real world and a spiritual practice. After all rituals, a little of your food and drink should be left outdoors as an offering to the Faeries or land spirits and any leftover salted water should be poured onto the ground.

Robins and Wrens

I welcome the robin to my garden at the beginning of the year. As the Witch's Year progresses, we will see that folkore attributes the growing half of the year that begins at the Winter Solstice to the robin, and the waning half of the year, that begins at Midsummer, to the wren. January is a tough time for birds. Robins like to be in close company with humans, so putting food out at the start of the year helps them survive and honours the magical bird, or little god, of the waxing year.

STARGAZING

The great glory of January in northern latitudes is the night sky. Long, dark January nights are the best time of the year for stargazing and deep, frosty blue night skies are often preceded by intense, fiery sunsets. Stellar magic is an important aspect of witchcraft. Even if you have no knowledge of the constellations, it is easy to recognise Orion the Hunter's distinctive belt of three stars that rises soon after sunset at this time of year and rides high in the sky. He is, as we shall see, the image of the witch's god in the heavens. Consult a night sky almanac that shows the constellations month by month, or a phone app that shows which stars are visible at your location, and you will soon learn to recognise not just Orion with Sirius at his heels, but the Plough and the polar stars, and other constellations including Taurus (the Bull) and the Pleiades (or Seven Sisters), both of which rise ahead of Orion in the January sky and can be seen very clearly at this time of year. These constellations are honoured all over the world and are woven deep into Celtic and Norse mythology and hold much spiritual meaning for witches. Humans have recognised Taurus for many thousands of years; its stars form the eye and facial features of a cave painting of a bull in the Palaeolithic cave of Lascaux, made some 17,000 years ago, so when I look up at these stars I am part of a long continuum of human experience.

The annual Quadrantid meteor shower reaches its peak on 4 January and if the night is dark enough you will able to see shooting stars close to the constellation of Draco in the northern sky. This is the time of year when the magnificent Aurora Borealis, or northern lights, may be seen, even as far south as the British Isles.

HOME WORK

Witchcraft has always been thought of as a domestic activity that belongs to ordinary people and takes place largely in the home, and everyday domestic activities can be full of magical power and meanings. If you seek out the many traces of historical witchcraft that can be found in museums, you will notice immediately that spells and magic are often made with herbs and food; that they can be baked, knotted, plaited, sewn, knitted and carved or burned onto domestic objects or kitchen walls. My house is full of things used to make magic; not just the ritual tools described above, but things with dual magical/practical uses. A knife which is used to cut and prepare the herbs for spells and magic is a friend with its own spirit. A battered old basket, rescued from a jumble sale many years ago, collects the herbs that must not touch the ground when gathered. A terracotta mixing bowl with a shiny black interior is a scrying bowl used to see into the spirit world. These things are ordinary, and anyone looking at them would think they were just everyday kitchen items, but witchcraft has made them special. Other household items (cooking and baking utensils, crockery, glass jars, cloth and thread) are pressed into use when needed. A spell might be a pinch of herbs sewn into a bag, a plait of red wool, a cloth heart stuck with pins, or a hawthorn twig tied with green thread. In witchcraft, the line between the domestic and the magical is a blurred one; this is part of the joy of it, and the simplest, most mundane activities are full of the deepest magical meaning when done with the right intent.

A Spell for January

Spell casting is practical, everyday magic intended to make something happen; it is sometimes referred to as operative magic, or results magic. This simple spell involves tying knots in a piece of red yarn or cord. It has been used by witches in many parts of the British Isles down the years. The use of knots in magic is very ancient, because tying knots in thread is one of the oldest human activities. Red symbolises fire, energy and, because it is the colour of blood, the life force. The trick, as with all spells, is that the most important part of the magic is your magical will; a kind of finely focused concentration on your magical purpose. The action of knotting is an aid to that will.

You will need

- A length of red yarn or wool (knitting yarn is ideal), measured from the tip of your middle finger to your shoulder with your arm outstretched.

Method

Decide on the purpose of your spell. Spells work best when you have a clear and achievable outcome in mind (succeeding at a job interview, for example, or doing well in an exam or passing a driving test). Concentrate your magical will on achieving the object of your spell; visualise the successful outcome.

Then tie nine knots in your cord or yarn, pulling the knots tight and reciting this charm as you go:

By knot of one, the spell's begun
By knot of two, it cometh true
By knot of three, so mote it be
By knot of four, the open door
By knot of five, the spell's alive
By knot of six, my spell I fix
By knot of seven, the gates of heaven
By knot of eight, the open gate
By knot of nine, the thing is mine!

Stop thinking about the spell immediately and let it go on its way and do its work.

Put the knotted cord on the altar and leave it there to help the spell on its way for a lunar month. After that, hang it up somewhere safe, or if it was made to help someone else, give it to them.

There are many variants of this rhyme. Like many spoken spells, it is doggerel and the words do not matter. They are an aid to your magical will. Sometimes a spoken spell is repeated, until the words lose all conscious meaning and become pure intent. The beauty and effectiveness of this spell lies in its simplicity. You can refine it by using it when the moon is waxing to make something grow or increase, or by casting it during the waning moon if you want something to lessen or fade away.

A Note on Measurements

All the measurements used in magical work in this book are based on the witch's own body rather than conventional measuring systems. This makes the magic personal to the witch, and increases its effectiveness.

As January draws on, the days become noticeably longer. Towards the end of the month, catkins have appeared on the hazel, alder and pussy willow branches, and the first snowdrops are appearing. On 25 January, the feast of Saint Dwynwen, the Welsh patron saint of lovers, is celebrated. After rejecting the attentions of an unwanted suitor, Dwynwen lived a life of solitude on Ynys Llanddwyn, a small tidal islet off the coast of Ynys Môn (Anglesey), a wild and very beautiful place where the remains of her shrine and well can still be seen. Llanddwyn became a great place of pilgrimage in the Middle Ages, and Dwynwen would grant happiness in love to those who honoured her. I like to remember Dwynwen on this day by making a feast in her honour for friends and family. She seems to me like the spirit of her wild home and of the wells. Wells will become increasingly significant as we move on the next month of our Witch's Year.

A Meditation for January: The Magical Study

The January meditation is designed to allow you to create a special interior space in your mind in which you can work your magic. It is based on an old technique that dates back to classical times, called the Art of Memory, that is widely used by creative people and by magical practitioners. You will create an inner room; a study or special place where you will find whatever you need to work your magic. You will be able to return to it again and again and use it whenever you need to. It will help you find answers to questions that may elude your conscious mind and provide a peaceful inner sanctuary. It is important that you notice as many visual details as you possibly can in this meditation. Do this meditation regularly and you will find that on each visit you see more details.

You are standing in a peaceful garden on a winter evening. It is January and the night is cold but the stars are bright above you. You can see Orion, Taurus and the Pleiades, and Corvus the Raven shining in the night sky. Somewhere above you an owl calls.

Follow a path through the garden until you come to a door. Stand in front of the door and look at it closely, Notice everything about it that you can. What does it look like? What is it made of? What colour is it? Is it old? New? Large? Small? Find the lock and the handle. Reach out and touch it if you wish.

When you are ready, take the key to the door out of your pocket, put it in the lock, use the handle (if there is one) and open the door. You step into a room. It is warm and comfortable. In one corner is a fireplace where a wood fire is burning. Gentle lamps provide all the light that you need. There is a curtained window, and you can sense, but not see, the night sky outside. The room contains an altar covered with magical objects. Look at these slowly and carefully, noticing each one in as much detail as you can; pick them up and examine them if you wish. Also in the room is a table on which are magical tools; everything that you might need to work your magic. Look at them all carefully. Pick them up, knowing that when you return again you will be able to use them.

Two of the walls of the room are lined with bookshelves. There are books on every subject connected with witchcraft and magic. Look at the books, noticing some of the titles. When you need answers to magical questions, you know that you will be able to come here and find a book containing the answer that you need.

Elsewhere is a cupboard full of jars and bottles containing herbs and other substances for making magical preparations. Take your time looking around the room, absorbing as many of the details as possible. This is your magical study, your inner working place. You can return here whenever you need to work and study in the inner worlds, and you will find whatever you need to know, even if your conscious, everyday mind is not aware of it. Your study is a magical being in its own right and has its own, indwelling spirit. As you stand in your study, sense this spirit, greet it and it will welcome you to your study. When you have seen enough, thank the spirit of the study and bid it farewell.

Take one last look around then open the door and leave your study, closing the door behind you. Gently return to your everyday waking consciousness and straight away write or draw as much as you can remember. Return to your magical study frequently. After several visits you will come to know it well and become accustomed to working there and using what it has to offer.

FEBRUARY

February

Cleansing and Purifying

The Year Quickens

Under the ancient yew trees the last remains of ice glitter on puddles at the edge of the road. The church sits on an egg-shaped mound; a site that was holy before the coming of Christianity. In the churchyard, the path threads its way amongst old gravestones. Rooks call loudly. Everywhere there are masses of snowdrops and early primroses greeting the returning daylight, and defying the last of winter. The wind tugs at leafless oak and ash trees; the holly trees alone retain their deep green leaves. Beyond the shelter of the churchyard, the path up the narrow valley is icy, wet and treacherous. The river is swollen with recent rain and somewhere across the valley, where the low sun shines on dead bracken, a deer barks and a buzzard circles slowly. The owner of this land is returning it to the wild and it is a haven for the more than human.

Half-frozen water drips down the rocky outcrops and onto the path. To walk this path is to leave the world behind, and enter a timeless peace. A well and its chapel nestle in the shelter of a low cliff. In the tiny well house with its steep roof, built over the spring at the base of the cliff, the water is still and clear in its granite tank. In this flood season it seeps through the stones and overflows down the steps, bubbling out over the path. It is biting cold to the touch and slips down the throat like cold molten fire. From the well house, the water flows in a stone channel under the base of the well chapel wall. Inside the chapel there is nothing but the quiet, insistent sound of the water as it runs from north to south in its trough behind the altar in the east and out of the chapel into another smaller well house on the chapel's south wall. The altar stone is a massive piece of granite; a repurposed megalith. It is incised with four ancient, equal-armed crosses that pre-date the saint who claimed this place. The altar window and the doorway in the west provide a pale, cool light. The taste and gentle sound of the water alter consciousness; to spend time here is to enter deep trance and be transported. The water brings not only peace but inspiration too.

Outside the sun is sinking low and fiery behind the hill across the valley

February Associations

Festivals: Candlemas (1st), Lupercalia (15th)
Figures: Bride, Juno Februata
More Than Human: Snowdrops, swans
Totems and Symbols: Wolf, white swan, hearth

and a thin skin of ice is returning to the water that lies by the path. This is the time of ice and fire, and the time of Bride, who throughout these Celtic lands is goddess of all the wells.

In February the year quickens; it comes alive. The month is named after the Roman goddess Juno Februata, mother of the god Mars. Candles were lit in her honour at the beginning of the month and our month begins with Candlemas; the Sabbat when witches celebrate the goddess Bride of the growing year; a joyous festival of fire and light. The earth tide continues to ebb away; Juno Februata also presided over rituals of purification and cleansing at the February full moon, and so February became the traditional month for spring cleaning, a custom that continues today. This is the month of hearth and home; we learn to protect the home with charms, make the witch's mirror and a house for the spirits.

CANDLEMAS

Candlemas is celebrated on 2 February. Some witches choose to celebrate the Sabbats on the eve (that is, the night before the actual date); others on the day itself. In practice, we all have to work these celebrations into busy lives, so be practical and, so long as you celebrate close to the 'right' date, do what works for you. In recent years Pagans have begun to call this festival by the Irish name of Imbolc, but I prefer its older name of Candlemas; a name which suits its nature and meanings very well. It is the midpoint between the winter Solstice and the Spring Equinox; the turning point between winter and spring. The days have been lengthening by a few minutes each day since the beginning of the year, but at Candlemas the return of the light becomes really noticeable for the first time. Snowdrops are in full bloom and the first primroses are greeting the world. Folk tradition in the West Country states that if Candlemas day is fine and fair, there will be more winter weather to come before the season ends; conversely wild and wet weather at Candlemas means that winter weather is over.

Candlemas is the festival of the Celtic goddess known as Bride or Brigid, the great goddess of Britain and Ireland who is revered throughout the Celtic lands and beloved of witches. Bride gave her name to the island of Britain: in Roman times the people living in the northern part of what eventually became England were known as the Brigantes and their kingdom was Brigantia. Bride is remembered in many place names, and the sacred river Braint on Ynys Môn is named for her. Christianised as Saint Brigid or Bridget, she was referred to as 'the Mary of the Gaels' and had an exalted place within Celtic Christianity, belying her Pagan origins. It was believed that she was the foster-mother of Jesus (an important role in medieval Celtic societies).

In the Gaelic-speaking areas of Scotland, a wealth of spells, charms and incantations called on her for protection and aid, and for her great healing powers. These spells and prayers can be found in the *Carmina Gadelica*, compiled by folklorist Alexander Carmichael. This massive compendium of folklore and magic, in which Paganism and Christianity are inextricably mixed, contains the remarkable *Genealogy of Bride*, which takes the form of a classic invocation, or recitation of words of power, seeking the protection of the goddess:

The genealogy of the holy maiden Bride,
Radiant flame of gold, noble foster-mother of Christ
Bride the daughter of Dugall the brown,
Son of Aodh, son of Art, son of Conn
Son of Crearar, son of Cis, son of Carmac, son of Carruin.
Every day and every night
That I say the genealogy of Bride,
I shall not be killed, I shall not be harried,
I shall not be put in cell, I shall not be wounded,
Neither shall Christ leave me in forgetfulness.
No fire, no sun, no moon shall burn me,
No lake, no sea, no water shall drown me,
No arrow of fairy nor dart of fay shall wound me,
And I under the protection of my Holy Mary,
And my gentle foster-mother is my beloved Bride. [1]

Bride is the supreme protective deity, who brings health and heals all manner of hurts and harms, not just for humans, but for animals too. She is protectress of the home. In Celtic belief she is a triple goddess, and her power is threefold. Invoked as the Three-in-One, she is mistress of the arts, poetry and music; of smithcraft or metalworking, and of healing. Fire and light belong to her and in medieval times in Ireland a perpetual fire was kept burning in honour of Saint Brigid at her convent in Kildare. Today in Ireland, Saint Brigid's day is acquiring an increasingly Pagan flavour; the goddess has returned and is being recognised once again. Distinctive Saint Brigid's crosses are woven from rushes and hung up in houses for protection; feasts and the blessing of wells take place. Healing wells are dedicated to Bride throughout the British Isles, with Bridewell still being a common place name, even in large cities.

Bride therefore presides over the elements of fire and water, and at this cold time of the year she is described as being of ice and fire. My Candlemas celebration begins with a visit to one of the many holy wells in the area where I live, and I honour the goddess Bride of the wells and drink some of the well water. I might visit the beautiful well of Saint Clether in North Cornwall, described at the beginning of this chapter, and one of the most truly sacred places I know, or Saint Nectan's Well close to the sea at Hartland Point in North Devon, or the well of Saint Augustine at Cerne Abbas in Dorset, in the village beneath the great chalk giant on the hill. A supply of well water for ritual use is collected on Bride's Day in blue glass bottles which will be left in the moonlight at the next full moon to be charged and blessed, then kept out of daylight. (Blue glass is always used when the blessing of the moon is needed.) The well water will be used at the Sabbats and other rituals throughout the year.

Candlemas is celebrated with white and golden foods symbolising fire and light. In Scotland and Ireland, round oatcakes (called bannocks in Scotland) are made and one is left on the doorstep as an offering for Bride, or for someone in need. The emphasis on hearth and home at Candlemas dictates that food should be shared in the name of Bride with those who have need of it. The life stories of the Irish Saint Brigid depict her sharing food, and working miracles to feed the poor and needy. There is a very old association of Bride with milk in Ireland and Scotland, where cattle farming has been at the heart of life since the Neolithic period. All dairy produce: milk, butter, cream and cheese, especially sheep's or goat's cheese, is eaten at Candlemas, because sheep, goats and some cattle produce their first milk of the year at this time. Honey is also offered to Bride. There are plenty of white and golden vegan alternatives.

Practice: The Candlemas Ritual

Like most major witchcraft ceremonies, the Candlemas ritual takes place at night, after the sun has set (the exceptions are Midwinter and Midsummer, when sunrise and sunset rites are observed). It is a ritual of fire and light and a festival when the goddess alone is celebrated. The season of growth is only just beginning, and the god is not invoked. He can still be seen in the starry skies, but is not yet present in the growing things of earth. He will be with us later, when the light grows stronger. Bride is welcomed into the home, and this is a festival at which the concepts of hearth and home are very important.

The Candlemas altar is decorated with snowdrops and pussy willow. Snowdrops are known as February Maids or Bride's Flower, and it is considered unlucky to bring them indoors on any day other than Candlemas. The goddess is embodied in the ritual in the form of the Bride; a large 'corn doll' made of a sheaf from last year's harvest gathered at Lammas in August, the festival that sits opposite Candlemas on the Wheel of the Year. (Sabbats that are opposites always have echoes of each other, even though they take place six months apart.) The Bride wears a white dress, trimmed with gold symbolising fire and the returning light. She will live with me until the following Lammas, when she will be replaced by a new Bride. In August when we gather our harvest, we will learn how to make the Bride. If you have not celebrated this ritual before, you can use a corn dolly or obtain a few stalks of wheat from a florist.

This is an intense and occult ritual that begins with a small candle flame and transports the participants from earth to the heavens and back again.

Preparation

The Candlemas Sabbat requires careful planning and preparation, both mental and physical.

You will need to have prepared some anointing oil. Use sweet almond oil as a carrier, and put a little in a small bowl then add a few drops of essential oils. Choose something sweet and floral; jasmine and ylang-ylang will both work well.

Take time before the ritual to plan how you will invoke or call upon Bride; the mental images and ideas you will use. You need be in a calm, focused state for this ritual and its intense visualisation, so find time to relax and meditate beforehand.

You will need

- Snowdrops and pussy willow to decorate the altar
- Three white candles for the altar
- A fourth white candle in a holder to place in your window
- A blue candle for each person present
- Matches and a taper
- A large metal (heatproof) bowl with a little sand or earth in the bottom (enough to stand the blue candles in). I use a small cauldron
- An anointing oil
- Bride (or corn dolly or ears of wheat)
- Fabrics and decorations for Bride's bed. Choose things befitting for the goddess of fire and the growing year

The ritual

After sunset, a single candle is lit and placed in the window so that anyone aware of the tradition will know that Candlemas is being celebrated in the house.

Prepare Bride's bed. Use fabric to make a little bed big enough for the Bride or corn dolly, and decorate it with whatever you think the goddess will like. I use spring flowers and ribbons.

Cast the circle and light the three white candles on the altar. As you do so, call upon Bride as the triple goddess of the growing year. To do this, you can weave together imagery drawn from Celtic myth as inspiration. Bride is a maiden with the rays of the sun in her hair, queen of the white hills, the rider of the white swan, guardian of the wells, and mother of the king of glory. In the Celtic nations, the white swan is sacred to Bride and is one of her supreme symbols. At this time of year migrating whooper swans return to the West Country, and to Ireland, where they gather around Bru na Boinne; the white-walled megalithic mound of Newgrange in County Meath.

Each altar candle represents one of the gifts of Bride. The first is the flame of creative inspiration – the inspiration of the artist, poet or musician or any other creative work. The second flame is the gift of Bride as mistress of smith-craft; itself a magical and sacred practice in the Bronze and Iron Ages that is understood as symbolic of purification through which dross, impurities and weaknesses are purged and cleansed, resulting in something that is true and tested. This flame is therefore the flame of truth. The third gift of the goddess is the flame of healing of mind and body, that brings peace and harmony. These gifts of Bride are given by the goddess for the year ahead, and Candlemas is therefore a time of creative inspiration. You will feel the presence of the goddess with you.

Each person takes a blue candle. Present the anointing oil to Bride and ask her to bless it. Stroke the candle with your finger, beginning at the centre, and then working to each end, slowly and deliberately covering it with oil until the entire candle is anointed, in a focused meditative state.

Place the candles in the metal bowl; stand them in the sand and light them from a single taper that is passed round.

Watch your candle flame; focus on it, and let your mind merge with it. Reach out as though taking the flame into yourself; visualise it filling your body as well as your mind. Become the flame; grow incandescent and brilliant. See yourself flaming like a star in the dark spaces of the universe; you are part of the light that originates from the stars and part of Bride, the source of all light. Experience this to the full.

Return to the circle and to your candle flame, knowing that you carry the light of Bride within you. Her fire will always burn in your heart and inspire and energise you, even in difficult or dark times. If there is a problem or something that is holding you back at this time when the year is quickening, project it into your candle flame, and see the problem burning away to ash and scattering to nothing on the wind. The blue candles are left in the bowl and placed somewhere safe to burn down overnight.

Candlemas concludes with the beautiful rite of Bride's Bed. The bed is traditionally placed by the hearth, at the heart of the home. Put Bride in her bed and repeat, over and over:

Bride is come, Bride is welcome
Bride is come, Bride is welcome.

Welcome the goddess and the returning light to the home. The circle is then closed and Bride should be left to sleep overnight in her bed, if possible close to the blue candles from the visualisation which will burn down to nothing during the night. The following day she is returned to her normal place in the house where she will live until it is time to make a new Bride with freshly harvested corn at Lammas.

Enjoy the Candlemas feast; it is important to eat and drink something to return fully to earth after journeying to the stars in such an intense visualisation. Inner images from this Sabbat will remain with you; reflect on them and use them creatively.

THE WITCH'S MIRROR

The mirror is an old-fashioned witch's tool. Mine is my constant friend and companion in everyday magic-making. It has many uses in witchcraft; its basic function is to act as a focus for the witch's magical will and to aid their concentration. It is used extensively in spell-casting and practical magic, often combined with candles to repel unwanted energies or magical intentions. Moonlight or sunlight can be focused, directed and reflected onto an object, a place or a person. It can also be used to see into the spirit world, and a dark or black mirror, which we will make later in the year, is a highly effective tool for scrying or divination. Mirror magic is unobtrusive; the mirror goes about its work quietly and unnoticed, and this is what makes it so effective. In *A Sea Witch's Companion* I described in detail the making of a Sea Witchcraft mirror and its role in moon and tide magic. The ordinary witch's mirror can be used in daylight and it often involves working with the sun.

Creating a witch's mirror is very simple and straightforward. An ordinary mirror tile or handbag mirror that will fit in a pocket is ideal for the purpose and can be bought for pennies. The mirror does not require any elaborate crafting or preparation. It should simply be cleansed and blessed with salt and water, passed through incense smoke and the flame of a candle, then rubbed with mugwort, the herb of vision. Keep your mirror covered when it is not in use.

In January we practised the self-dedication ritual of bathing the face and body in the light of the full moon. When you have made your witch's mirror, work this ritual again, but this time, at the February full moon, use your mirror to focus the moonlight and reflect it on onto yourself. This intensifies and deepens the magic.

A HOME FOR THE SPIRITS

Every witch's home should contain a house for the spirits. This will become a home for different kinds of spirits: visiting spirits that will find a place to rest for a while, and the household and familiar spirits that will take up more permanent residence and become the witch's constant friends and companions in the making of magic. 'Familiar' in this sense means part of the family. The spirit houses I describe here are very different from the ones used in the practice of feng shui, which can be bought. The spirit house used in witchcraft must be made by the witch themself, otherwise it will not work. As your practice of witchcraft develops, and your contact with the spirit world grows, you may find that visitors to your home remark on its atmosphere. Visitors to my home, some of whom are unaware that I am a witch, will often remark on its warm and pleasant atmosphere. This has nothing to do with heating; it is because of the spirits that share the house with me, and the positive relationship that I am lucky to enjoy with them. A house with no spirit presences can feel dull or tired, and of course, a house with unhappy spirits will have a troubled atmosphere. Making a spirit house is an essential part of building your relationship with the spirits in your home. By doing it, you will announce your presence to them very directly. They will become aware that you care about them, and will start to announce their presence to you in various small ways. Day by day, your awareness of the spirits around you will become heightened, and you and they will begin to communicate. We will begin working with the world of spirit in February by creating a home for the spirits that you will work with later in the Witch's Year.

I was first taught how to make a spirit house many years ago by Cecil Williamson, the founder of the Museum of Witchcraft at Boscastle. Cecil was a skilled magical practitioner and wise teacher; I was fortunate to know him in the last 15 years of his life, and most of what I know about traditional witchcraft I learnt from him. To make a spirit house using Cecil's method, you will need a large glass jar. It must have a lid, as it will be sealed, and should have a wide neck so that you can put a variety of things into it.

An old sweetshop jar is ideal, as are large pasta jars or glass food storage jars. All of these can be found at car boot sales, junk shops or recycling centres. You will find that if you tell the spirit world you are looking for something to make a spirit house and ask for help, the right thing will turn up, probably in a very unexpected way. The jar should be thoroughly cleaned inside and out, and dried. Then you fill it with things that you think a spirit might like to have in its home. Cecil's recipe included small quartz pebbles, sea shells, shards of mirror, sea glass, ears of dried barley and wheat, plaited corn stalks, dried rosebuds and cornflowers, and red thread; all of them items used in the kind of traditional witchcraft that he studied and practised. My first spirit jar, made under Cecil's watchful eye, contained all these things. It is still with me many years later, and is lived in happily by a spirit friend. That is all I can tell you, because spirit working is a private matter, and the witch must not reveal details of their relationship with 'their' spirits or betray confidences. To do so would cause the spirits to depart. 'To know, to dare, to will, to keep silent' is the magical practitioner's maxim, and in the case of spirit working it absolutely should be respected.

The jar should be between a quarter and a third full of its contents. Any plant or vegetable matter must be thoroughly dried before use, so that it cannot rot or decay in the jar. The lid is then placed on the jar, and it is sealed with thread and candle wax. In Cecil's version red thread and wax were used. The jar is now ready for use.

In March we will learn how to attract a familiar spirit to it. It is important to understand that a spirit house is not a prison that traps the spirit; it is a resting place and the spirits may come and go whenever they please. I never command or compel spirits, as some magicians do; that is not the witch's way. I ask respectfully and if they choose to work with me, that creates a close relationship of trust and friendship. Once you have made your spirit jar, please keep it clean. A dusty, neglected spirit house is a sad sight, and if its inhabitants are not cherished, they will soon leave. Unless it has been designed to attract spirits of the darkness, the house should be kept in a light sunny place, but not somewhere where visitors can see it; it should not attract questions or be an object of curiosity. Never be tempted to show it off to other people. A pleasant location in your bedroom or a quiet work room will work well.

Over the years I have experimented with the contents of spirit jars and learnt that the contents will closely reflect the character of the spirit that takes up residence. A sea spirit will be attracted to a house containing items connected with the sea; a spirit of the woodlands may like to live in a house furnished with twigs, leaves, nuts and other forest items. A crow or magpie spirit might like a house with glass, marbles, sequins and shiny things. A house for an ancestor spirit could contain family mementos. The permutations are endless, so before you make a spirit house, think carefully about the kind of spirit you would like to attract to it, and then find contents that will suit them. Spend plenty of time on this and experiment until you are happy with the result, then seal your jar ready for use. You can choose colours of thread and wax that are appropriate – red for health and positivity, green for earth and growth, blue for the sea; again, experiment until it feels right.

Other items can be used to make houses or resting places for spirits. I treasure a perfect, tiny abandoned bird's nest, beautifully made of moss, twigs, grass and downy feathers, that I found on the ground in a remote churchyard. It lives under a small glass dome to keep it clean, and I am blessed with visits from the spirits of the air. A large sea shell, a branch of twisty hazel wood hung from a beam, a hollow rock with tiny crystals found on a beach on the Jurassic coast of Dorset; anything that feels right to you can be used. Spirit houses should always be found, made, recycled or scavenged. Spending a lot of money on something will defeat the object of the exercise, because spirits cannot be bought or sold. Let the spirit world and intuition lead you, allow your magical creativity free rein and you will make, find or discover something that is perfect for you and for the spirits.

HOUSEHOLD MAGIC

In February, when the days are still short and the weather may be cold and wet, I focus my magical attention on my home. I honour Juno Februata by giving my house a thorough spring clean. Spirit houses and resting places are given special attention, so that the spirits in my home feel respected and cherished. A few drops of a suitable essential oil or herbal tincture can be added to the cleaning water to bless the home and its spirits. I like to use cedarwood or lavender for purification, or tincture of vervain, the enchanter's herb, which is beloved of the spirits. In May, we will learn more about herbcraft, plant spirits and how to make your own tinctures.

There is one place that I do not clean. My house is an old one and has a large fireplace with a beam over it and a big chimney. I use these, not just in Sabbats and major rituals, but in spell-making and everyday witchcraft, and much of my magic happens at the hearth. I have always tried to live in houses with an open fire, because so much of my domestic magic requires the use of the fire and all the activities that go with it. It is a witch's tradition that cobwebs should be left in the chimney. It is a dark and liminal space, between the inside and the outside, and the spirits who live in it are betwixt and between the worlds. They have an affinity with spiders and other creatures of dark places, and like to be left to themselves and not disturbed by cleaning. The chimney itself is swept once a year before winter comes, but otherwise it is left as it is so that its own spirits can work their magic there.

Ensuring that the house is happy and safe is an important and continuing part of my witchcraft. Protecting the home has always been important. It can be protected from intruders and also from harmful energies or unwanted magical intent. The key places that should be protected are the openings in the home. Charms are the magical equivalent of locks on doors and windows, and over the course of the year you will learn how to make various household charms using seasonal materials. We begin in February, the month of Bride, goddess of fire, by thinking about the hearth. The hearth or communal fire is where humans have always gathered and since we first lived in houses, the chimney has been recognised as a place where spirits and magic may enter and leave the home. The hearth is considered particularly vulnerable because, unlike doors and windows, it cannot be closed, and because in the days of 'real' fires, it was also a dangerous place where a damaging fire was most likely to start. Until stoves became widespread in the nineteenth century, the hearth was also where most people did their cooking, and the bubbling cooking pot that was hung over the fire and the witch's cauldron are one and the same thing. Since the invention of central heating, most of us don't think about these things, and fewer still have open fires or stoves that require a chimney. The element of fire is a fundamental part of my witchcraft on a very physical as well as a symbolic level, and my fireplace is used for all kinds of magical activities. Spells are written or made, then burnt and activated as the resulting smoke goes up the chimney. Different types of wood (oak, ash, hazel and apple, for example) have their own ritual uses. Ashes from ritual fires are used in magical preparations; incenses are made and used, wax is melted or I may scry by gazing into the flames. If you have access to an open fire in your home, you may wish to try all of these activities; if you do not, there will be creative alternatives.

Protection charms for the hearth and chimney take many forms, and you can see good examples in museums of charms that have been found when old houses have been renovated, although the best advice is to leave such things *in situ*; they may still be working, providing protection, and creating a happy atmosphere in the home, so removing them could take that protection away and change the atmosphere. There is a growing understanding of traditional household magic, and old charms are now recognised and their purpose acknowledged, instead of being thrown away as rubbish. If you live in an old home, there may be old charms quietly working their magic in hidden corners. Examples of old charms found in chimneys include shoes, especially children's or baby shoes, and horseshoes, all of which were believed to protect the health of the family and bring good fortune, and also some rather gruesome sheeps' hearts stuck with pins and nails and dried by years of chimney smoke, bird skulls and bags or bundles of herbs, which were used to stop unwanted spirits from entering.

February is the time to make charms to protect the hearth, using materials that can be found at this time of year. If you do not have an active fireplace, you can still put charms in a disused chimney or you may be able to find another suitable place in your home;

use your imagination and creativity and find a hiding place where charms can do their work undisturbed. Most of the charms in my home are my own interpretations of traditional ones, so my hearth contains a wooden heart, painted black and with iron nails hammered into it; a plaited and twisted length of black wool, measured from the tip of my middle finger to my nose, with the sharp, dried thorns from a blackthorn branch woven into it; a large and very old iron nail about 4in/10cm long; and a circle of naturally holed witch stones collected from local beaches and threaded on strong wire (*see* July for the magic of witch stones). The colour black works well for chimney charms that will live quietly in darkness. Friends who recently built a new house continued the old tradition by making a special niche in their chimney in which a pair of their baby's old, outgrown shoes were placed and have been left undisturbed to bless and protect the hearth. You can make similar charms to mine, or invent your own. You will find, as you venture more deeply into witchcraft, that you develop your own 'witch senses' and creativity related to your craft, which you will learn to trust. As you begin to work with the spirit world, the spirits will lead you too, and you will begin to create your own very individual charms and spells that feel right to you. Learn to trust those witch senses, and use what feels right, and you will discover your own, very personal practice of witchcraft.

The most effective protection charm for a door or window is a small mirror that will reflect back unwanted attention or energies, and prevent them from entering your home. A small handbag mirror or even a tiny piece of mirror mosaic is ideal for this purpose. Whatever you use should be small and unobtrusive; you do not want it to attract attention. Prepare the mirror in February during the moon's waning phase. The waning phase is always used for magic which will repel or banish; as the moon wanes away, so will whatever you wish to get rid of or repel. Ritually cleanse the mirror, just as you did with your witch's mirror. Ask the blessing of Bride on the mirror then place it on your altar and focus your magical will into it. As you do so, ask a protective spirit to take up residence in the mirror. The mirror should then be left on your altar to charge until the next new moon when it will be ready to use. You should be able to sense the presence of its spirit guardian. It can be placed near the door or window, facing outward so that it can reflect away from the home, and if possible where it cannot easily be noticed.

You may sometimes notice witch balls in the windows of old houses. They look like giant Christmas tree baubles, and are usually made of silvered glass, although green or blue ones are also sometimes found. Witch balls were placed in windows in the eighteenth and nineteenth centuries to protect against malefic witchcraft and reflect back and repel what was not wanted from entering the home. They can sometimes be seen in old cottages in Devon and Dorset, and by the sea an old green glass fishing float may be used for the same purpose. Most people pass them by without understanding what they are for. Old original witch balls are becoming very rare and sought after, and can command high prices in antique shops or at auctions. New ones are now being made in different kinds of glass, they are more affordable and fulfil their traditional magical function, and can be a beautiful addition to a witch's home.

Candles

Candles are used in all the Sabbat rituals and in spell-casting and practical magic. Candlemas is the festival of the returning light and Bride is very much a fire goddess, so February is the right time to think about using and making candles for your rituals. Making your own candles for use in rituals is a very enriching process; burning a candle that you have made yourself creates a very direct, experiential and personal link with the meaning of the ritual, and with the gods and spirits too. I do not use candles made of industrial paraffin wax because it is a by-product of the fossil fuel industry. Making candles using liquid wax, moulds and essential oils is a highly skilled craft but simple candles can be made from sheets of beeswax (obtainable from a beekeeper or craft supplier). The beeswax is laid flat on a piece of paper or craft mat, and a length of candle wick placed at one end of it. The wax can be softened very slightly using a hairdryer and is then rolled tightly around the wick to form a candle. Beeswax has magical importance, which we will learn about in June.

The Frost and Fire Charm

An old West Country curing charm that calls on the threefold goddess can be used at this time of year. This is a spoken charm:

> *There were three ladies came out of the west; one for frost and two for fire.*
> *Out with thee frost, and in with thee fire!*

In this form, it should be spoken at sunset while facing west. It can be used as a charm against persistent colds that won't go away, or chilblains. A small piece of cloth is rubbed on the nose in the case of colds, or on the chilblain; the charm is spoken three times, and the cloth is burnt.

The charm can also be used in reverse form, and spoken facing east at sunrise:

> *There were three ladies come out of the east, two for frost and one for fire.*
> *Out with thee fire, and in with thee frost!*

Used in this form, it is a charm against burns or scalding.

LUPERCALIA

On 15 February the Romans celebrated the festival of Lupercalia; the festival of wolves, one of the most important festivals in the Roman calendar. This ancient rite honoured the she-wolf who suckled the twins Romulus and Remus who founded Rome. It also became associated with the god Pan in later Roman times, and was both a ritual of purging and purification, and also an increasingly orgiastic fertility festival in which young men ran naked or semi-naked through the streets of the city in the name of the goddess, blessing crowds who gathered, especially women, whipping them with thongs cut from the skin of a sacrificed goat. This festival was intended to ensure fertility and could possibly be the Pagan origin of Saint Valentine's Day.

I mark Lupercalia in my own way with a magical ritual in honour of wolves and other animals driven almost to extinction by human activity. So many species, including wolves, bears and eagles, that have been at the heart of our mythologies and magic for aeons, are struggling to survive. We invoke them and call on their power in our rituals, so we owe them our help. I invoke their spirits, and work spells for their protection and increase, and for the people who are working to save them. Perhaps a new vision of Lupercalia; one that honours and celebrates threatened wild creatures, could become part of the Pagan calendar.

The month will end for me with another visit to one of the holy wells to drink the pure water as the ice melts away. The days are noticeably longer now, and a little warmer. The snowdrops that greeted Bride at Candlemas will be long gone, and daffodils and other early spring flowers will be joining the hellebores and primroses. Buds will be starting on some of the trees. As March approaches the golden honey-scented flowers of gorse or furze will be opening to welcome the first bees on the moors. The Witch's Year has truly quickened.

A Spell for February: Candle, Needle and Mirror

The February spell works with the element of fire, with light and with your witch's mirror. Decide on the purpose of your spell. If the purpose is for growth, or to increase something, work the spell when the moon is waxing; if it is to lessen or decrease something, work it when the moon is waning.

You will need

- A candle (dinner or table candle size) in a candle holder. Use a beeswax candle if possible
- A good-sized darning needle

- Your witch's mirror
- Matches or a taper

Method

Focus on your intention and the purpose of your spell. Maintain this focus throughout the work.

Use the needle to scratch something that represents your intention into the candle. This should be something simple: a letter or sign that means something to you. Stick the needle through the candle, about half way down. The needle should pierce right through the candle, so that it protrudes on both sides. As you do this, visualise your intention being achieved and the spell succeeding.

Place the unlit candle in the holder, in front of the mirror, somewhere it can burn safely, because the spell requires you to leave it unattended. I put the candle holder in a large bowl of water or sand. Make sure that the candle is positioned so that you can see its flame reflected in the mirror.

Light the candle with a match or taper and watch it burn. As the flame grows, focus your magical will on the flame and on achieving your objective. Do this silently and with absolute concentration until you sense the moment is right. Then let the spell go. Visualise it going on its way and stop thinking about it. It is important in spell work to trust the magic to do its job and not keep worrying about it once the spell is made, as this will interfere with its effectiveness.

Leave the candle and mirror alone to do their work. When the candle has burnt down so that the needle falls out, the spell is done. The needle can be used again, but any remains of the candle used in the spell should be returned to earth. I do this by burying them in a quiet corner of the garden or putting them on my compost heap (both the cotton wick and beeswax stub are biodegradable).

You can refine this spell by choosing the colour of the candle. A yellow candle (representing air) can be used for purposes connected to the mind or intellect, a red candle (fire) for creative matters or purposes that require passion, a blue candle (water) for spiritual, emotional or relationship purposes, or a green candle (earth) for material matters such as finance or property, or anything related to the environment.

A Meditation for February: A Vision of Bride

The meditation for this month is an encounter with Bride as the triple goddess of the arts, of smithcraft or purification, and of healing. It will enable you to develop your own personal image of the threefold goddess and forge a link with her that will grow and deepen. It calls for you to visualise a fire burning in a hearth; if you live somewhere with a fireplace, you can light an actual fire and look into the flames to work this meditation. Otherwise light a candle. The meditation should be worked during the hours of darkness.

Light your candle or gaze into the fire. Focus on the candle flame or the flames of the fire. Take plenty of time and do this for as long as you need, until your concentration is entirely focused on the flame. Let it fill your vision so that you can see nothing else. Let it fill your thoughts until there is nothing else. Let the flame fill your mind and body.

As you gaze deeper into the flame, a vision of the goddess Bride grows within it. Look at her and notice everything you can about the goddess of fire and light. Around her are the beginnings of growth: snowdrops, green hellebores and primroses and catkins of willow, hazel and alder. She is crowned with golden flames and behind her the ice that wreathes a frozen spring is starting to melt into trickles of fresh, cold water. By her side are two white swans and in the far distance a golden sun is rising between two snow-capped hills.

Greet the goddess and take in every detail of her that you can. As you look, you become aware that she stands at the centre of a great company of people: artists, makers, craftspeople, poets, musicians, creative people of every possible kind, carrying the tools of their arts and crafts. Look closer, and you will see yourself somewhere among them. You are making or creating something. Bride shows you this creative vision of yourself. She holds out her hands to you and gives the art or craft that this new self is making as a gift to you. You take this gift of the goddess of the arts into yourself and keep it safe, and thank the goddess for it.

As you watch, the company of artists fades away and is replaced by a smith or metal-worker who stands next to Bride, working with metal and surrounded by the heat and fire of a forge or furnace. Look at them. Look at what they are making. The smith asks you to look closer and you see that the metal they are working is a version of yourself. You are hot, molten metal in the hands of the smith, but you feel no pain. The smith works the molten metal that is you, passing it through the flames until all impurities and dross fall away from it.

The smith holds out to you a new, tried, tested and pure version of yourself. Bride gives this self as a gift to you; take it into yourself and thank the goddess. As you watch, the smith fades from view and Bride stands alone before you. Cupped in her hands is pure, golden fire. She holds it up to your head and passes it down your body until it fills you. This is the flame of wellness of mind and body. It is the third gift of the goddess. You let it fill your body and mind and bathe in its warmth and light in the presence of Bride and thank her.

You look at Bride again; the threefold goddess. Sometimes she is one, sometimes she is three. Now thank the goddess for all the gifts she has bestowed on you and promise that they will be used to do her work. Bid Bride farewell. As you watch, she fades slowly away until you are once more gazing into the flame of the candle or your fire. Return slowly to the plane of earth.

When the meditation is over, think about how Bride's gifts will become part of your witchcraft. The art or craft skill that you were given may be something that you already do, or it may be something new and unknown that you will decide to learn.

MARCH

March

Awakening and Honouring

The Return of the Light

It is Spring Equinox and a force nine gale is blowing. The year is balanced between darkness and light and the Equinox coincides with a new moon; this morning will see the highest tide of the year. Bursts of sunshine and blue sky alternate with leaden clouds, blown by the storm. At Aberffraw, the tide has been powering up the river estuary for hours and water is lapping around the gardens at the bottom of the street. The medieval bridge has been engulfed and stands, with its arch just above the tide, in the middle of a wide expanse of water where the swollen river has spilled onto the saltmarsh and dunes. All along this side of the island the gale is increasing the power of the Equinoctial tide and forcing water inland. At Porth Trecastell, watched over by the megaliths of Barclodiad-y-Gawres on the headland, the beach has disappeared completely. At Porth Nobla, on a tiny strip of beach by the dunes, a big flock of crows, the winter birds of Bendigeid Fran and the Morrigan, are feeding at the sea's edge, dodging the waves when they come too close, wheeling on the wind, riding the storm and calling to each other as the year moves on into the light and their season ends. Further along the shore the tide is crashing into the sand dunes and eating them away. The wind will rebuild them when the tide has receded. I watch the sand collapse into the water from a vantage point on a very ancient granite outcrop, thought by geologists to be over 600 million years old; it began its life on the bed of a long-gone ancient ocean in the southern hemisphere, and has travelled right around the earth as our planet's tectonic plates move. It is impossible to imagine how many tides and Equinoxes it has seen on its journeys around the earth and through time. Huge waves, several times my height crash onto the rocks, dying away into foam at my feet and soaking me with spray. It feels cold but good. Hundreds of crows and jackdaws, cawing loudly, start up in front of me as more waves crash over the summit of Lion Rock, the highest point on this shore. Suddenly the clouds are gone and

March Associations

Festivals: Isis Navigidium /Festival of Isis of the Ships (4th), Spring Equinox (21st)

Figures: Andraste, Young Sun God/ Horus/ Belinus/ Mabon/ Maponus

More Than Human: Primroses, gorse, hares, catkins, Equinox high tides

Totems and Symbols: Hare, Tinners' Rabbits

the sunlight turns the sea to gold. From the cromlech of Ty Newydd, a little way inland, I can see the peaking spring tide pushing its way up headlands and washing over reefs and islets, all the way from Rhoscolyn in the west, past Cymyran and Rhosneigr and round to Barclodiad. The relict landscape of Tywyn Trewan, stretching for miles between me and the sea, and now interrupted by the runway of a military airfield, is an endless mass of gorse blossom, the flower of the Equinox, that greets the young sun god as the Equinox passes and the darkness of winter recedes.

March sees the return to the earth of the lord of growing things when the light grows greater than the dark at Spring Equinox. It is the month of mad March hares and of the first buds and golden flowers that greet the growing light when life awakens from the long sleep of winter. The elemental tide of the year begins anew. We honour the power and beauty of the young sun at the Equinox, find a familiar spirit and make a wand for magical work. Witchcraft moves outdoors as we plant seeds and plan a witch's garden. A walk in the woods will provide treasures for the seasonal rituals that lie ahead.

At the beginning of March in Greek and Roman times, the great festival of Isis of the Ships (Isidis Navigidium) was celebrated all around the Mediterranean Sea. The worship of the Egyptian goddess Isis had spread throughout the Graeco-Roman world. One of her many titles was Stella Maris, or Star of the Sea, and she was protectress of ships and sailors, including the ships that brought the grain from North Africa to feed the people of Rome. On 4 March, the first day of the sailing season, great processions and feasts took place, and model boats, laden with offerings of flowers and fruit for the goddess, were floated out to sea.[2] Begin the month by honouring Isis at the seashore or by a lake or river. Undertaking a beach clean or removing rubbish from a riverbank is a great way to celebrate this festival, or a physical offering can be made to Isis.

THE MONTH OF GOLD

Primroses, celandines, daffodils and gorse are in full bloom. The weather may still be cold but the golden flowers of March attract the first bees which are just awakening. In Devon and Cornwall, primroses line the lanes and pathways and grow like garlands around the old holy wells. In the Celtic lands the primrose is considered to be the passport to Faerie or the Otherworld, and a primrose flower picked in March will grant you admittance to the hollow hills (the megalithic mounds and tombs) to feast and dance with Tylwyth Teg/Fair Family (Wales), or the Sidhe (Ireland), or just the Others, on the magical nights of May Eve or Midsummer's Eve. Primroses are believed to grow profusely in the Otherworld. Working with the Faeries, the spirits of the land, by whatever name you wish to call them, is a key part of the practice of witchcraft. If you can come to know and understand them, then your witchcraft will be enriched, often in unexpected ways. (We will learn more about the land spirits in April.)

Gorse or furze blooms everywhere in March, especially on the moorlands and heaths. It is said that gorse is in flower somewhere on Ynys Môn (Anglesey) every day of the year, but in March, its blossoms cover great swathes of the dunelands and moors, giving off a subtle honey scent that is full of enchantment and has erotic associations. In Wales it is associated with the Faeries and land spirits; it represents the young sun at the Equinox and gorse was burned in his honour at this time. It is visited by the first bees of the season and mead made with gorse honey was highly prized for its magical properties. It is very unlucky to bring the flowers indoors, but they make a good yellow dye that can be used to colour eggs at Equinox and Easter.

Primrose Anointing Oil

Making primrose anointing oil is a good way of harnessing the magical power of this Faerie flower. Made during March, it will be ready for use on May Eve and throughout the magical year. Three drops placed on the forehead will act as a passport to the hollow hills and facilitate encounters with the Others. It can also be used to anoint wands and other tools for magical work with the Faeries. This preparation is for external use only.

An anointing oil is different from an essential oil, in which the essence of the plant is extracted using steam. It is an oil infused with the plant and is easily made at home. I use sweet almond oil as a base oil when making anointing oils. It is light, non-greasy and does not have a strong scent. It is also inexpensive. Olive oil or other greasy cooking oils are not recommended.

Primroses can be gathered from special places, especially those associated with the Faeries or the spirit world, to increase the magical effect of the oil. I have made oil from primroses growing under a hawthorn tree on the edge of my village, and from a beautiful churchyard in mid-Wales built on a mound that was sacred in pre-Christian times. The colour of the finished oil will vary according to where the primroses are gathered.

You will need

- A clean and dry glass jar with an airtight lid (a preserving jar is ideal)
- Sweet almond oil (or another base oil of your choice)
- Primrose flowers (the quantities are up to you).

Method

Pick your primrose flowers, asking permission of the plants first. They should be picked on a sunny day in March when the moon is waxing, and should be dry (damp flowers may go mouldy). Do not be greedy; take only what you need, and pick the flowers carefully so that you do not damage the plants or their roots.

Put the flowers in the jar and cover them with the oil. The amount of oil and flowers you use is entirely up to you. Fasten the lid tightly on the jar.

Leave the flowers to infuse, at least until the next full moon (longer if you wish). Sunlight will help the infusion process. Turn the jar and give it a gentle shake every few days. The oil will gradually take on the colour of the primroses.

Strain the oil (compost or recycle the flowers) and put it into clean, dry bottles for use. It can be used throughout the year, especially on May Eve and Midsummer Eve, the traditional times for visiting the hollow hills. I return any leftover oil to the earth in March before making a new batch for the coming season.

EQUINOX: THE RETURN OF THE LIGHT

The Spring Equinox is the culmination of the magical work of March. It occurs three quarters of the way through the month and many of the activities and customs of March prepare for the Equinox. Whilst the last Sabbat, Candlemas, was a festival of the maiden goddess, at the Equinox we celebrate the young god in all his growing glory. To the Egyptians the young, virile sun god was Horus, lord of the eastern horizon, and many witches and occultists still honour him with this name. To others he is Frey, Arthur of the shining spear, Belinus, Lleu or Lugh, or Cernunnos, the lord of all that grows, the stag with the sun between his antlers. The new astrological great tide of the year begins at Spring Equinox when the sun enters Aries, the cardinal sign of fire. The fire tide will flow or rise until it peaks at Midsummer; for the next three months the earth will experience its maximum period of energy and growth. The god has returned to the earth, so the constellation of Orion, our image of the god in the winter sky, now rises during the hours of daylight and sets much earlier. At the Equinox he can still be seen in the west in the evening after sunset; by Beltane he will no longer be visible in the night sky.

Perhaps more than any other Sabbat, the Spring Equinox has a profound and often unacknowledged effect on the psyche and the emotions as well as the body. The Equinox itself is a very strange moment; a point of complete balance, when the world hangs poised between the powers of darkness and light. Experiencing this to the full can bring a deep occult understanding and strength on a physical level as well as emotionally and spiritually. Once the moment of balance is passed, the world embraces the light and springs into growth. The awe-inspiring power of the young sun god is overwhelming; it is the life force itself and it changes everything. These effects are even more pronounced if a new or full moon occurs at, or close to, the Equinox. The gravitational pulls of the sun and moon combine together to create very high spring tides which affect humans wherever they live, because the water in our bodies is affected by the tidal pull. Observing a very high equinoctial tide can be a marvellous experience that will bring an instinctive understanding of the Equinox; a visit to the coast at this time is highly recommended. Because of this combination of effects, Spring Equinox can be quite a difficult time. The sun is driving light and growth forward, trying to push the world through the point of balance and banish the dark part of the year, and it can feel as if the light is struggling with the dark. Equinox may make people aggressive, or over-emotional, or accident-prone. It can be a very edgy time, or an exhilarating rollercoaster ride for the psyche. Witches understand this; our Equinox rites and customs are designed to bring us a deep and rewarding understanding of its power and beauty, and to let us experience to the full the moment of perfect balance between light and dark and celebrate the leap forward into joyous light and growth as the wheel of the year turns.

Modern Pagan Equinox rituals can sometimes seem less significant than those of Beltane or Midsummer, but it is important to understand that to the peoples of Northern Europe the moment when the light became greater than the dark was amongst the most important and auspicious days of the year, when rituals were enacted to ask the gods to make the land fertile for the coming growing season, and the fields and flocks were ritually blessed. If you have a garden, this is therefore the time to ask the goddess and god to bring fertility and good health to all that you grow. Before the Equinox, make sure the garden is clean and tidy and ready for the burst of growth that is about to start, then make an offering to the goddess and god in the garden, and process slowly and purposefully around it, walking sunwise, thanking the goddess and god and the spirits of the land, and asking for their blessing on all the plants and trees and the ground itself.

Plan what you intend to grow in the coming season and prepare the ground for a witch's garden of your favourite magical plants. If you have room, you may wish to design an area of the garden dedicated to the goddess and god. This need not be expensive: I have a pillar stone that represents the god and a small circular pool that catches the light of the full moon as a shrine to the goddess. A witch garden can be created almost anywhere; one of my favourites is on the tiny balcony of a friend's high-rise city apartment. During March I sow most of my flower and herb seeds. Seeds should always be sown during the moon's waxing phase. If you do not have access to a garden, acknowledge the season and seek the blessing of goddess and god on the green spaces that you visit, and by sowing a pot of sprouting salad seedlings on a windowsill just after the new moon that precedes the Equinox.

THE MARCH HARE

The month of March belongs to the hare. 'Mad as a March hare' we say, because their exuberant, exhibitionist behaviour at this time makes them fitting symbols for the crazy growth surge of the Equinox. My father and I once watched a hare race across a beach and leap and frolic in the waves at the edge of the sea on a wild, windy March day in Ynys Môn. All round the world, hares are associated with the moon, and in China and India people see the image of a hare in the moon. The 'madness' of the March hare is essentially mating behaviour, and is a spectacular sight if you can witness it.

The hare can be a potent symbol of the Spring Equinox. The idea of a Saxon goddess called Eostre associated with both the hare and the Equinox appears to be a recent development (the veneration of Eostre is, of course, a lovely thing). There is just one historical reference to her, by the Saxon historian Bede, which actually associates her with April, and has no reference to hares, so we will return to her, and to eggs and the magic of birds and flight, next month. In fact, Bede mentions a different goddess, Hretha, in connection with the Equinox. In Roman times the British tribes, especially the Iceni of East Anglia led by their queen Boudicca, venerated a goddess called Andraste. Boudicca invoked Andraste before her decisive battle with the Romans, when she performed divination by releasing a hare from under her cloak. It is therefore reasonable to assume that the hare was associated with Andraste, and if we are looking for a goddess to link with this time of year, then the warlike nature of Andraste fits well with the edgy energy of the Equinox, and fighting, boxing mad March hares do indeed appear to be under her influence.

The Welsh saint Melangell is the patron saint of hares and a protectress of animals, who is honoured by many witches and Pagans. In a story that seems more Pagan than Christian in its symbolism, she sheltered a hare from pursuing hunters under her cloak. Her remote church at Pennant Melangell in Powys is a beautiful place of great peace and sanctity.

Hares have always been associated with shape-shifting as well as with the moon, so witches feel a close affinity with the hare. At her trial the seventeenth-century Scottish witch Isobel Gowdie recounted the spell she used to transform herself into a hare:

> *I shall go into a hare, with sorrow and sighing and muckle care,*
> *I shall go in the devil's name, aye while I come home again.*

A well-known folk tale tells of a party of hunters who chase a hare. Their hounds almost catch it, and one of them bites its leg before the terrified hare manages to escape. They come to the cottage of an old woman and find that she is breathless, exhausted and is bleeding from a wounded leg.

The design of three hares with their ears meeting in the centre of a circle is found across the world. It is a visual puzzle in which the hares actually only have three ears between them, with their points meeting in the centre of the image, but on first glance they appear to have two ears each. This is an ancient image that occurs in Buddhism, Islam and Christianity; the oldest known version comes from the Buddhist Mogao cave temple in China and dates from the sixth century CE. The three hares are also found at the medieval cathedral at Paderborn in Germany and on other ecclesiastical buildings in Europe. The image is particularly associated with Dartmoor in Devon, where it is known as the 'Tinners' Rabbits', because of its historic associations with local tin mining. The Tinners' Rabbits can be found carved on 28 churches on and around Dartmoor including those at Chagford, Widecombe-in-the-Moor and South Tawton, and elsewhere in Devon at Broadclyst and Sampford Courtenay, and are the emblem of the Dartmoor town of Chagford. They also occur in Dorset, Somerset and Cornwall. The Tinners' Rabbits have become a part of the folklore and magic of Devon; new and beautiful images of them proliferate and the Grimspound Border Morris dance side created a dance in their honour which is danced throughout the West Country. The web of poetic connections between hares, the moon and Spring Equinox makes the Tinners' Rabbits or Three Hares a potent symbol for witches and Pagans, so March is a good time to go looking for them in Devon and elsewhere in celebration of the Equinox.

Many witchcraft activities in March involve working with wood, and preparing it for use later in the year. Trees have started into growth and their sap is rising, but they have not yet come into leaf. Wood that is cut during March will be strong and supple and will dry and season well. On an elemental level, working with wood in March is very appropriate. Wood springs from the earth, but is primarily associated with fire. Before the Equinox, the great tide of the year is the earth tide and is almost at its lowest ebb, and at the Equinox it turns and becomes the flowing tide of fire. Working with wood unites both elements within us, and our spell this month also involves creating a wooden talisman. Find time to visit woodlands in March, feel the first stirrings of growth, and with the blessing of the tree spirits, gather wood for use in your witchcraft.

The Witch's Wand

The wand is an extension of the witch's magical will and has many different purposes. It is used to cast the circle, in ritual, and to make spells. It is interchangeable with the athame, or ritual knife, used by Wiccans. The advantage of a wand is that the witch can, and should, make it themselves. It should not be used or touched by anyone else without the witch's permission.

Making a wand is a long process that cannot be rushed; the wood is cut at Spring Equinox when the sap begins to rise, and is left to season over the summer then finished and consecrated at Autumn Equinox. The first task is to choose what kind of wood to use. Any wood can be used; the choice is entirely up to the individual witch. Each tree has its own magical significance and virtues and it is important to choose something that reflects your personality and intentions.

The Celtic Tree Alphabet is a complex magical system that can provide a wealth of knowledge to help you make your choice. The Tree Alphabet is also a ritual calendar in which each tree is assigned to a month, so if you wish, you can choose a tree that aligns with your birthday or some other significant date. On a practical level, some woods are much easier to work with than others. You might wish to let the gods or spirits make the choice for you. The woods most commonly used for wands are:

Ash: The ash is a very vigorous, strong-growing tree that signifies clarity of thought, understanding, and the energy of growth. In the Northern tradition, Yggdrasil, the World tree, is an ash. It is a link between the outer and inner worlds, and embodies both male and female energies, and both sun and moon. Deities associated with the ash include: Odin, Gwydion, Math, Arianrhod, Mars, Poseidon, and Nemesis.

Oak: The oak signifies strength, courage, the doorway to the mysteries, and rules the light half of the year from Midwinter to Midsummer. The Greek oracle at Dodona was an oak tree; the words of Apollo were heard in the sound of its leaves rustling in the wind. Deities associated with the oak include: Cernunnos, Herne, Zeus/Jupiter, Apollo. Dionysus, Thor, Pan, the Dagda, Bride, Diana/Artemis, Demeter and Athene.

Hazel: The hazel signifies wisdom, magical knowledge, intuition and divination, and it is the wood traditionally used for magicians' wands or staffs. Deities associated with the hazel include: Mercury/Hermes, Thoth, Thor, Aengus.

Willow: Willow is the tree of the moon goddess. It signifies psychic powers, lunar magic, and the power of the waters and the tides. All moon goddesses are associated with the willow, including Luna, Selene, Diana, Hecate, Persephone, Circe, Artemis, Hera and Ceridwen.

Apple: The apple signifies inspiration, fruitfulness, love. Deities associated with the apple include: Aphrodite, Ishtar, Ceridwen, Eros and Dionysus.

Hawthorn: The hawthorn is the supreme Faerie tree and is a doorway to the Otherworld. It signifies enchantment and all aspects of Faerie magic. Deities associated with the hawthorn include Olwen, Blodeuwedd, Cardea, Hera, and also the hosts of Faerie and spirits of the land.

Rowan: The rowan signifies protection against sorcery and strengthens psychic powers. Deities associated with the rowan include Bride and Freya.

Holly: The holly rules the dark half of the year from Midsummer to Midwinter. It signifies protection, courage, the magic of dreams, and fire magic. Deities associated with the holly include Taranis, Thor, Gwyn ap Nudd, Holda and the spirits of the Wildwood.

Blackthorn: The blackthorn is a powerful wood that is used for banishing, cleansing and purifying. It signifies the powers of fate and the Underworld. Deities associated with the blackthorn include Saturn, Nemesis, Lucifer, the Morrigan and Morgan le Fay.

My own wand is made of pale, almost white ash wood from a local forest. Tendrils of honeysuckle had twisted themselves tightly round the tree, making it grow in a series of spirals that seemed like an embodiment of the vigorous strength of the ash. I removed the bark and the honeysuckle, leaving a twisted spiral wand with its own intense energy. The sap was rising so strongly when I cut the wand that I was able to gently peel the bark away from the wood with just my fingers, leaving the surface free from marks or cuts.

When you have chosen the wood you wish to use, find a suitable tree. Remember its location, because in autumn you will return to it to consecrate your wand and work with the tree spirit. The wand must be cut from a living tree because dead wood is dry and brittle. The only exception to this is driftwood found on the seashore which, if left to dry out, can make a good wand.

Method

Ask permission of the tree first, and seek the blessing of its indwelling spirit. Cut only the piece that you need; never be greedy or take more than you need. Cut the wood cleanly with a sharp blade, being careful not to damage the bark or harm the tree. The wand should measure from your elbow to the tip of your middle finger.

When you have cut your wand, cut off a lock of your hair and leave it at the base of the tree as a token of your gratitude. It is important to give a gift of a physical part of yourself to the tree in return for its gift of a part of itself to you. Gifts such as money or food will not create a bond with the tree.

Then sit peacefully for a while with the tree, meditating and thanking its spirit for the gift of your wand. You may see a vision of the tree spirit.

If you intend to remove the bark from your wand, it should be done straight away as the rising sap will make this task easier. If not, leave the wand just as it is. It should be stored in a cool, dry place where it will season over the summer months, ready for you to finish at the Autumn Equinox.

PREPARING WOOD FOR RITUAL FIRES

The Beltane festival at the beginning of May calls for a ritual fire made of nine different kinds of wood. These should be gathered and prepared around Spring Equinox so that they will dry and make a good fire at Beltane. For the Beltane fire you will need to gather twigs of birch, oak, ash, hazel, willow, hawthorn, rowan, apple and holly, measuring from the bottom of your palm to the tip of your middle finger. There is no need to cut living wood for this; fallen wood can be used and a woodland walk on a March afternoon should provide most of what you need. Gather the twigs into a bundle and bind them with ivy. If your Beltane tradition calls for two fires (*see* May), make two bundles. Keep the bundles somewhere dry, so that they will be ready to use at Beltane. In witchcraft nothing is wasted; the ashes from ritual fires can be saved and used in spells and other practical magic.

Practice: The Spring Equinox Ritual

The Spring Equinox Sabbat should celebrate the magical moment when the light grows greater than the dark and the whole earth springs into growth as the great tide of the year flows into the element of fire. It is a festival of the young virile god who is both the sun and the lord of all that grows, and includes a small fertility ritual. The goddess is present too as the dark, endless power of the tides and the moment of balance itself. This ritual should be celebrated as close to the actual Equinox as possible, so that you can experience the physical as well as the spiritual aspects of the season.

Preparation

The altar is dressed with yellow flowers (daffodils are best; do not bring primroses or gorse blossom indoors), a phallic pine cone (a symbol of the god) and hawk feathers if you can find them. The ritual calls for a yellow candle, a dish of earth and some sunflower seeds. Food for an Equinox feast should be golden and can include honey in celebration of the first bees of the year. If you have alcohol at your feast, use mead, ideally made with gorse blossom honey.

The Equinox ceremony takes place at night, but during the hours of daylight, take your witch's mirror and use it to reflect the light of the sun onto your body, from head to foot. This creates a physical link with the growing sun god and prepares you for the ritual. Honour and welcome the god as you do it.

The ritual

First cast your circle, then call on the goddess as lady of the tides to be present. She is the lady not only of the tides of the sea, the moon and the sun, but of the great tides behind birth, death and rebirth that rise and fall ceaselessly and that govern all things. The occultist Dion Fortune wrote of her:

I am that soundless, boundless, bitter sea,
All tides are mine and answer unto me,
Tides of the air, tides of the inner earth,
The secret, silent tides of death and birth.[3]

She is the lady from whom we are all born, and to whom we all return. She has many names: Veiled Isis; Binah (the dark supernal mother of the Qabalah), Hecate, Persephone, Levanah of the moon, and Luna are just a few of them, and she can be invoked with one or all of them, or with whatever name feels right to you. The goddess in this guise is the balance of the Equinox itself and watches over us as the great tide turns. Her presence is felt as a calm stillness; the moment when the world hangs poised between darkness and light.

Then the yellow candle is lit on the altar and the god is welcomed. The following invocation can be used as the candle is lit:

Thee we invoke, O light of life
Be thou a bright flame before us
Be thou a smooth path beneath us
Be thou a guiding star above us.

The god can be honoured as the Celtic sun deity Lleu (Wales)/Lugh (Ireland), who is pictured as golden-haired and bearing a shining spear, as the Egyptian god Horus, Hawk of the sun and lord of the eastern horizon and the sunrise, as the Romano-British god Belinus, as Cernunnos, the antler-crowned horned god, or as all of these.

Next the sunflower seeds are planted. If you are working with a group, one person should hold up the dish of earth while another, representing the god, ritually plants the seeds in the earth. As this is done, concentrate on the seeds and visualise them germinating, trees bursting into leaf, and animals giving birth. Bless the seeds in the name of the god. After the ritual they should be nurtured carefully before being shared and planted outside at Beltane. Later in the summer, with the blessing of the sun god, you and your friends should have bright golden sunflowers to enjoy.

Then seek your vision of the god. This is an intense moment of inward meditation when all who are present visualise the god at the moment of Equinox, stepping into the light under the guardianship of the goddess as lady of the tides. The

Equinox has come; the dark part of the year has passed and the new great tide of fire has begun. From this moment on, life and growth will return in full force. Goddess and god are thanked and depart, and the circle is closed. Then the feast of golden food and drink can be shared.

A Spell for March: The Rowan Cross Amulet

The rowan cross is a very traditional protective amulet, and there are numerous versions of an old charm that goes:

Rowan tree and red thread, puts the witches to their speed.

This spell makes a great witch gift. Amongst other things, it will be effective against pesky chronic ailments, especially arthritis and all pains in the joints, lightning strike, venomous snakes, mischievous spirits and malefic witchcraft. It should be kept about the person, and is usually carried in the pocket or wallet. It is best made in March when the sap is rising but the tree is not yet in leaf. The trick with this spell is to find and identify a rowan tree before its leaves appear. The rowan, also called the mountain ash, is a small, hardy upland tree that thrives in rocky ground and poor soil. It bears beautiful red berries at the beginning of August that are also used in witchcraft, and is common in mountainous areas, and on Dartmoor and Exmoor close to where I live. Cultivars can increasingly be found in city parks and gardens too, but finding a rowan tree in March can be something of a magical initiative test, especially as the old witches' tradition specifies that, when working magic with rowan wood or berries, the witch must always work with a tree they have never used before.

The equal-armed cross was an important magical symbol long before the advent of Christianity. It signifies the four cardinal directions, the four seasons, the four elements, the four lunar quarters and the unity of male and female principles.

You will need

- Two rowan twigs the same length as your middle finger
- A length of red woollen thread, measured from the tip of your middle finger to the point of your nose (with your arm outstretched). As with all magic, using measurements based on your own body personalises the magic and increases the power of the spell

Method

Politely ask the rowan tree's permission to cut your twigs, and thank it for its gift. Cut the twigs cleanly. Do not damage the tree, and take only what you need.

Take the two twigs and hold them together so that they form an equal-armed cross. Wrap the thread round the centre of the cross, securing the twigs, concentrating on the idea of protection. Repeat over and over 'rowan tree and red thread' until almost all the thread has been wrapped around the twigs.

Secure the cross and seal the magic by tying three knots in the thread, with a final burst of concentrated magical intent as you do so.

Keep the cross on your altar until the next new moon, when it will be ready to use.

FAMILIAR SPIRITS

In this month's meditation, you will meet your first familiar spirit who will accompany you and aid you in your magic-making. Working with a familiar spirit is a central part of witchcraft; active engagement with the world of spirit is what distinguishes the witch from those who simply follow the Pagan spiritual path. Study this section carefully; allow plenty of time for the meditation and find a quiet place where you will not be disturbed.

Witches often have several familiar spirits. The first familiar is traditionally an animal from the spirit world. You will build up a relationship with your animal familiar, and they will soon become a trusted and valued companion. They will help with your spells and may be invited to your rituals; they will rest in the spirit house that you made earlier in the year, and become an important part of the magic that you will make throughout the year.

Working with the spirit world means learning to expect the unexpected, so you should not have any preconceptions about what kind of animal will come and join you. At the beginning of my own journey into witchcraft, my initiator shared with me the following visualisation. I was completely surprised by what came to me; it was not from a species that I had previously felt connected to in any way, but it has become my lifelong guide and magical companion. It is especially important to put aside any thoughts of spirit contact with earthly pets that you have known and loved that have passed away, or with living species that you feel a close affinity with. This is about something very different because the animal familiar carries within it all the magical essence and meanings of its species. Just empty your mind and accept whatever comes to you.

Finding a spirit companion is an exciting and beautiful thing, and it is tempting to tell everyone. You will notice that I have not described my familiar to you, or told you what kind of animal it is. The relationship between the witch and any spirit is an intensely personal and private one. If you speak of it to others, your familiar spirit may leave and not return. We mentioned earlier the magical advice: 'To know, to dare, to will and to keep silent', and in this, as in many other magical matters, it is a very wise one.

As soon as you have returned from this meditation, take your journal and write or draw everything you can remember about your meeting with your familiar spirit. Do not rush this; take as much time as you need. You may be surprised at the amount you can remember. When you have finished, eat or drink something to earth yourself fully. This meditation can be a very intense experience and it is quite usual to feel tired afterwards.

Once you have your first familiar spirit, it will become a central part of your witchcraft. You should work regularly with the familiar. Make time at least once a week (that is, in each of the lunar quarters) to meet with the spirit. Repeat the meditation journey if you wish; when you get used to meeting the spirit, you may not need to do this; you will be able to relax and close your eyes and the spirit will come to you.

Each time you meet, you will learn more about each other. Invite the familiar to rest in the spirit jar that you made in February. You may notice that the spirit jar has a strong and very different energy when the familiar is there. The familiar may also come to you in dreams or visions; this is a real sign of the strength of the bond between you that should be welcomed. You can use your witch's mirror to call to the familiar. It is very important to keep up contact with the spirit; if you neglect it, it will assume that you do not wish to work with it any more, and will leave and not return. You may find as the connection with your familiar deepens, that you take on some of the characteristics of that animal in your everyday life. This is quite natural and a positive thing.

After several meetings, it will be time to ask the familiar spirit to work magic with you. There is no set way of doing this; it will come naturally to you. You can ask it to help with your spells by adding its magical will to your own. When a spell is made, ask the familiar to charge it with its own spirit force. Always be respectful and polite when working with the familiar spirit, and treat it as you would expect to be treated by a close friend. You can also ask your familiar spirit to be present at your Sabbats and other rituals. It will become your closest magical companion throughout the rest of the Witch's Year. In the future you may acquire other familiar spirits (usually not in animal form), but the spirit animal will be your first and your lifelong friend and will be with you always.

Meditation for March: A Spirit Friend and Guardian

Picture yourself in an open country landscape on a sunny March day. A gentle breeze is blowing. You are walking on a pleasant path over the brow of a hill towards woodland. There are gorse bushes with golden flowers in full bloom and primroses and celandines line the path at your feet. As you walk towards the woodland, the sun disappears behind clouds and the wind begins to blow more strongly. The sky grows darker and you hurry towards the trees. As you reach them it starts to rain heavily. Rain spatters on the bare branches and you press deeper into the woodland, looking for shelter. Straight ahead of you is a huge, ancient oak tree, the biggest tree in these woods. At the base of its gnarled trunk is a cavity large enough for you to shelter, and you crawl inside out of the rain. The space is surprisingly large. It carries the rich scents of leaves, wood and earth, and you can hear the innumerable rustlings and scrapings of countless tiny creatures. Ahead of you a narrow passage leads down into the earth, dimly lit by a greenish light. Follow the passage down, down, into the depths of the earth. After a while it levels out, and you are walking along a passage with rocky walls. Keep on walking. The light grows dimmer, until eventually you reach the end of the passage. The light fades away completely and you are standing alone in total darkness and silence. You can see and hear nothing. Wait here; you are not afraid of the darkness; it feels full of magic.

Now call silently. Call for a spirit to come to you. Call silently in the darkness. Call with all your magical will. After what seems like a long time, two eyes appear as points of light in the distance. As you call, they come closer. You can see nothing else, only the eyes. Let your eyes meet the spirit's eyes; make eye contact. Immediately a strong bond is made between you and the spirit animal. The animal comes closer and closer, and as it does so a light grows around it until it stands or perches beside you and you can see it clearly. Look at the spirit animal and notice everything that you can about it: its size, shape, colour; look at every detail that you can. Use all your inward senses. Reach out and touch your animal and the bond between you will grow deeper. Project a feeling of love and trust, as you would with a living creature. Tell the animal your name (this should be the name that you use in witchcraft and magical work). It may tell you its name, but this may happen at a later time, after you have worked magic together. Ask the animal if it will consent to be your familiar spirit. If the animal speaks to you; listen carefully to its words (whether or not they make sense to you), but do not try to interpret them; just take them into yourself. Pledge yourself to work with your new familiar. Stay here a while together, enjoying the spirit's company.

Now it is time to return. Your familiar moves away along the passage and you follow. If it is a large animal or bird, it may let you ride on its back. You travel with it back along the passage in the earth until you can see in the distance ahead of you the light at the entrance under the great oak tree. You reach the entrance and step out into the woodland with your familiar spirit. The rain has stopped and the sun is shining through the bare branches of the trees. Look once more at your familiar. Then thank it. You bid each other farewell, knowing that you will be together again soon. The animal spirit disappears back into the cavity in the oak tree. Walk slowly back across the landscape and back into your everyday self.

APRILE

April

Growth and Blossoming

Great Alchemy at Work

At the beginning of the month there was the blackthorn winter; freezing cold winds and delicate white blossoms on dark bare thorny stems. Now the weather is warm and it is the time of the hawthorn. Everything is growing strongly now. Cow parsley, mares' tails and iris stems are springing up in ditches and on riverbanks, and on the hedges and the paths every plant and herb jostles for space. The hawthorns are everywhere, in the hedges, woodlands and heaths: they dot the exposed fields and find a foothold in the sand on the dunes, or grow in cracks in the rocks where no other trees will grow. They are so commonplace and unassuming that most of the time, we don't notice them at all.

In all the Celtic lands they are the supreme Faerie trees that must be honoured and respected because to disrespect or damage a hawthorn would be a grave insult to the Tylwyth Teg, the Fair Family or the Little People. The most special trees are honoured with offerings and must be greeted when passing by. There are some rare trees which bear deep pink or red blossom, and these are especially blessed. Now, suddenly, the hawthorns have become visible. Their fat buds have burst open and the creamy white blossom is appearing everywhere. From the megalithic mound of Bryn Celli Ddu the fields in all directions are a mass of white, interrupted by small patches of green. The woods look as if snow has fallen on them.

Blossom drifts along the hedgerows and rings the tidal pools. The narrow paths that head along the riverbank to the stepping stones are drenched in it, and close up it has its own distinctive scent; sweet and sour at the same time. The whole land is transformed by the blossom; it is intoxicating. I make my way onto the vast expanse of dunes that stretch for miles opposite the mountains of Llŷn on the mainland. In this desert of sand dunes and saltmarsh everything is pared back to its essentials and the landscape is constantly torn away and remade by the wind. Paths disappear and dunes spring up, only to be dismantled again.

April Associations

Festivals: None
Figures: The Others/Faeries/Tylwyth Teg/Aos Sí
More Than Human: Birds, eggs and feathers, hawthorn blossom
Totems and Symbols: Egg, hawthorn

Skylarks constantly call and a lone marsh harrier rides the wind. Here the hawthorn trees are stunted and bent over by the incessant wind into fantastic shapes. A solitary crow leads me to two perfect blossoming hawthorns: one is upright and its crown is level with my shoulders; the trunk of the other bends downwards and hugs the ground. Here I sit and wait, offer thanks and ask the blessing of the Tylwyth Teg. Out of the corner of my eye, I glimpse something watching me, and somewhere, amidst the calling skylarks, I catch the sound of wild laughter on the wind.

In April the goddess of dawn and light presides and the magic of birds, eggs and feathers is everywhere. Hawthorn trees show the way to Faerie and we learn the old art of 'sitting out' and how to See. This is a busy month in which everything is growing strongly. A place is prepared for the magical plants that will become friends and allies. A new broom sweeps us into spring and the hollow hills await the brave.

As we saw last month, Eostre was the Saxon goddess of dawn and light. She was associated with April, and gave her name to Easter, which usually (but not always) falls in April.[4] Find time to salute Eostre at dawn in April and greet her with bright colours. It is impossible to sleep through the dawn chorus as the sound of birds fills the morning and nesting has begun in earnest. In the Northern Pagan tradition, birds link the three worlds: they carry messages up Yggdrasil, the World Tree, from its roots and from our world to the home of the gods.

The egg is a symbol of creation, of potential and of new life at this time of year. It is central to the Orphic Mysteries of Greece, and symbolises the Great Work in alchemy. The use of eggs in springtime rituals predates Easter in many places. Ukrainian *pysanky* are beautifully decorated eggs that are given as gifts and eaten at both Pagan and Easter feasts. They are painted with liquid wax using traditional patterns and then placed in dye. After they have been dyed the wax is removed to reveal the patterns. Eggs can be used to decorate your altar in April. They can be painted or dyed with food colouring.

A wreath of feathers is easy to collect at this time of year and makes a good addition to your altar. Like much of the more than human world, birds are struggling to survive. In many places, their habitats and food supplies are under threat from human activity. Witches have always befriended animals and birds, so if you are attracted to the idea of bird magic, and especially if your familiar spirit is a bird, spend some time getting to know more about the birds that live in your neighbourhood and try to help them in practical ways, perhaps by providing habitats and food for them. They will reward you not just with their presence, but on a subtle magical level.

A MAGICAL FLYING BOX

This very special charm is based on something I once bought by accident at a jumble sale. I was attracted to a very battered little 'treen' wooden box; the kind made for tourists in the early twentieth century, with a picture of the Scottish Highlands on the lid. It called to me magically and I bought it for pennies. Inside, nestling on a bed of cotton wool were the remains of three broken grey-blue speckled eggs, two tiny feathers and two battered 1930s cigarette cards depicting a yellowhammer and a moorhen. It was an old flying spell from who knows where, and it exuded a quiet magical power. I have kept it safe on an altar ever since and use it when I want to communicate with bird spirits or to travel in vision through the air with them. If you are lucky enough to find the remains of birds' eggs on the ground after the chicks have hatched, save them carefully. Find some small feathers and whatever else seems right to you. Search out an old box or tin from a junk shop, car boot sale or similar, and make your own little nest of bird magic.

Birds lead us to the elemental spirits of air. The spirits of air are ephemeral, fleeting creatures that may wink or flutter into our consciousness for a few brief moments and then be gone. To sense their presence is a strange and profound magical experience. The spirits of air can be experienced outdoors on a windy day. Focus your magical will on your breathing and on the air that surrounds you, and you will sense their fluttering invisible presence. To attract the spirits of air and light into your home, obtain a few old loose pieces of broken chandeliers. These pieces of old glass contain prisms that refract and reflect light and they can be bought very cheaply in antique or junk shops. Hang them in a sunny window, and as the sunlight falls on them, they will shine rapidly moving rainbows around the room and onto your face and body, and you will immediately feel the presence of the spirits of air and light. Letting the intensely coloured light flow over you can be a health-giving experience. On a magical level, air is the element of thought and the mind, so the magical atmosphere that is generated will bring clarity and new ideas.

SPIRITS OF THE LAND

In April, as the trees come into leaf and spring flowers and blossoms open, you will sense that everything around you is alive and that the spirits of the land surround you. It is time to get to know these beings we call Faeries, the Tylwyth Teg, the Sidhe or just the Others. 'Away with the fairies' is an insulting term used to describe someone who does not live 'in the real world'. Over many years I have had enough experience of the spirits of the land and other beings to have great respect for Faerie. It is from the spirit world that much of the power of witchcraft comes, and I am grateful for all that the spirit world has taught me. 'Away with the fairies' is a description I am happy to own.

By whatever name they are known, belief in the land spirits who coexist and interact with us has been pretty universal in most times and places. Especially in the more remote places, we have lived alongside them time out of mind and their stories are central to our myths and folk tales. We find accounts of Faerie lore and magic in the records of historical witch trials and in the practices of the cunning men and wise women of the eighteenth and nineteenth centuries[5], and working with the spirits of the land is still at the heart of traditional witchcraft.

It is important to understand that Faeries are not the tiny, gossamer-winged, pretty little creatures portrayed in Victorian children's books. I was brought up to know these spirits as the Tylwyth Teg, or Fair Family, who shared the land with us and were respected and honoured at particular places, usually hawthorn trees, rocks or pools of water. Some places were recognised as gateways to their world, and most people, other than witches and cunning men, avoided these. My next-door neighbour's very elderly father, who was known to the whole village just as *Taid* (grandfather) was a *dyn hysbys* (cunning man) and taught me how to speak with the Tylwyth Teg and not to be afraid of them, as most of my childhood friends were. The Welsh name for the otherworld, *Annwn*, has the sense of a world that coexists with our own and is somehow inside it. The witch learns to sense these spirit beings who are always present, and to work with them. They live by their own rules and laws and do not share our ways of doing things. Their world is beautiful but very different, and full of danger for unsuspecting mortals. The old folk tales contain a lot of wisdom about Faeries and how to behave in their company. If you wish to work your witchcraft with the Faeries, you would do well to study the folk tales.

Time operates differently in the Otherworld, or Faerie. A mortal who spends even a very brief time there may return to this world to find that much more time has elapsed. They may find that centuries have passed, and that all those they knew are long gone. Worse, they may crumble to dust on their return. Returning from the Otherworld can be difficult, if not impossible; the best way to escape is usually to be rescued by a faithful mortal lover. In the Welsh tales mortals stepping into a Faerie ring of toadstools were caught up in a wild dance with the Tylwyth Teg, and disappeared from mortal view. When they were rescued, usually a year and a day later, they did not realise that they had been 'away' and thought that they had been dancing for just a few minutes.

Mortals should never accept food or drink in Faerie, or they will be unable to return, and they should never make promises or bargains with Faeries as the consequences will usually be both unexpected and very difficult. Faeries will punish greed and broken promises, and mortals who talk about them or betray their secrets. Faeries' moral codes are different from mortal ones and their punishments can be very harsh and painful. One tale found in many places tells of a woman who told a Faerie in a crowded marketplace that she could see him. He asked which eye she could see him with, and when she told him she instantly became blind in that eye and never saw Faeries again.

The land spirits must always be treated with the greatest respect and venturing into the Otherworld should be undertaken only with the utmost caution. I know this from personal experience. On one occasion in a forest in Devon on an early autumn morning, I wandered into the Otherworld unawares. Although I knew these woods well, curiosity led me down a path under two arching oak trees that I had never seen before. It was very pleasant: the birdsong seemed louder and sweeter and the flowers more colourful. I quickly realised something was not right; the light was a strange grey-greenish colour that I had not seen before and the sky was a deep midnight blue. I could see lights in the distance and hear faint voices singing and urging me to go deeper into the wood. Then something broke the spell; I realised the danger and quickly ran back along the path back to the arch of trees and onto the path I knew. I thought I had been there just a few minutes and was shocked to find the sun was setting. I had arrived there in the morning and the whole day had gone by. Try as I might, I have never been able to find those trees or that path again.

On the second occasion I deliberately chose to cross into the Otherworld with a spirit whom I had come to know well. It was at a remote place on the coast, known locally as a gateway into the spirit world, and a very high tide was rising. It was a foolhardy thing to do. We walked together for a very few brief minutes along the tideline in the Otherworld. Everything was different and intensely beautiful: light, sea, sky and land; it was timeless and blissful. Then I was suddenly made to leave by my spirit companion who understood the danger, and instantly found myself lying on the beach I had left just a few moments earlier, but at least an hour had elapsed and the tide was falling rapidly. I felt bereft; I knew I had no option but to leave that beautiful but very dangerous place, but was devastated at the same time. I understand why the tales say that those who return from the Otherworld are said to be betwixt and between the two worlds and never fully return; the sadness at losing that beautiful land and the intense happiness it brought did not leave me for several weeks and I felt lost for a long time. I would advise against deliberately visiting that world and urge great caution if you find yourself there unawares.

Working with the land spirits in our own world is a different matter, if you keep your wits about you. It is possible to befriend Faeries by leaving gifts for them. Where I grew up, the usual gifts for the Tylwyth Teg were cream, milk and honey. There are tales of people who provide clothing for Faeries, a seat at the fireside, or food when they are hungry. They appreciate their share of the feasts consumed at Sabbats and I always leave a little of the food we have enjoyed under the hawthorn tree in my garden for them. If you are kind to the spirits and befriend them, they may reward you, although you should never ask for anything. They may help mortal friends who are in dire need and have nowhere else to turn by providing money or food, or helping with work. Never, ever speak about Faerie help or gifts, or these will be withdrawn and the Faeries will leave forever. Never threaten a Faerie or raise your voice to them. You may never see the Faeries who leave gifts or help you, but if you do, it is likely to be 'out of the corner of your eye' and when you are not looking. Working with the Faeries should be approached without any specific desires or expectations. I have outlined some gentle and safe ways to do this below. It is a very individual business; different for everybody, and once you have embarked on this path you will have to find your own way. Always keep the wisdom of the old tales in mind.

THE FAERIE TREE

Hawthorns have been around for a very long time; pollen analysis has revealed that they were thriving in Britain at least 8,000 years ago, and deposits of hawthorn have been found in megalithic tombs. Hawthorns were sacred to the Roman goddess Cardea (the White Goddess), who protected babies and young children. She was propitiated at weddings where torches of hawthorn were burned in her honour, and the powerful taboo against bringing cut hawthorn blossoms indoors is likely to have originated with the Romans. The hawthorn has a special place in British history and mythology; it became the emblem of the Tudor dynasty after the defeated King Richard the Third's crown was found under a hawthorn bush at the battle of Bosworth Field and used to crown the victorious Henry Tudor.

The Glastonbury Thorn is a local variant of hawthorn that flowers on Christmas Day. According to a medieval Christian legend, Joseph of Arimathea travelled to Glastonbury and planted his staff on the top of Wearyall Hill, where it miraculously sprang into bloom. The original thorn on the hilltop died or was destroyed several times down the centuries, notably by Puritans during the English Civil War, but was always replaced by new cuttings. In recent times it became an important part of Glastonbury's 'New Age' identity. Sadly, the tree was reduced to a limbless stump by vandals in 2010, and after replacements were also vandalised, has now been permanently removed. Glastonbury Thorns grown from cuttings can still be seen at various locations in the town, and a sprig of the tree in bloom is still presented to the British monarch at Christmas. In the Welsh tale 'How Culwch Won Olwen' in *The Mabinogion*, which has strong Pagan elements, the name of Olwen's father, the terrible giant Yspaddaden Pencawr, means 'Giant Hawthorn'.

Hawthorn is the Faerie tree *par excellence.* Although it is sometimes called the May tree, it comes into its own during April when its flowering season begins. In my childhood in Ynys Môn there were some particular hawthorn trees that had to be greeted whenever you passed them, because they were places where the Tylwyth Teg lived. Ignoring one of these trees was to risk the wrath of the Fair Family; an aunt of mine, realising she had forgotten to say good morning to a Faerie hawthorn, once walked a mile back to the tree to put things right. Hawthorn trees with deep pink or red blossom were very special and as children we left offerings of milk, cream and honey for the Tylwyth Teg under the red hawthorn tree. In Ireland it was believed that felling a Faerie hawthorn could cause serious bad fortune, illness or even death. In the West of Ireland, where belief in the Others is still strong, the taboo against cutting down Faerie hawthorns is still carefully observed and in recent years the routes of new roads have been altered to avoid damaging them.

In both Scotland and Ireland, clouties, or small pieces of cloth, are tied around the branches of special hawthorn trees. Often these are hawthorns growing by holy wells. These clouties are curing spells: as the cloth decays away, so the illness will leave the affected person. One such tree is Saint Patrick's Thorn at Tinahely in County Wicklow (Ireland), where clouties are tied on the tree on 4 May (*see* July for more about holy wells).

A kind friend gave me a beautiful deep pink flowering hawthorn for my garden that has pride of place in its own special corner. It arrived on a cold winter day and was planted with the blessing of the Faeries, and green, red and black silk ribbons were tied in its branches. The red hawthorn is thriving and has become a focus for Faerie work in my garden. Offerings are regularly left at its feet and every year in April when its leaves have unfurled and its buds are opening, I replace the silk ribbons with new ones.

Begin your own Faerie magic with a hawthorn. If you have room, plant one in your garden in honour of the Others, and work with them there. Hawthorns are small, shrubby trees that grow in hedgerows and at the edge of woodland. They can be kept small and make a useful part of a wildlife hedge. The birds will thank you for the berries in autumn. If you do not have room for a hawthorn tree, why not adopt one in a field, woodland or park as your Faerie tree? Visit it regularly, make small offerings to the Faeries of milk and honey, talk with the tree and spend as much time with it as you can. You may be rewarded not only by the tree itself but by contact with the Others too.

Hawthorn Blossom Anointing Oil

Hawthorn blossom is central to Faerie magic. Its power is immense, so it should be used sparingly and with care. The method for hawthorn blossom anointing oil is the same as the one we used last month for primrose oil, but hawthorn blossoms are used instead of primrose flowers. Only a small amount of this precious oil should be made because none must be leftover or wasted. Prepare it as soon as the hawthorn flowers open fully, on a dry sunny morning in April.

This oil has powerful energy and should be used one drop at a time in magical operations where you wish to enlist the help of the Faeries. A single drop of hawthorn blossom oil on your forehead can be used to increase contact with them.

You will need

- A glass jar with an airtight lid (a preserving jar is ideal); the jar should be clean and dry
- Sweet almond oil (or another base oil of your choice)
- Hawthorn blossom
- Nine small glass bottles

Method

Take a glass jar with you as the blossoms must not be allowed to touch the ground. Approach the tree with great respect and ask it and those who dwell within it very politely if you may have some blossom.

Carefully pick just nine hawthorn blossoms because nine, being three times three, is the best number for Faerie magic. Taking care not to damage them, put the blossoms straight into the jar.

Cover them with sweet almond oil to a depth no greater than the distance from the top of your thumb to its first joint.

Put the jar on your altar and leave it to infuse until the next new moon.

When it is ready, pour the oil into very small glass bottles and place one of the blossoms in each bottle.

Practice: Sitting Out

Sitting out is an old practice that has always been part of witchcraft. Like all the best magic, it is simple but has profound effects. It is also sometimes called hedge sitting, or hedge riding. It takes time and a little patience. At its most basic it means sitting quietly somewhere and meeting the spirits of the land. If you practise it regularly in the same place, you will find you can communicate with the spirits there. They may speak with you, and you may see them. I have on several occasions been rewarded with a glimpse of Faeries and land spirits.

This practice can be done in your garden or any landscape that you feel an affinity with. It doesn't require any complex magical equipment – just comfortable clothing. You should also take a small amount of simple food (bread or biscuits or fruit are good) and a little water to help you return to the plane of earth when you have finished.

April is a good time to begin as it is warm enough to spend hours outside. Like many magical practices, sitting out doesn't happen in human time. It will take as long as it takes, so do not set a time limit on it or be tempted to rush it, and if it works properly, you will have no idea how much time has passed.

First, find your place. The best places for sitting out are liminal or 'thin' in some way; for example on the boundary between two places, such as hedgerows, riverbanks or the edge of woodland, or the kind of places you might walk past without noticing. Some of my favourite sitting out places include a line of old beech trees (a hedge gone wild) between two fields, a little-used path along the edge of a small wood, a quiet place on the shore between two beaches, and beside the hawthorn tree in my garden. You can find these places everywhere; I know witches who sit out in parks in the centre of cities. Sitting out is such a quiet, unobtrusive activity that it unlikely that anyone will notice you.

You will know the right place when you find it; just empty your mind and wander until you find a place. The place will make you feel welcome and you should feel a quiet but positive energy. You may find that this energy varies around the seasons and that different places will work for you at different times of year. If you sense that a place does not want you to be there, then respect its spirits and move on until you find the right spot.

Once you have found your place, sit down and make yourself comfortable. If you have a mobile phone or similar device with you, make sure it is silent and stow it away where you will not be tempted to look at it. Now you are ready to begin. I like to ask my familiar spirit to be with me when I sit out, to protect me and make sure that if I meet beings from the Otherworld I observe the safeguards described above. Sitting out is deep magic, so protect yourself. If you feel nervous about trying it, in addition to calling on your familiar spirit, cast a simple circle round yourself. Put yourself in a calm but focused state and relax by breathing deeply and slowly. Sitting out is the opposite of most forms of meditation in which you completely detach yourself from your surroundings. Your aim here is to blend completely with the land around you; to become part of it. Look at everything around you as closely as you can.

First look at the big things (trees, for example), then focus your attention closer and closer on the small things until you are looking at blades of grass, tiny creatures, pebbles; whatever is around you. Do this for as long as you can. Then listen to everything around you. Begin with any loud sounds (animal or bird calls, running water), then focus in on every little sound you can hear. Then do the same thing with your senses of touch and smell. Do not attempt to define or analyse anything, just experience it as closely as you can. Your aim is to connect with the place on as deep and close a level as possible.

At some point in this process, you should reach a point where you have no separate conscious mind any more. You will have become part of the land itself; its senses will become your senses. It is in this state that you will sense, hear or even see spirits. Do not force anything; just take what comes. The nature of this contact will vary from witch to witch. You may receive answers to questions or creative inspiration, or help with spells and operative magic. You may just experience the pure joy of being with the spirit world.

While sitting out I have met with animal spirits: fox, hare, toad, viper and jackdaw. I have spoken with the indwelling spirits of rocks and trees and met discarnate spirits and distant ancestors. On one occasion on the coast of Ynys Môn the spirit of a young girl began talking with me about how easy it was to catch fish in a net here, how to weight the net with stones and carry the catch back to camp. I realised later that I had been speaking with an ancestor from Mesolithic times, when hunter gatherers lived on this shore. Unbeknownst to me, I had been sitting out at a place where archaeologists had found evidence of one of their camps. Next to my garden hawthorn I once glimpsed a little being, about half as tall as me, wearing a coat of green leaves, on the periphery of my vision or 'out of the corner of my eye' as the old tales have it. We made eye contact briefly; he smiled and was gone.

A sitting out session will usually end naturally when you start to feel tired or uncomfortable, or it can be cut short more suddenly by a change in the weather. You will find that the spirit world gently withdraws and that your everyday perceptions return. You must always thank the spirits and the place as you return. It is normal to feel a little betwixt and between as you come back to the everyday, and you may also find that, although you think you have been sitting out for just a few minutes, that many hours have passed. Complete your return by eating the food you brought with you and drinking the water. Leave a little of the food and water as an offering before you leave.

You can also use your witch's mirror to spend time with the spirits of the land. Take the mirror to your favourite hawthorn tree and simply sit and meditate by looking into it on a sunny April day. You may sense spirit presence in the shifting patterns of light. Increase the bond between you and the tree by reflecting sunlight with the mirror onto yourself and onto the tree. If you are finding it difficult to sense the presence of the spirits, anoint both your mirror and your forehead with a single drop of hawthorn anointing oil.

Some Faerie Names

Faeries/the Fae/Faerie, the Otherworld – England

Tylwyth Teg/the Fair Family, Bendith y Mamau/Blessing of the Mothers, Annwn/The Otherworld – Wales

The Sidhe/Aos Sí/the Little People/The Others, Tir na nÓg/the Land of Youth – Ireland

Sith (Gaelic)/Seelie Court, Elphame – Scotland

The Witch's Broom

The popular image of the witch is not complete without the broomstick; the traditional witch's form of transport. The broom, or besom, still plays an important role in witchcraft. Like the cauldron, it is a great example of an everyday domestic item invested with magical meaning and power, and like many domestic items it was also gendered; historically the broomstick belonged exclusively to women. The witch's broom is made from the wood of three forest trees: its handle is made of ash, the brush is made of birch twigs, and the brush is bound to the handle with flexible willow twigs or bark. As we have seen, each tree has its own magical and spiritual meaning in contemporary witchcraft; these are derived from the Celtic tree alphabet which has its roots in Welsh and Irish bardic poetry and mythology. This is a complex area of magical practice; it is a wonderful thing to explore and can lead the witch deep into the magic of the land itself.

The ash handle of the broom symbolises the god, lord of all that grows, and witches who make their own brooms may carve a phallus on the end of the handle that is hidden within the brush of birch twigs. Riding the broomstick therefore contains an important element of sexual symbolism. Birch is the birth tree and is associated with the goddess as mother of the year. Willow is the tree of the moon goddess, so the broom holds within it two aspects of the goddess and one of the god, and considerable magical power.

The broom is used at the beginning of Sabbats and other rituals to sweep the circle. As the witch physically sweeps the perimeter of the circle with the broom, they visualise sweeping all psychic dirt, negativity and unwanted energies away from the circle. Unlike most witch's tools, the broom is kept in plain sight and not hidden away. It can be kept near the hearth and may be decorated with ribbons and a holed witch stone. I like to keep a small broom that I have made hung up in the fireplace. Different coloured ribbons may be added to the witch's broom to mark the changing seasons. It is a potent object and full of power, not least because of its sexual symbolism. It plays a specific role in some Sabbat rituals, and in initiation ceremonies, where it forms a symbolic gateway to the circle through which the initiate must pass. A handfasting, or witch wedding, concludes with the couple jumping over the broomstick three times for luck. The handfasting broom is decorated with red, white and green ribbons and with flowers, and can be presented to the couple as a gift after the ceremony.

Make a small replica broom to grace your altar, for use in personal rituals, or as a witch's gift.

You will need

- A piece of ash wood
- Birch twigs
- Secateurs or a sharp knife
- Garden twine
- Young, thin willow stems
- Ribbon for binding (optional)

Notes

The ash handle should measure from the tip of your middle finger to your elbow and the birch twigs for the brush should be half this length. As with the wand that you cut in March, you are using your own body to make the measurements, and putting your own very personal and concentrated will or power, which cannot be replicated by anyone else, into whatever you measure. Understanding the importance of small details such as this, that pass unnoticed by most people, and working with them, is the essence of effective magic-making.

Method

As you did when making your wand in March, ask permission of the ash tree before cutting the handle, and thank the tree respectfully. Leave the bark on the broom handle. Similarly, ask permission of the birch tree and give thanks for the birch twigs. The quantity is up to you.

The brush must be attached securely to the handle. Bind the birch twigs as tightly as possible to the ash handle with garden twine, and then let the broom rest for a week somewhere cool but dry before adding the willow bindings, as both the handle and brush may dry and shrink after you cut them. Wood should always be left to dry away from central heating, as hot dry air may make it split.

Cut at least three very thin, whippy lengths of willow the same length as the ash broom handle and immediately bind them tightly around your broom. Young willow is very flexible and should not split. It can be secured with a knot and the loose ends woven into the broom.

If you wish, finish the broom by binding it with ribbon. The most usual colour for this is green, but choose something that reflects your magical intentions.

Later in the year, you may wish to make another small broom for more specific magical work, substituting dried stems of vervain or mugwort for birch twigs (*see* August).

THE WITCH'S GARDEN

In April, work in the witch's garden begins in earnest. Everything will start to grow this month. Any changes to the layout and any soil preparation should be completed. I hoe and weed as necessary (although a lot of plants that others consider to be weeds are magical plants and are left in peace) and tidy up. My witch's garden features several kitsch concrete toadstools and a gnome rescued from the local tip, and these are spruced up and given a fresh coat of paint. Magical plants and herbs that will be grown in pots can be planted and existing plants in pots should be tidied and any dead growth removed. Most flower and herb seeds for direct sowing can be sown into the ground in April and tender seeds that were started earlier can be planted out, once danger of frost is past.

In the coming months of the Witch's Year we will learn more about magical plants and how to work with them. Choose the plants you wish to work with in your witch's garden and plant them where you wish them to grow. When you do this, make sure you welcome them to the garden. Learn as much as you can about how they grow and the conditions they like, ready for the season ahead.

As April nears its end, the primrose anointing oil that you made in March will be ready to use. On May Eve, the last night of April, take your primrose oil to one of the old places. This can be anywhere that is associated locally with the land spirits or Faeries and the working of magic. The folk tales will tell you where to find such places. In the Celtic lands the hollow hills, or megalithic mounds and cromlechs are such places, or perhaps there is a hill or a wood or other place that tradition associates with witches. When you have found the right place, and if you dare, anoint yourself with a few drops of primrose oil, call upon the spirits, and see what happens …

A Spell for April: The Witch's Ladder

The witch's ladder works on the principle of repetition. A spoken spell is repeated over and over again until maximum magical power has been achieved and is then sent on its way. The witch's ladder is a device that gives a structure to the repetition of the spell and aids concentration.

You will need

- Thick thread or yarn. Stand with one arm outstretched and measure a length of thread from the tip of your middle finger to your nose. The colour is up to you
- Thirteen birds' feathers
- Holed stone (optional)
- A simple form of words expressing your purpose

Preparation

As with all spells, pay attention to the lunar calendar: if the spell is for growth or increase, work it during the waxing phase of the moon. If it is for banishing or to lessen something, work it when the moon is waning.

Choose a colour of thread that suits the purpose of your spell. You could choose green for growth, or to contact the Faeries, for example, or black for banishing and purification.

Any feathers can be used. Again, you might wish to choose them to match your magical intent: gulls' feathers for sea magic, for example, or just use what you can find. Feathers should be easy to find, as the nesting season is in full swing.

For the verbal element of this spell, use a few simple words that you can repeat over and over, for example 'Wart be gone' or 'seedlings grow'. If the spell is for someone else, include their name in the wording.

Method

Empty everyday thoughts from your mind and focus on your magical purpose. Ask your animal familiar spirit to help if you wish.

Take the thread and, leaving a good length at the top to make a hanging loop later, tie a knot around the shaft of the first feather.

As you pull the knot tight, focus as hard as you can on your magical purpose. Repeat this process with the remaining twelve feathers, descending down the length of the thread, until all the feathers are attached. If you wish, to add extra power, add a holed witch stone to the base of the thread to weight it. (See July for more on the magic of holed stones.)

Make a hanging loop at the top of the thread big enough to put your hand through easily.

Now take your witch's ladder and, holding the hanging loop in your left hand, grasp the knot around the first feather gently in both hands and speak your spell as you do so.

Move your hands to the next knot and repeat the spell again. Repeat the process with all the feathers, and then repeat it over and over; again and again, speaking the spell every time you reach a knot. As repetition is crucial, do this for as long as you can.

Then send the spell on its way and don't think about it any more.

If you used a holed stone to weight the ladder, you can also stand with it held out in front of you over a bowl of water, and swing it with a gentle circular motion like a pendulum, repeating your spell over and over. The water acts as a conductor for the spell and will help its transmission.

Leave the ladder on your altar until the next full or new moon. Then, if you have made it for somebody else, you can give it to them, or if it is for a specific place such as a garden or a workroom, hang it up there.

A Meditation for April: The Faerie Hawthorn Tree

This month's meditation is designed to help you meet the spirits of the land and to help with the process of sitting out. You might like to try this interior journey to increase your confidence before practising sitting out in the landscape.

You are walking along a rocky path by the bank of a small stream on a pleasant April day. The path leads gently uphill; and the stream flows over small waterfalls. Listen to the sound of the water; you can also hear birdsong, and you notice that a robin is perched on a rock just ahead of you. As you approach, it flies on, as if leading the way for you.

Keep following the path uphill until you come to a stone wall with a gate across the path. Open the gate and go through. You have reached the source of the stream; a clear, fresh spring that flows into an ancient stone basin. Growing next to the spring is a small hawthorn tree in full blossom; the guardian of the spring. Its flowers are white with pale pink centres and smell intoxicating. The robin who led you here is perched on a hawthorn branch. As you watch, the breeze blows stray blossoms into the spring; they look like snow falling as they float down onto the water and are carried away by the stream.

Cup your hands and take a drink of the cold, clear spring water, then thank the spring and the tree for this gift. Rest peacefully by the hawthorn and look at it closely. Notice every little detail of its trunk, branches, leaves and blossoms. Blossoms drift down onto you. Listen to the sound of the breeze whispering among the leaves, the water flowing down the hillside and the robin singing. As you look and listen you see there is a gateway behind the tree and beyond it a path winding over the hillside. The land on the other side of the gate looks different; the colours are more intense, there are flowers that you have never seen before and the sky is silver. This is the Otherworld, Faerie, Annwn. You are at a place where the two worlds meet.

You look away from the gateway and as you do so, you catch a fleeting glimpse of someone out of the corner of your eye; a being from the Otherworld; from Faerie. They look directly at you and smile. Notice everything you can about them as quickly as you can. Some hawthorn blossom falls onto your eyes and you blink. When you look again, the being has gone and the gateway has disappeared.

Thank the tree for this glimpse of the Otherworld. Leave the spring, go back through the gateway and down the path by the stream. Return gently in your own time to the everyday. When you have finished this meditation, write or draw your vision of the Otherworld being in your journal.

MAY

 May 

Celebration and Passion

The Joyous Flowering

May Day, when we celebrate the union of goddess and god, is the best day of the year for a wedding. I am up before dawn ready for the long journey to North Cornwall and the omens are not good; heavy rain is falling. It rains all the way. For the last ten miles, the road passes through a seemingly endless bluebell wood; a massive carpet of bright blue flowers gleaming in the wet early morning light and the home of innumerable spirits. The rain hammers down. Then, within two miles of the coast, the sky clears and the sun shines brightly. The bridegroom, who comes from Padstow, and who chose this place, had told me all along that the sun would shine on us. Everything feels washed clean by the spring rain.

The field next to the sea at Trevone is bounded by a thick Cornish hedge of hawthorn and bramble; a mass of white and pink blossom. The sky and sea are intensely blue. I am nervous; it is the first time I have done this. The bride is waiting, garlanded with flowers. I ask the guests, coven members and friends, to gather in a circle with the bride and groom hand in hand at its centre. An older couple walking their dog stop to watch. He says it's some kind of devilish ritual; she says, 'Don't be silly dear, anyone can see it's a wedding' and asks if they can watch. Several other interested people join them.

The circle is cast and the ritual proceeds. As the bride and groom make their vows, I am overtaken by something timeless and very powerful; a kind of spirit possession. Something speaks through me and moves for me; it is wonderful and beyond anything I have previously experienced. I can see that the bride and groom are held by it too. I do not look up but I can sense a large crowd of people watching, urging me on and offering their blessing. The couple's hands are tied together and the ceremony ends with them jumping over a broomstick three times for luck. The spirit possession melts away and I look up, expecting to see

> **May Associations**
>
> **Festivals:** Beltane/ May Day/ Calan Haf (1st), Obby Oss (1st), Flora Day (8th)
> **Figures:** Maia, Flora, the Green Man, Obby Oss, Jack in the Green
> **More Than Human:** Bluebells, plant allies, spring flowers, trees in new leaf
> **Totems and Symbols:** Maypole, willow

the crowd I had sensed so strongly. There are only our guests and the dog-walking couple, who are eagerly asking questions about Pagan weddings.

Full of abiding joy, we all make our way to Padstow to celebrate May Day with the Obby Osses capering through the streets and crowds singing and dancing in the traditional raucously sensual manner. Years later I learn from a folklorist that the field we had used for the handfasting is known locally to be haunted by a host of largely benevolent spirits and that several Bronze Age ritual deposits were found there.

At the beginning of May we celebrate the marriage of goddess and god at the glorious festival of Beltane and bring in the May with joyful and raucous folk customs that celebrate the coming of summer and continue throughout the month. The world revels in the energy of growth; we make garlands, learn about plant allies and celebrate the flowers of the season.

May Day, or Beltane, is a joyous time of celebration and rejoicing. The fire tide flows very strongly through everything with its immense energy and growth is at its peak. The trees are bursting into leaf; bluebells, cowslips and other spring flowers are in full bloom, baby birds are hatching and new life is everywhere. If you are living by witch's time, you will really feel the power and happiness of this season. Experience it to the full, bathe in the marvellous energy of it and allow the tide to carry you into summer.

> *Unite and unite, and let us all unite*
> *For summer is a-come unto day*
> *And whither we are going, we will all unite*
> *In the merry morning of May.*
> (The Padstow May Day song)

The Romans celebrated the Floralia, the festival of Flora, goddess of flowers, for four days at the beginning of May and also venerated the goddess Maia at this time. Flora Day is still the name given to May celebrations at Helston in Cornwall. Maia was one of the Pleiades, the mother of Hermes/Mercury and a goddess of growth who gave her name to the month. Pagans have adopted the Scottish name, Beltane, for this festival. In Wales May Day is Calan Mai, or sometimes Calan Haf (*haf* means summer), and along with Calan Gaeaf (Samhain, 31 October) it marks one of the two divisions of the year in the old Welsh calendar. Beltane means good or bright fire, and like most of the other festivals of the Wheel of the Year, it was celebrated with bonfires. A widespread Celtic custom was to light two fires and drive cattle between them to purify them. Calan Mai fires were still lit in Wales at the beginning of the twentieth century at Tan y Bryn (Fire Hill) in Carmarthenshire and elsewhere in South Wales.

> *Hal an tow, jolly rumble, O*
> *For we are up, as soon as any day, O*

For to fetch the summer home
The summer and the May, O
For summer is a -come, O
And winter is a-gone, O.
('Hal an Tow', as sung by the people of Helston on Flora Day)

FOLK CUSTOMS

Folk customs abound in May, especially in the West Country where May is the most important time in the ritual calendar. In Devon, Cornwall and Dorset, it feels as if the whole world has turned Pagan this month and Bringing in the May happens everywhere. Homes and streets are decked with greenery and flowers. Mostly people use whatever is to hand: bluebells, cowslips and apple blossom. Elder leaves and rowan are hung over doorways to bring blessings and protection too, as May Eve is a time when the Faeries are abroad. Hawthorn is used, although never, of course, brought inside the house. These customs have a timeless quality. They work because they embody the energy of the season, the life force and fertility. 'Maying', one of Henry VIII's favourite customs, meant going out to the woods at night to celebrate the May and it was widely accepted that the normal moral restrictions and sexual boundaries did not apply at this time. For witches, Beltane is a love feast; the marriage of goddess and god, so these May Day customs are full of meaning and provide a wonderful opportunity to celebrate the season with others. There is sometimes a wild and anarchic edge to the May customs; the energy of the season cannot be contained.

The Obby Oss

At Padstow in Cornwall the Obby Oss celebration that takes place on 1 May is the most powerful and extraordinary folk custom I have experienced and is a must for any witch seeking the full May Day experience. It is celebrated with passion, vigour and all the raw energy of an ageless fertility ritual by the people of Padstow, despite the presence of crowds of onlookers.[6] The music and drumming are hypnotic. The dance of the Oss, as it capers around then dies and is revived by its Teazer to a thumping drum beat, is strongly and knowingly erotic, and it is said that any woman caught under the skirts of the Oss will be pregnant within the season. A member of my coven who had difficulty conceiving tested this by deliberately putting herself in the way of the Oss, and can testify to the 100 per cent efficacy of the custom. Whatever its age and origins, it is a very special and intense spiritual experience that exudes a truly Pagan sexuality and engages the body and emotions as well as the mind.

At Minehead on the North Somerset coast, the traditional Sailors' Hobby Horse dances from 30 April until 4 May, greeting local people at their houses and performing 'booties' (holding someone under its skirts and then dancing with them) that bring health and fertility. Both the Padstow Oss and the Minehead Horse have their own songs and tunes that are unique to them and to May Day, and the music at both is an integral part of the ceremonies. Like Padstow, Minehead can be raucous and anarchic; both these events celebrate the power of life and growth in ways that are a million miles from the genteel folk revivals of Victorian times, and are all the better for that. It is telling that both towns resisted attempts by Christian priests in the nineteenth century to end the Oss/Horse customs. In Padstow, when food was short and the townspeople were faced with starvation, the local vicar offered roast dinners to anyone who would give up dancing with the Oss; there were no takers.

These traditions embody the spirit of their towns and of May Day in a very special and unique way that has to be experienced to be believed, and witches love them. Hobby Horse customs were once much more widespread and were not just confined to May Day, with many appearing at Christmas and New Year too. Salisbury Museum in Wiltshire contains Hob Nob, the town's rather sad hobby horse imprisoned in a glass case, together with a splendid giant. Perhaps the local people might like to liberate their horse and start celebrating the May again?

Flora Day

Flora Day at Helston (also in Cornwall, on or around 8 May) has a very different vibe. After the Hal an Tow pageant and Mummers Play that recounts the mythic history of the town and includes Saint George, Saint Michael and a fearsome dragon, the stately Furry Dance (not the Floral Dance, please!) weaves its way through the town and in and out of shops and houses all day, with men and women in formal dress (the men sport top hats and tails and the women wear brightly coloured dresses and big hats), led by Helston's brass band playing the famous tune. Although less wild than Padstow, the Furry Dance has its own slow and powerful spiral energy, which builds throughout the day, and puts me in mind of the great ourobouros serpent, coiled around the world, biting its own tail.

Another flower-related celebration takes place in the villages of Kingsand, Cawsand and Millbrook, on the Cornwall shore of Plymouth Sound, where the Black Prince procession sees the launching onto the sea of a model boat bedecked with flowers.

May Day

Morris dance sides welcome the May by dancing at dawn in city centres, on village greens, at the seashore, and at hillforts and stone circles. Amongst many other places, they can be found bringing in the May on the magnificent Cerne Abbas Giant in Dorset, at Hay Tor on Dartmoor in Devon, Cabot Tower in Bristol, Primrose Hill in London, and at Plymouth

Hoe (Devon), Ely Cathedral and Wandlebury Rings (both in Cambridgeshire), Adlington (Cheshire), Chapel-en-le-Frith (Derbyshire), Chelmsford (Essex), Leicester, Birmingham, Nottingham and Oxford, where a choir also welcomes May Day with a Latin hymn sung from the tower of Magdalen College (but local authorities have done their best to end the dangerous custom of jumping into the shallow river Cherwell).

May Day traditions grow and evolve. Jack in the Green, a person wearing a conical framework covered in green leaves, originated as part of chimney sweeps' and milkmaids' May Day celebrations in London and South-east England in the seventeenth and eighteenth centuries. Chimney sweeps were considered lucky, doubtless because they worked in the dangerous liminal space of the chimney (*see* February). May Day marked the last time fires were lit and chimneys swept until the following autumn. The Jack in the Green May festival at Hastings is a four day event (3–6 May) with its own unique character, attended by thousands of people. The concluding Jack in the Green procession includes giants, drummers and hundreds of green men and women and May Day revellers dressed in their own unique costumes. It has a wonderfully anarchic atmosphere and concludes with Jack being ritually slain to 'release the spirit of summer'. Other Jacks in the Green appear at Rochester and Whitstable in Kent, where they are part of chimney sweeps' processions, as well as in London and Bristol. The Jack in the Green custom is being enthusiastically espoused by Pagans and lovers of folklore and is spreading rapidly. It can now be found at May celebrations in Oxford, Ilfracombe in North Devon, and Evercreech in Somerset, and in a growing number of locations in London and Kent.

Garland Day

Abbotsbury in Dorset has its Garland Day on 13 May. Two large May garlands are carried from door to door by children collecting money. In small rural communities, these 'collecting' customs were an accepted part of life; a way of helping others in hard times, rewarding creativity, and providing treats for children who didn't have much. An officious local policeman tried unsuccessfully to stop the custom in the 1950s by arresting the children using laws against begging, and confiscated the funds they had collected. Local people were not amused. The garlands used to be taken out to sea by fishers to ask the sea's blessing on the new fishing season.

The garland tradition is now spreading to other nearby villages in Dorset. May garlands and May bushes (hawthorn boughs, usually in full bloom, cut and decked with ribbons) were formerly widespread throughout England and were usually, as at Abbotsbury, made by children who collected funds. The garlands would often have a doll in their centre, possibly to represent the Virgin Mary. May garlands are still made at Bampton and Charlton-on-Otmoor in Oxfordshire. The tradition has been revived in Cambridge and, like Jack in the Green, is spreading.

Castleton Garland Day (Derbyshire) takes place on 28 May. The Garland King is a man completely encased in a conical framework of flowers who parades through the town on horseback with his female consort. A procession of dancers; children dressed in white and carrying garland sticks led by the town's silver band, follow them.

Beltane

The Edinburgh Beltane celebration held on May Eve on Calton Hill, founded in 1988 by the Beltane Fire Society, is a major modern fire festival inspired by ideas of ancient Pagan celebrations. It is a large-scale arts event, featuring dancers, drummers and fire with a central procession led by a May Queen and a Green Man.

A Bealtaine Fire Festival that celebrates the coming of summer and Ireland's cultural heritage, has been established at the Hill of Uisneach, the traditional site of Bealtaine fires and the ancient sacred centre of Ireland in County Westmeath. Uisneach has been inhabited for at least 5,000 years, and there is archaeological evidence for the lighting of ritual fires there. Both these festivals are very popular ticketed events that usually sell out in advance. Local witches and Pagans are reviving the custom of lighting the Beltane fires elsewhere in Scotland and Ireland.

Maypoles

Maypoles were found across Northern Europe and Scandinavia in medieval times, although arguments for them as survivals of older Pagan traditions are not very convincing. The first recorded instance of a maypole in Britain was at Llanidloes in mid Wales; mentioned in a fourteenth-century poem by Gryffydd ap Adda ap Dafydd, and they became popular in Tudor times across England, Scotland and Wales. The Puritan parliament, horrified by the licentiousness and drunkenness of Maying, banned maypoles in England in 1644 and ordered them to be destroyed. They became legal again with the restoration of Charles the Second in 1660; Oak Apple Day (29 May) was created as a new holiday to celebrate the restoration of the monarchy and is still part of May festivities in some places, but most current May Day celebrations involving a maypole and May Queen in Britain date back to the reign of Queen Victoria.

The May Queen

Tennyson heralded the vogue for these 'medieval' customs with the publication of his poem 'The May Queen' in 1832 and the first 'revived' celebration took place at a London theatre in 1836. They spread across the country and soon became much-loved customs. The essential elements were a maypole, a May Queen (usually a young girl), and a procession. John Ruskin even devised a May ceremony in 1881 for a Church of England women's teacher training college. Whether or not the maypole can be linked to Yggdrasil or Germanic Pagan sacred trees, it is certainly phallic in appearance and fits well with a Pagan understanding of the world. Permanent maypoles can be found in England at Welford on Avon in Warwickshire, where the maypole is a grade two listed monument, Dunchurch (also in Warwickshire), Wadworth in South Yorkshire and Wellow in Nottinghamshire, where the maypole dates back to 1856. Barwick in Elmet near Leeds in Yorkshire boasts England's tallest maypole, which puts in an appearance once every three years. Dancing around these maypoles mainly takes place at the end of May, rather than at Beltane.

Probably the biggest and best-known May Queen ceremony takes place at Knutsford in Cheshire, with others happening at Lustleigh and Great Torrington in Devon, Chislehurst in Kent and Endon in Staffordshire. Maypoles and May Queens are decked in flowers and the traditional May colours of red, green and white.

Well Dressing

The custom of well dressing takes place in villages in the Derbyshire and Staffordshire Peak District throughout May, June and July. Village wells and springs are blessed and large pictures created from thousands of flower petals pressed into wet clay. These are usually images of saints or biblical stories, but the impulse behind them, of venerating wells and springs, and giving thanks for clean, fresh water with the flowers of the season, is one that resonates with witches. Well dressing is said to have originated as a thanksgiving custom when Peak District villages were spared during the Black Death and other outbreaks of plague.

Other May Customs

The Calan Mai bonfires in Wales were made with the wood of nine different trees; streets were decorated with hawthorn and spring flowers and May carols were sung in the morning, followed by dancing throughout the day. Calan Mai was one of two great *Ysbryd Nos* or spirit nights (the other being *Calan Gaeaf*/Samhain); doors and gates were garlanded with rowan branches to stop harmful spirits entering. It was a traditional time for divination, especially for young women seeking marriage partners.

> *Arise, arise you pretty fair maids*
> *And take your May bush in.*
> (May carol)

In Ireland the May bush custom was widespread. May bushes, decorated with ribbons and traditional gold and silver balls, are still placed outside some houses and in town centres and are left in place until the end of May. Flower garlands were hung around the necks of cattle to prevent them from being 'overlooked' (harmed by someone with the

Evil Eye or by the Sidhe), and flowers were spread on thresholds to prevent unwanted spirits entering.

Dairy produce was especially important and offerings of milk and butter were left for the Tylwyth Teg in Wales and for the Aos Sí in Ireland, both as a mark of respect and to prevent them stealing or souring dairy goods. Like their Celtic counterparts in Scotland and Ireland, Welsh witches and Pagans are taking a lead in reinstating the old May customs.

The wildest and most dangerous English May custom is the notorious annual cheese rolling at Cooper's Hill in Gloucestershire, in which people race down a precipitously steep hillside in pursuit of a wheel of Gloucester cheese. This one is absolutely not for the faint-hearted. It takes place on the late May Bank Holiday Monday.

BRINGING IN THE MAY

Use May Day customs to inspire you, bring in the May and create your own unique Beltane celebration. This can be both a very creative process and a profound experience. As with so many aspects of witchcraft, it is practical and experiential; meaning and magic are found as much in doing things and making things as in more formal rituals.

Prepare for Beltane by making May garlands to hang on your door and around the home and garden, or to wear as crowns in Beltane rituals. These are very simple to make. Make a circular frame of wire or weave and twist pliable willow twigs together and tie them, and attach bunches of green leaves and May flowers to the frames, remembering not to bring hawthorn inside the house. Willow is very appropriate as it is the tree of the moon goddess and is sacred to Hecate, Demeter, Persephone, Ceridwen and Blodeuwedd, amongst others, and has been used for making baskets (one of the most ancient crafts) for thousands of years. Ready-made wreath bases can be used if you prefer, but, as with all practical witchcraft, the effort involved in making them yourself increases their magical power. If you feel the need to protect your home against Faerie or spirit incursions, tie leafy rowan or elder boughs over the door. Rowan should be tied with red thread and elder with green. May garlands and boughs are usually kept until Midsummer and then burned on the Sabbat fire, but they can be burned at the end of the Beltane Sabbat if you prefer.

I begin May Day with the old custom of bathing my face in the fresh dew at sunrise which is believed to be very good for the skin. The sensation of cold, fresh dew on the face is exhilarating and connects me instantly with the more than human world around me. Waking early on May morning is not difficult because the dawn chorus is in full flow. Going out early on May Day, standing with your feet on the earth and your arms raised to the sky, feeling the energy of the season, letting the strong pulse of the earth flow through you, connecting with all that lives and with the spirit world, and invoking goddess and god is the absolute heart of Beltane.

I then ask the goddess and god of the May to bless my garden and the land around me and all that grows. Asking for blessing on the land can be done anywhere, whether you have a garden or not. I walk slowly around the garden, looking at everything and greeting all the plants, then set up my Beltane staff at the centre of the garden. The staff is a straight hazel pole, as tall as I am, that I have had for many years, with a forked top in honour of the horned god. I pick a small posy of herbs and May flowers, wrap the stems in tinfoil to keep them moist, and tie the posy to the top of the May staff with red and green yarn. It will remain there until the following day. A May staff can also be made from ash, or any strong, straight wood, and will acquire its own Beltane magic.

Beltane sits opposite Samhain on the Wheel of the Year. Like Samhain, it is a liminal time when the Otherworld comes close and its inhabitants are all around us. It is a traditional time for entering the hollow hills and communing with the Others. If you wish to meet them on May Day, my best advice is to visit a bluebell wood. Bluebell woods are liminal, transitory places and in this lies their special magic; the flowers are short-lived and only with us during May. Wandering through bluebells underneath trees just coming into leaf and experiencing the colour and scent of the massed flowers can be both intoxicating and entrancing, in the true sense of the word. Anoint yourself with your primrose oil before you go, and protect yourself with rowan if you wish. Let your mind as well as your feet wander, and who knows what or who you may glimpse out of the corner of your eye?

> *Oh do not tell the priest of our plight,*
> *For he would call it sin*
> *For we have been out in the woods all night*
> *A-conjuring summer in*
> *And we bring you good news by word of mouth*
> *Good news for cattle and corn*
> *Now is the sun is come up from the south*
> *With oak, and ash, and thorn!*
> (Rudyard Kipling, A Tree Song, from *Puck of Pook's Hill*, as used in witchcraft Beltane rituals)

Practice: The Beltane Ritual

The Beltane ritual has three key elements:

- It is a fire festival: the flowing tide of fire heralds the coming of summer and the fire protects and purifies

- As at Samhain, the Otherworld comes close and Faeries and spirits are welcomed
- At the heart of Beltane is the union of goddess and god; it is a passionate Sabbat that is celebrated to the fullest extent

In this ritual, you will feel the power of the season, when growth is at its strongest all around you. It will energise you and carry you forward in the weeks to come. The mood of the ritual should be one of joy and sensuality; everything should be enjoyed to the full.

Preparation

- Beltane should be celebrated outdoors, as the sun is going down in the evening. As with Candlemas and other Sabbats, you may choose to celebrate on May Eve, or on May Day itself. Witches like to celebrate Beltane in woodlands and sometimes at the seashore.
- When choosing a site, be mindful that Beltane calls for ritual fires and observe safe working principles. I prefer to celebrate Beltane in my garden; May flowers such as foxgloves and cowslips will be in bloom, and I can light two fires safely in fire baskets and use big outdoor garden candles or flaming torches to mark the quarters. I put candles in glass jars to light the way to the circle. Planning how to incorporate fire and light creatively and safely into the ritual is a very practical consideration when preparing for Beltane. It sounds very basic, but organise dry kindling and reliable lighting materials, and work out in advance exactly how fires will be lit and who will light them; there is nothing more dispiriting than struggling unsuccessfully with damp paper and matches in a high wind. If you have two fires, leave plenty of room for people to pass safely between them. You will need the bundles of twigs of the nine ritual woods that you made in March. These should be dry and ready to use now.
- When I celebrate in the garden, the May staff that I described above acts as an altar pole for the ritual. It is placed in the north quarter and I hang a May garland on it. Your May garlands can be placed around the working place or worn by participants.
- If you are working with others, choose people to represent the goddess and god. Doing this can be a profound experience as they will really feel the power of the deities; make sure the people you choose are prepared for this and will welcome it.
- Allow plenty of time for the ritual, not least because the Beltane feast can be a lengthy business that should be savoured and not rushed.
- The Beltane feast can consist of anything that seems right to you. I like to cook it over the ritual fire so I choose things that can be barbecued on skewers or

roasted in the embers. There will also be oatcakes (the traditional bannock) and a green salad, if possible made of fresh new leaves and shoots in honour of the god of growing things. Foods with aphrodisiac properties such as cherries and chocolate would be appropriate to celebrate the marriage of goddess and god.

The ritual

The fires are lit and the bundles of twigs placed on them. Cast the circle.

Invoke and honour the spirits of the land, then invoke and honour the more than human: the animals, plants and all that lives. Take time to do this and think about it; sense all the live and spirit presences that are with you and welcome them to your Sabbat.

The spirit of summer is then awakened and set free. This can be done by singing or chanting. Create a form of words for this or simply visualise the spirit of summer waking and rising from the earth while chanting 'Awake, awake, awake'. The spirit of summer could be visualised as a Green Man or wodwose (a medieval spirit of the wild forest), as a plant or animal, or in whatever way you wish. Traditional May songs can be used; some covens use adapted forms of the Kipling poem quoted above. Drumming and circle dancing are good ways to raise energy to wake the spirit of summer. Put your concentrated magical energy into it, and the spirit of summer will be present with you, and throughout the summer season.

Invoke the goddess and god of the May. There are many forms of goddess and god that can be used at Beltane: perhaps Flora, Maia, Diana or Artemis, Ceridwen or Maid Marian for the goddess, and Pan, Cernunnos, Mabon or Maponus, Robin of the Greenwood or Herne for the god. Choose whatever inspires you or fits with your tradition. The goddess is invoked as all that is beautiful at this time. She is the warmth, the dew, the wind amongst the trees, the lady of flowers, and mother of the mysteries. The god is invoked as the lord of all that grows, the god of the greenwood, goat-foot Pan and antler-crowned Cernunnos. A form of the Irish 'Song of Amergin' can be used:

I am a stag of seven tines
I am a wide flood upon a plain
I am a wind on deep waters
I am a shining tear of the sun
I am a hawk on a cliff
I am fair among flowers
I am the god who sets the head aflame with smoke.

Once invoked, goddess and god are present with you. The culmination of the rite is the union of goddess and god. If you are working alone, this can be visualised. If you are working with others, the people you have chosen will enact it. This is usually done symbolically; they join hands and then embrace, but again, the way you choose to do this is up to you. The ritual can conclude with more circle dancing.

The Beltane feast follows. When darkness has fallen at Beltane, you will sense the presence of all those from the Otherworld who are with you. Offer some of your food to them. When the feast is done, thank the goddess and god. You will feel them withdrawing their presence gently from your circle. Then thank all the spirits and those who have joined you and bid them return to their own worlds. Close your circle. The spirit of summer has been awakened and is now wild and free.

The Green Man

The Green Man is becoming very popular with contemporary Pagans and some like to think of him as a god, especially at Beltane. As a witch working with the spirit world, I prefer to see him not as a deity to be invoked and worshipped, but rather as the presiding spirit of the woods and forests; indwelling and always present in the green places, who can be called upon when working magic, as a guiding spirit in the woods, or to protect trees.

PLANT ALLIES

In the witch's garden, everything will be growing strongly now, and it is time to learn about plant allies. Everything I describe in this section can be achieved in a very small garden, and most of it can be achieved with just a few plant pots. Most people think of plants as things we grow and use to eat or make things, or as medicines; as commodities that we use. Witches who work with growing things, and who understand that everything has its own indwelling spirit, take a very different approach that is not transactional, or about treating plants as resources to be used.

The plants that I grow are my friends and allies; powerful magical helpers akin to familiar spirits, but also subtly different. I grow them because I want to gain their trust and friendship, and work magic with them as partners. This is very different from conventional herbal medicine, and also from most of what is termed magical herbalism. I may sometimes harvest them, with their permission, but sometimes I may not; just watching them grow and spending time with them will be enough. The magic worked by plant spirits is strong and very direct. Gaining the friendship of a plant ally is not easy, but it is a wonderful thing when it is achieved.

Knowledge of the curative properties of herbs has been built up over thousands of years. Some of them (willow and meadowsweet, foxglove and yew, for example) still form the basis of modern medicines. At the same time, complex systems of magical correspondences were developed linking the properties of herbs to the astrological planets, days and hours. If you wish to delve deep into herbalism, these can be studied. What I advocate here is a much simpler approach that requires the witch to engage directly with the spirit of the plant. This is a slow process that cannot be rushed; it will take as long as it takes, and will require patience and persistence.

What plants can be plant allies and how can you discover your own plant allies? The answer to these questions is both simple and complicated. It is simple because in the first instance, a plant ally is a plant that you feel attracted to. This does not mean seeing an image of a plant and thinking that it is pretty and might look good in the garden. It means being in the physical presence of a plant and feeling an irresistible compulsion to grow it. The spirit of the plant is attracting you, and you do not really have any choice in the matter. It has enchanted you, and you must acknowledge that it has you in its power. Any plant can be a plant ally if its spirit enchants you like this on a first meeting. Plant allies may be beautiful flowering plants or aromatic herbs, but they may just as easily be plants with more subtle charms, or plants that most people dismiss as weeds. When discovering your plant allies, it is therefore very important to be honest with yourself, and not to reject a plant because it is a weed or looks ‘unattractive’. A plant ally may a plant that grows in the wild.

A Word About Foraging

Years ago I used to go out picking a few wild field mushrooms and other fungi in autumn for stews and soups, and wild garlic to eat in spring; it was a normal part of rural life. When foraging first became a popular phenomenon some years ago it seemed an innocent thing that would allow more people to enjoy the earth's gifts. Sadly, human greed intervened. There are no mushroom fields where I live any more because people uprooted every last mushroom to sell to restaurants; and once gone, they can't grow back. Whole banks of wild garlic are trampled and destroyed and everything, leaves, flowers and roots, taken away in industrial quantities and sold or put in freezers. People on expensive foraging weekend workshops strip hedgerows of every last 'wild vegetable' or edible plant. Even at this local level, the earth, which gives so generously, is being pillaged by the greedy for profit. It is sad, but I can no longer recommend foraging as a practice. Berries that are plentiful everywhere in autumn are the only possible exception, but even then, please only take what you need for immediate use and never be greedy. I grow all my plant allies myself; some are grown from seed, others are purchased from nurseries or swapped with other witches. A witch who works with plants should be generous; when plants get too big or self-seed they provide witch gifts for others who need them.

The complicated part of plant ally work is that you will have to learn how to grow the plant and provide it with the conditions it likes, and then that you will have to spend time getting to know its spirit. In my small garden, most of the plants, in addition to the Faerie Hawthorn, the place where I meet the Others, are plant allies. Over the years they have taught me how they like to be looked after and what they need to grow well. Garden manuals are helpful, but a plant will let me know if it is in the wrong place or needs different soil or light or shade. Getting this right can take a while, but a happy garden full of plants growing strongly in May is a marvellous thing. Some of my plant allies have deep roots and need a lot of space; others are happy in pots or even growing in the cracks in paving stones.

To get to know the spirit of a plant, practise sitting out with it (as described in April). Sit with the plant for as long as it takes; empty your mind of extraneous everyday thoughts and focus just on the plant. Look at it as closely as you can and notice every detail about it. Remember that sitting out is a process that engages all your senses; when working with plant allies this may mean using senses you didn't know you had. Carry on sensing the plant to the exclusion of everything else until its spirit rewards you by communicating. Keep doing this until you become allies. You have to learn how to leave human-centred thinking behind and enter the plant world. This is very rewarding if you persevere with it. The plant will teach you how to work magic with it, and this may owe nothing to conventional ideas about herbalism or magic. Do as the plant spirit tells you. When working with plant allies it is important to learn how to be quiet and passive and to always let the plant spirit take the lead. Never try to impose your will on a plant ally, because it won't work. If you want to use part of it (a leaf for a charm, for example) ask politely and only take it if given permission. When I do harvest parts of my plant allies, it may be to use dried leaves in spells or charms, or to make tinctures or anointing oils. We will return to this in June.

Some of my plant allies are, unsurprisingly, plants that have recognised magical properties.

Vervain, sometimes called enchanter's vervain, is a superb magical herb. The Roman writer Pliny noted that the Celts used it in their magic. Its spirit aids me in magical workings, and in enchantments. I have a pot of vervain close to my back door and I spend a lot of time in summer just sitting with it. Year by year it has taught me much and deepened my magical practice. It is an unassuming plant with small violet flowers in late summer that look like tiny lights at twilight. A vervain plant must never be bought but should always be given. Fortunately, when vervain is happy, it seeds itself everywhere, which means I always have plants to give away to witches who need them. Vervain allows me to make anointing oil and tincture to use in the winter season while the plant sleeps.

Solomon's Seal captured me with a powerful enchantment and has never let me go, so much so that I keep adding to my stock of plants. In May it has beautiful white-green pendulous flowers hanging from arching stems and contemplating them is profound magic in itself. It was known in Egypt as the backbone of Osiris and its spirit brings strength and stability and access to very deep magical worlds. Its dried flowers resemble small phalli so are used in generative magic. It allows me to make small amounts of tincture and anointing oil which are used in curing to give strength.

Mugwort is the herb of vision. It is named *Artemisia vulgaris* in Latin after the goddess Artemis and is sacred to her. It is an aid to dreaming (a sachet under the pillow will promote dream recall) and visualising. With the spirit's permission, it can be used to consecrate scrying mirrors and other witch's tools. It can have a very mild psychoactive effect on some people when drunk as tea and has a faint, minty smell that can be a little intoxicating. I work with the mugwort spirit to develop my scrying and divination abilities and when seeking dreams.

Vervain, solomon's seal and mugwort are all herbaceous perennial plants that die back in autumn and remain dormant until the following spring. This means they will allow me to harvest their leaves and stems at the end of summer before they die. Mugwort and taller varieties of Solomon's seal need to be planted direct into the earth.

Foxglove is the ally that teaches me the way to Faerie. Looking deep into its flowers in May and early June and merging with the patterns on its petals takes me out of the human world. This is intense work that is only possible for the short time the flowers are in bloom. It is a biennial that spreads its seeds everywhere and makes new plants every year, so once you have foxglove in the garden it will always be there. The leaves and seeds of foxgloves contain a substance (digitalis) used in medicine to treat heart conditions and should not be ingested.

A Word on Working Safely with Plants

None of the plants I have described in this book, other than foxglove (above), which I suggest you simply look at, has any known toxicity or potentially harmful effects. Please always work responsibly with plants. If you use plants other than the ones I have described here, then do so responsibly and research them first. I suggest the use of plants for magical purposes only, and not for medicinal use. The methods described throughout the book (anointing oils, tinctures, infusions and incenses) use plant materials in very dilute quantities. I do not recommend any other uses of these plants. Please act responsibly and sensibly when working with your plant allies.

A Spell for May: The Goddess and God of the Trees

This charm is for strong growth and fertility. It should be placed in a garden or growing place, or given to woodland to work there. The last one of these charms that I made nestles in a hollow in the trunk of a very old oak tree in woodland at one of my working places, an Iron Age hillfort in East Devon, as an expression of gratitude for all the magical help and visions the tree has given me.

This is a very simple spell. The oak twig symbolises the god of the greenwood, and the willow twig the goddess of the moon.

You will need

- A fresh, green oak twig the length of your ring finger
- A fresh, green willow twig, the length of your ring finger
- A length of green thread measured from the tip of your middle finger to the bottom of your palm. Use an organic/biodegradable material such as wool. Do not use artificial fibre that will not decay

Method

Cut your green thread in two and bind the two twigs tightly together at each end. As you do so, concentrate on the meaning of the Beltane ritual; of the sacred greenwood marriage of goddess and god.

Visualise the goddess and god, and ask them to bless growth and fertility this spring and summer.

Just after dawn on a May morning, while the dew is still on the ground, place the charm in the home you have chosen for it and let it do its work.

A Meditation for May: The Lord and Lady of the Greenwood

In a great forest on a May evening the trees are just coming into leaf and dappled sunlight filters through their pale green leaves. A path leading into the forest is framed by overarching oak trees and in the shade birch, ash and hazel trees all reach upwards, together with evergreen hollies with their deep green glossy leaves. Tendrils of honeysuckle twine around trunks and branches. The ground is carpeted with bluebells that stretch away into the distance; their colour and scent are entrancing. At the edge of the path ferns are unfurling in spirals of new growth. Walk along the path; somewhere ahead of you there is a sound that might be birdsong or distant laughter.

As you travel further into the forest the shade grows deeper; you have left the outside world far behind. Journey on along the path beneath the trees until you come to a clearing. It is lit by a silvery light, although the sky above is a deep midnight blue. At the centre of the clearing stand two figures: the Lord and Lady of the Greenwood; Queen and King of the May. They are both clothed in green and crowned with flowers and leaves. On the Lord's head are tiny curving horns and roses grow in the Lady's hair. The Lord and Lady embrace and as they do so, flowers open all around their feet and plants spring into leaf. The first butterflies and moths flutter around their heads. Birds sing loudly and you see that the trees are full of their nests; everywhere chicks are hatching and fledglings are flying for the first time. Across the clearing a mother hare and her young leverets play. Behind the Lord a roebuck stands and two fauns run from beneath the Lady's skirts. A viper slithers through the grass.

All the new life of summer has begun at once. The Lady holds out a golden cup to the Lord and he drinks deeply. Then he gives the cup to her and she drinks. She holds out the cup to you. You take it and drink the wine of summer. Drink deeply. It seems to contain the essence of all the flowers, trees and plants of May and fills you with the wild joy of the season. You kneel before the Lord and Lady and receive their blessing; the blessing of the Greenwood at Beltane. Thank them. They fade from your sight and you are alone in the beautiful clearing with the animals, birds and flowers. Enjoy this vision of all the life of the forest for a while, then return along the path and out of the forest, full of energy and joy.

June

Power and Beauty

The Zenith of the Year

The longest day began at first light with a quiet ceremony to greet the sunrise on the Jurassic cliffs of East Devon. At noon, the sun's zenith was marked too, with drawings made with a burning glass. The day has been warm and sunny, and we assemble in the peace of evening at the working place we love on the southern slopes of Dartmoor to celebrate a ritual for the bountiful goddess of earth and the sun god at the height of his powers. Midsummer herbs have been gathered, strawberries and raspberries picked, and roses brought from our gardens. The place is a small copse of old oak and ash trees with a circular level place at its centre, carpeted with woodland flowers. We are welcome here. North of us is a granite tor and in the west a small stream tumbles noisily over mossy boulders in a series of waterfalls. The fire is lit in the fire bowl, spirals of smoke float lazily up through the trees, and Midsummer incense is offered to goddess and god. Water from the stream and the herbs of Midsummer are placed in the cauldron. Spirits of place are greeted and honoured, the circle is cast and we are outside everyday time and space. The goddess is invoked into a priestess, and the god into a priest. This ritual is joyful but peaceful and serene; everyone shares a sense that they are guided by the deities and by the spirits of woodland, water and the Moor. Circling our fire, we become part of the dance of sun, moon and planets. Priestess and priest, full of the presence of goddess and god, embrace over the cauldron as the year reaches its fullness. Roses are used to sprinkle water from the cauldron over everyone, conferring the blessings of Midsummer.

As the sun sets, we share our feast of Midsummer berries and fruits. We are enveloped in a deep peace; the year and the sun stand still for a timeless moment until we thank our goddess and god and bid them farewell, and the night and the year move on again. Light lingers in the west as the first stars and planets begin to show. No one wants to move or leave this magical time and place.

June Associations

Festivals: Midsummer (21st), Golowan/ Feast of John (21st–28th)

Figures: Sun God, Ceridwen, Juno

More Than Human: Bees, roses, Saint John's Wort

Totems and Symbols: Sun, sun wheel, flaming arrow, oak

As we gently stir ourselves, someone points across the stream to the west. To our astonishment, a big brock badger is standing stock still, watching us. We have no idea how long he has been there. We silently greet him, Tanglefoot, beast of the woodland, who has shared the Midsummer magic with us. Eventually he turns away slowly and disappears into the growing darkness. A bright, blue earthlight shines in the western sky late into the night; the year has turned once more.

In June the Witch's Year reaches its peak at Midsummer when we honour the sun god at the height of his powers. The year turns once more; the Holly King replaces the Oak King, the wren takes the place of the robin, and we look into the cauldron of Ceridwen. In the month of bees and flowers, we learn an alphabet of trees, and make more plant magic, make a sun wheel and experience the power of the Midsummer sun.

Like May, June is named after a Roman goddess: Juno, wife of Jupiter and mother of Mars. Juno presided over marriage, childbirth, and all aspects of women's lives, and so the Romans considered June a propitious month for weddings. Juno was honoured with roses, as was Aphrodite in Greece. The association between roses, which are in full bloom at Midsummer, and their perfume, and goddesses, especially those associated with love and sexuality, is widespread, and I like to decorate my altar with roses in June in honour of Juno, Hera, Aphrodite, Isis and other goddesses appropriate to the season. Wearing rose essential oil or rose perfumes is another way to honour these goddesses in June.

MIDSUMMER MYTHOS

At Midsummer witches celebrate the god as the Oak King; the lord of the waxing year at the height of his powers. The oak is the biggest tree in the forest. Its roots are said to reach as far below ground as its branches do above. It is also the strongest tree; its wood is long-lasting and hard-wearing, and was traditionally used to make doors, roof beams, the masts of ships, shields and barrels. Oak was the tree of Zeus and Jupiter, the chief gods of the Greek and Roman pantheons respectively, and the chief sacred tree of the druids (the word 'druid' derives from the same root as word for oak in the Celtic languages). The oak tree flowers at Midsummer when the oak is king. Midsummer sits opposite Yule on the wheel of the year and is its mirror image. Like Yule, it is a solar standstill and a hinge on which the year turns, and when the days start to grow shorter after the Solstice, the Oak King will be replaced by the Holly King, the lord of the waning or dark half of the year. In some traditions the oak and holly do battle at Midsummer, and the holly vanquishes the oak. The waxing and waning parts of the year are also embodied in the robin, the bird that rules from midwinter until midsummer, and the wren, who rules from Midsummer in its turn. At the end of the year, we will see these rivalries enacted in mummers' plays and other folk customs.

The goddess who presides over Midsummer for me is Ceridwen, the lady of the cauldron, who is revered by witches, druids and Pagans alike. Her story is well-known and is found in the Welsh *Hanes Taliesin*. Ceridwen was an enchantress who brewed a cauldron of herbs that was the source of mystical poetic inspiration (poetry was both magic and an art) and that would confer all knowledge of past, present and future on the first person who drank from it. It was intended for her son Afagddu and the cauldron had to be stirred for a year and a day before its magic would work. Ceridwen placed it on an island in Llyn Tegid (Bala Lake) and employed a local lad, Gwion Bach (Little Gwion) to stir it. On the last day of stirring, three drops of the hot liquid fell on Gwion's finger, and, without thinking, he put his finger in his mouth, thus instantly gaining all the knowledge meant for Afagddu. Gwion fled from Ceridwen's anger, in a shapeshifting chase in which they each took many forms, and which has been interpreted as a pursuit through the seasons of the ritual year. Gwion became a hare in the autumn and Ceridwen transformed herself into a greyhound and pursued him. He became a fish and she an otter; then he became a bird and she pursued him as a hawk. Finally, in the harvest season Gwion hid as a grain of corn amongst thousands of grains on a threshing-room floor. Ceridwen became a black hen, searched through all the grain with her beak and claws, found Gwion and ate him. When she returned to her own shape, she was pregnant with Gwion and nine months later gave birth to a baby boy who became the greatest poet, Taliesin (shining or radiant brow).

The idea of a mystical cauldron is central to Welsh and Irish myth. The Cauldron of Bran had the power to bring dead warriors back to life[7], and the poem *Preiddeu Annwn* tells of an Otherworld voyage made by Arthur and his companions to a series of forbidding, mysterious castles in search of a cauldron of great power. These stories are used in our own time as the basis of ritual and magical practice.

The cauldron is the source of inner vision, prophetic powers, and inspiration as well as magic, and Ceridwen is the deity who presides over all of this. The story of Taliesin demonstrates that she is all-powerful, and those who would practise magic must respect and honour her. She is also mistress of the seasons; her shapeshifting chase with Gwion is also the story of the seasons of the year, and the deity of all herb craft. She is venerated throughout the year, but Midsummer, more than any other time, is Ceridwen's season. She is at the heart of the Midsummer ritual, and presides over all the work done with herbs and plants in June. If you are lucky enough to possess a cauldron, consecrate it and dedicate to Ceridwen and use it at Midsummer. Familiarise yourself with the stories of Ceridwen; fill the cauldron with pure, fresh water from a stream or spring and ask her blessing on it. Cauldrons can be bought at antique shops, but if you do not have access to a cauldron, any large bowl or vessel that inspires you can be used for the Midsummer ritual.

The Welsh story of Blodeuwedd, told in the *Mabinogion*[8], also relates to Midsummer. The enchanters Math and Gwydion made a wife out of the flowers of oak, broom and meadowsweet for Lleu Llaw Gyffes, who was destined not to have a mortal wife. They called her Blodeuwedd, or Flower Face. She was unfaithful to Lleu, and he was ritually

A Word of Warning About Cauldrons

Do not be tempted to light a fire inside your cauldron, as I have seen some modern witches try to do. This may damage it, especially if it is old and rusty. A cauldron is a cooking pot and is designed have liquid inside it and to be used over a fire, and preferably hung from a tripod.

destroyed by her lover Gronw Pebyr, and left for dead, but then revived through Gwydion's magic. Lleu ritually killed Gronw in his turn, and Blodeuwedd was turned into an owl. 'Blodeuwedd' is still a name for the little owl in Welsh. She was made of Midsummer flowers, and Lleu and Gronw are the two halves of the year who fight for the love of the goddess. At Tomen y Mur, high in the mountains of North Wales, where Blodeuwedd and Lleu lived together, an oak and a holly tree, bent by the mountain winds, grow entwined together. Blodeuwedd is a strange and rather ambivalent character, but I honour her at Midsummer with a reading of her story and a quiet meditation.

CELEBRATING MIDSUMMER

The solar year reaches its peak at the Midsummer Solstice on 21 June. The Solstice is a time of deep magic when the sun appears to 'stand still' for several days; it rises and sets in the same place and there is little variation in day length. Each of the Equinoxes and Solstices affects us physically as well as spiritually and emotionally in different ways, and Midsummer has its own very strong atmosphere. It is a time when our bodies as well as our minds feel the magnetic power of the sun as well as its light, and this effect will be magnified if the Solstice coincides with a full moon. The sight of a full moon rising on a Midsummer night brings a feeling of all-encompassing joy and a strong sense of union with all of nature. Midsummer should be celebrated to the full, not just on the actual longest day, but throughout the Solstice period. The energy felt if a new moon occurs at Midsummer will be subtly different and have a focused intensity. As Midsummer is a time that is felt strongly in the body and the emotions, pay attention to how it makes you feel and allow it to be a physical and emotional experience. Like Midwinter, the Summer Solstice builds gradually on a magical level and you will start to feel its approach as June begins. Allow the energy of Midsummer to build within you throughout the month; focus on it and make your preparations with deliberate magical concentration, so that when the Solstice arrives you will be full of its intensity. It is a time chosen for initiations in some witch traditions, and is also favoured for witch weddings or handfastings.

At Midsummer, the great tide of the year will turn as the sun enters Cancer, the cardinal sign of water, the sign of the waters of life. It will move from the element of fire and become the ebbing tide of water; the element of the spirit and of love. The ebbing tide is a peaceful one that will be with us until the Autumn Equinox, and will fall gently away throughout the rest of summer and the harvest season. Midsummer is sometimes called Litha by witches and Pagans. The name originates from the Anglo-Saxon name for the two months of June and July; June was First Litha and July was Second Litha.

Midsummer is especially important in the northernmost latitudes where the hours of darkness are very short. It is celebrated throughout Scandinavia with a wealth of traditional customs and some beautiful Nordic Pagan ceremonies, and in Finland and Sweden it is a national holiday. Bonfires are the universal Midsummer custom. In Christian times in Britain the celebrations took place between Saint John the Baptist's Day on 24 June and Saint Peter's day on 29 June, thus marking the whole of the solar standstill period. In Scotland the Johnsmas fires were lit at sunset and kept burning until dawn, and the celebrations were greatest in the far north, with big bonfires of peat and heather lit in Orkney and Shetland. Shetland, close to the Arctic Circle, has very brief night hours of dusky twilight rather than darkness at Midsummer, known as Summer Dim. Puritans banned the Johnsmas fires in the seventeenth century but many were reinstated again in the eighteenth century. Midsummer fires were also celebrations of the harvest of the sea in the fishing communities of North and East Scotland. The village of Whalton in Northumberland has its midsummer custom of Burning the Baals on 4 July; a huge bonfire is lit and a big Kirn Baby or corn dolly wearing a long white dress is burned (*see also* August and Lammas).

Midsummer was celebrated with bonfires, torches made of blazing tar barrels on poles, and fireworks in Penzance in Cornwall until the late nineteenth century. In recent years the town has reinstated its medieval Golowan (Feast of John) celebration as a full-on community and arts festival with local Pagan input and elements. Its climax is the Mazey Day procession on Saint John's Day (24 June), with traditional serpent dancing, Penzance's Obby Oss Penglaz (a figure with a horse's skull, similar to the Welsh Mari Llwyd that we met in January), and dragons and other mythical beasts.

In Celtic belief, Midsummer is a time of deep enchantment, when normal rules do not apply, and it is fraught with dangers from the Otherworld. In Ireland and Wales it is a time when the old gods and spirits walk in this world. Midsummer Eve, like May Eve, is a time when the Faeries are abroad and wandering in the woods can be risky. Shakespeare knew this well – think of *A Midsummer Night's Dream*. It was also a time when witches and magicians would go out and seek the company of the spirits and Faeries, and ask for their help with magic. If you are tempted to go and meet the Others, anoint yourself with primrose oil and take your rowan cross for protection. The hollow hills; the burial mounds, megaliths and stone circles and other sacred places of the ancestors are the traditional gateways to the Otherworld and you may meet the land spirits celebrating Midsummer there. Remember not to join their dances, or you will be spirited away.

Fern seed (fern spores) confers invisibility if gathered at Midsummer, and will allow the bearer to go wherever they wish unnoticed. To be effective, it should be worn in the left shoe, but be careful, because fern seed belongs to the Faeries and if you try to take it, you will incur their jealousy and anger. They will try to stop you from getting it, using every trick they can think of. Saint John's wort, with its bright golden, sun-like flowers, is the great herb of Midsummer. Hung over doorways, it will prevent mischievous spirits from entering. In Scotland it was burnt on the Midsummer fires. It was believed to ward off the evil eye, malefic witchcraft and all enchantments and it was customary to sleep with it under the pillow on Saint John's Eve.

Plant Tinctures and Anointing Oils

In June my plant allies will be growing strongly. Tinctures are a staple in my magical work; they contain a little of the plant's spirit and, together with anointing oils, they are the best way of working with my plant allies in the winter months when the plants themselves are dormant. I dedicate this work to Ceridwen and ask her blessing before beginning. Tinctures are easy to make; the leaves of a plant are simply steeped in alcohol. Two or three drops can be drunk in a large glass of water for curing and conjuring; this is an extremely diluted safe dose of 'homeopathic' strength. Tinctures diluted in water can be used to cleanse objects and places, or increase their magical energy. I make tinctures of mugwort, vervain and Solomon's seal before Midsummer, while the days are still lengthening, so that they will contain all the magical energies of the season, and while the moon is waxing.

You will need

- Fresh plant material
- Alcohol: this should be a spirit (not wine or beer). Vodka works best as it is relatively tasteless and odourless. The amount depends on the jar you use, but a 750cl bottle of vodka will fill an average size preserving jar. Do not use fancy flavoured alcohol; basic is best
- A glass jar with an airtight lid
- Fine mesh sieve
- Large bowl or jug
- Small funnel (optional)
- Bottles with stoppers for the finished tincture

Method

Pick your plant material on a morning when the moon is waxing and as close to the Midsummer Solstice as possible. Work with your plant ally first to ensure that you have its blessing. There should ideally be enough plant material to half fill your jar. Ensure that the material is clean. Put the plant material in the jar.

Pour the alcohol over the plant material until the jar is full and put the lid on. Place the jar out of direct sunlight and leave the tincture to steep for about a month, shaking the jar gently every few days. The tincture may change colour as the herb infuses; this is a natural part of the process and a sign that it is working. Mugwort, for example, makes a deep brown tincture; vervain will be a delicate golden green.

When the tincture is ready, strain it through the sieve into a large bowl or jug to remove the plant material, which can be composted or recycled.

Pour the finished tincture into clean glass bottles and stopper them tightly.

Plant-based anointing oils should also be made at this time, using exactly the same method used in March for primrose anointing oil. For an anointing oil, use less plant material than you would for a tincture; only a little is needed. Unlike tinctures, while making anointing oils, leave the jar containing the plant material in sunlight to infuse, as the light and warmth of the sun help to release the active properties of the plants. Tinctures and oils can also be made later in the summer if you wish.

Store tinctures and anointing oils away from light. They should be used within a year, so do not make more than you think you will need; throwing excess away is wasteful and bad magical practice.

THE CELTIC TREE ALPHABET

In June the trees are in full leaf, so it is the best time to make a Celtic Tree Alphabet as the trees will be easier to identify. As we saw in March, the Tree Alphabet is a system of tree magic. It is both a calendar and an alphabet. It is descended from the Gaulish Coligny Calendar and from several early medieval sources from Wales and Ireland. It owes its current form to the poet Robert Graves[9] and subsequent work by magical practitioners, especially witches and druids. As we noted in March, it is a complex system that can be studied in great detail and that weaves myth and magical practice together in an enchanting way. It is linked to the Ogham system of writing that can be used both to empower wands, magical tools and objects, talismans and charms, and also as a system of divination[10].

Make your own tree alphabet by collecting a twig from each tree of the alphabet. Each twig should measure from the tip of your middle finger to the base of your palm. This sounds like a difficult task, but I was able to find almost all of my twigs in a single large area of accessible native woodland in Devon, except for rowan, gorse and heather (which came from Dartmoor), yew (from a churchyard), apple (from an orchard), and a reed (from a river bank). I set this as an exercise for new witches and several have completed it successfully using city parks, botanic gardens and urban green spaces as sources. There are several variants of the tree alphabet that fit the trees around the year in slightly different ways, and some trees are omitted from some versions. As with many aspects of witchcraft, there is no one 'correct' version, and it is up to you to choose the one that suits you best. The letters are the initial letters of the names of the trees in either Irish or Welsh (the names are similar in both languages and have the same initials). The consonants represent lunar months, and the vowels represent days (Solstices, Equinoxes and Sabbats). In all versions the alphabet begins with the birch tree at the start of the year in January, and Midsummer belongs to the oak. I have included here all the trees listed in different versions, in the order that they usually appear, so that you can make your own choices.

	Consonants	*Vowels*
B Birch	C Hazel	A Fir or Pine
L Rowan	M Vine or Honeysuckle	O Gorse/Furze
N Ash	G Ivy	U Heather
F Alder	Q Apple	E White Poplar or Aspen
S Willow	P/NG Reed	I Yew
H Hawthorn	R Elder	
D Oak	Sz/Z Blackthorn	
T Holly		

Collect your twigs in a respectful manner and leave them somewhere cool to dry. The initial letter for each tree can be written with black ink on the ends of its twig, or lightly burnt into it. Keep the alphabet wrapped in a cloth or make a bag for it. Take it back to one of the woodland places where you collected the twigs and conduct a small ritual. Ask Ceridwen and the spirits of the woodlands to bless your alphabet. When you pick your tree alphabet and use it, it will feel as if you have the essence of woodland in your hand, and the spirits of all the trees will be with you. Subtle variations in the colours and textures of the twigs will be accentuated as the alphabet ages.

The Sun Wheel

There are two types of sun wheel that are made for the Midsummer ritual. Both should be made at the beginning of June. The first is burnt during the ritual. An equal-armed cross made of two pieces of oak is fitted into a willow wreath base to form a cross within the circle. Flowers, herbs (including Saint John's wort and vervain) and oak leaves are threaded into the wreath base, together with dry straw or scraps of paper which will help it catch alight. The wheel is then left to dry so that it will burn well at Midsummer.

The second type of sun wheel originates in Scandinavian Midsummer ceremonies and has been widely adopted by witches and Pagans. It is made with wood, yarn and fabrics and is not burnt during the ritual but used to decorate the working place or your house or garden. This is magic through making; a great witch's craft project for June, and one that children will enjoy. It can be made in any size, from something that is small enough to fit into the palm of a hand, to something larger than a person. It is a good group activity; a coven may get together to make one very large sun wheel for the ritual, or individuals could each make their own.

You will need

- Four sticks or small branches of wood. Any kind of wood can be used, or garden canes, but I prefer to use oak if I can get it. For a small sun wheel, the pieces could measure from the tip of your middle finger to the bottom of your palm. For a very big sun wheel, they should measure from the end of one of your outstretched arms to the end of the other. There is no need to stick with these sizes; this is entirely up to you but do remember that the bigger the wheel, the more fabric and other materials you will need
- Strong garden twine
- A mix of yarn, ribbon, raffia or strips of fabric cut into lengths in fiery sun colours. Choose whatever looks good. The quantity needed will vary according to how big a sun wheel you want to make. Old materials from recycling centres or jumble sales are ideal. A mix of materials will look good. For a small sun wheel, you may prefer just to use yarn and ribbon

Method

There are two important principles here. The first is that you use your magical will throughout the process and concentrate on Midsummer. Bring images of the sun or the deities of the season to mind as you work. The second is that you use your creativity, enjoy the process, and create colour combinations that please you.

Bind two of the sticks together with twine at their centres and tie them tightly to form a secure equal-armed cross. Make a similar cross with the other two sticks, then bind the two crosses together securely to form an eight-spoked wheel.

Starting at the centre of the wheel, and tying one end securely to one of the spokes, weave a length of yarn, thread or fabric around the cross, wrapping it once round each spoke as you go. Weave tightly to make a secure sun wheel.

When you reach the end of the length, tie another one to it. Continue in this fashion until you have filled the cross with your materials, leaving just a small amount of wood (not longer than from the tip of your thumb to its first joint) showing at the outside edges. Tie the last end of material tightly to a spoke to finish the cross.

Make a secure hanging loop if you wish.

After the Midsummer ritual, the sun wheel can be placed on your altar or in a garden or other outdoor space. It can be left until it fades and falls apart naturally, or burnt at Lammas. Make a new one every year.

THE SUNFIRE CHARM

This is an intense form of embodied magic that creates a very personal link between the witch and the sun at Midsummer. It is difficult, slow work that requires concentration and perseverance, and can only be undertaken on a hot sunny day in June. It calls for a burning glass (a small magnifying glass works well), and it should always be done outdoors for safety reasons. First the outline of a sun symbol is drawn on a piece of wood or thick cardboard with a pencil. The witch then focuses the sun's rays onto the drawing using the burning glass and burns the image of the sun over the pencil outline into the wood or card. The witch concentrates their magical will with the sun's rays in the burning glass, and a deep magical connection with the sun is made. Making the sunfire charm requires immense concentration and should be done with great care. Once made, the sunfire charm is a powerful talisman full of the warmth and blessing of the sun.

BEES

Bees have played an important role in some Pagan mythologies and in magical ritual down the ages because humans have interacted with bees, and used honey and beeswax since very early times. Honey was used to sweeten foods, but it also had curative properties and was one of the oldest preservatives; in Egypt, both honey and beeswax were part of the embalming process and had many medical uses. Bees were said to be the tears of the Sun god Ra.

The Bronze Age Minoans of Crete worshipped the goddess Potnia, whose symbol was a bee. The Greeks wove a complex web of myth and magical symbolism around bees and honey; they used bees as oracles, and the priestess of the sun god Apollo at Eryx was called the Melissa, or Queen Bee, and carried a golden honeycomb. This title was also applied to the priestesses of the goddesses Demeter and Persephone who celebrated the Mysteries at Eleusis. Nymphs were referred to as Melissae; the first Melissa had fed the infant Zeus with honey and milk.

Beekeeping is both dangerous and a magical art in its own right, and beekeepers possessed their own secret magical knowledge and powers. There is much folklore about bees. In Devon where I live, the custom of 'telling the bees', which is widespread throughout Britain, persists to this day. Bees must always be told of a death in the family; the beekeeper goes to their hives and announces the sad news. Customs grow and change, and local people now tell the bees about births too.

Cecil Williamson, founder of the Museum of Witchcraft at Boscastle in Cornwall, collected a good luck charm given to a new baby consisting of two bumble bees (dead) in a charm bag. This lovely custom can be continued by presenting the parents of a newborn baby with a charm bag containing two enamel or ceramic bees.

Beeswax is the basis for herbal ointments and balms. It can be used to polish and protect the witch's wand or staff. It is also the material traditionally used to make poppets; the dolls used in image magic, and it continues to have many uses in witchcraft.

As pollinators, bees play an essential role in food production. They collect pollen from flowers grown in the light of the sun, which they then turn into honey and wax. To the witch, beeswax is stored sunlight, so that burning a beeswax candle in a ritual will release the stored power of the sun for magical purposes. This is one of the deeper reasons behind the burning of beeswax candles in so many spells as well as rituals; you are harnessing the power of the sun in your work. Even the simplest actions can be full of layers of meaning and symbolism that can be used to great magical effect.

Honey was the source of the sacred drink of mead, given to mortals by the gods, in both the Northern tradition and Celtic Paganism. Mead is made from fermented honey and may be the oldest form of alcohol made by humans. Archaeological traces from China of a beverage made with honey date back 9,000 years. It was made in Egypt, Greece and Rome. The oldest conclusive evidence of mead in Europe comes from a pot found on the Scottish island of Rhum that has been dated to 2500BCE. Mead was the drink of choice in early medieval times for the Celts, Saxons and Vikings alike. Its making and use were regulated in the tenth century CE Welsh laws of Hywel Dda; in Ireland it plays a part in the legend of the children of Lir and one of the largest structures on the Hill of Tara, the seat of the High Kings of Ireland, is named the Tech Midchuarta or Great Mead Hall.

The mead hall was the place where communal feasts were held in Saxon England and there are references to mead and to mead halls in Saxon poetry and riddles. Mead held an important place in Norse Pagan belief: the *Prose Edda* (written in Iceland in 1220CE) relates how Odin stole the mead of poetry, the source of poetic inspiration and knowledge from Suttungr's daughter Gunnlod and gave it to the gods and to gifted poets. It is little wonder that mead is a popular drink with modern Pagans and is *de rigeur* at Northern Tradition gatherings. If you want to have alcohol at your Midsummer feast, mead is the obvious choice.

Practice: The Midsummer Ritual

Of all the Sabbats, Midsummer carries with it an atmosphere of deep mystery, and you may feel the goddess or god moving and speaking through you at this time. The ritual can bring a kind of joyous inner calm. It holds strong memories for me, as I was first initiated into a coven, a truly life-changing moment, at Midsummer.

Preparation

Midsummer garlands are made from oak leaves, Saint John's wort, vervain and mugwort, picked early after sunrise on Midsummer Day. Use a willow wreath base or just weave and tie the herbs together. The garlands can be worn at the Midsummer ritual or used to decorate the working place or altar. They contain the herbs of enchantment and vision, and will strengthen the connection with goddess and god.

A good fire to honour the sun and the Oak King is at the heart of the Midsummer ritual. The Midsummer fire should include oak wood, even just a few dry twigs collected from the woodland floor. The old garlands from the Beltane ritual and any old charms that have finished their work should also form part of the Midsummer fire. It is important to get rid of them to make way for the new harvest season that is about to start. The altar can be decorated with roses and other Midsummer flowers. The ritual also calls for a single rose and a cauldron (see Ceridwen, above), or other large bowl filled with water. Use fresh stream or well water if you can.

The Midsummer feast consists of seasonal foods: summer fruits, edible flowers, fresh vegetables, salads; anything that is in season and can be picked or gathered on the day, plus anything else you enjoy. As well as mead, the juice of summer fruits, elderflower cordial or champagne, and fresh spring water are good choices for Midsummer drinks.

The main Midsummer ritual takes place as the sun sets, but there are a number of other observances that can take place throughout the longest day. Midsummer usually involves being awake from sunrise until late at night (unless you can plan for a siesta in mid-afternoon). Celebrating the sunrise is an important part of Midsummer, whether it is done alone on a hilltop or with thousands of others at Stonehenge, or even in the pouring rain if needs must. Witch friends on the North Sea coast of England, which faces the sunrise, fire a flaming arrow from a high cliff into the sea to greet the rising sun. Salute the sun: catch the sunrise in your witch's mirror, and bathe your body from head to foot in the sun's golden light. In the morning, fresh oak leaves, Saint John's wort and vervain for the garlands should be gathered. An old witch tradition is the lighting of the Midsummer fire at noon with the sun's own fire, when the sun reaches its zenith. A burning glass is used to kindle a flame from dry leaves and straw. A candle is then lit from the flame and nurtured carefully in a lantern until it is time for the ritual.

The ritual

Place the fabric sun wheel somewhere in the working place where it can be seen and enjoyed. If you have made an oak and willow sun wheel to burn, either fasten it to two poles so that it can burn safely, or put it on the fire at the end of the ritual. The altar is placed in the north and decorated with flowers and garlands. As with all outdoor rituals, a tall staff can be used instead of a conventional altar. The fire should be in the centre of the circle, and the cauldron or vessel full of water and the rose should be placed in the west. If you are working with others, you may choose two people to call upon the goddess and god. They should be garlanded.

Light the fire, remembering that you do this as the great tide of fire reaches its peak, and cast the circle. Then walk around the circle to each of the quarters (this can be done by one person alone or by everyone present):

> In the east say: 'May the winds blow cool and clean.'
> In the south say: 'May the sun bring warmth and light.'
> In the west say: 'May the waters flow bright and pure.'
> In the north say: 'May the earth bloom and her creatures thrive.'

The person chosen should call upon the god; they may create their own form of words for this. Call upon the god as the lord of the sun; as Helios, Lugh, Lleu, Belinus and by any other names you like to use. He is the lord of light and the king of glory, the golden bearer of the shining spear of light. Welcome him to your ritual and thank him for all the blessings of Midsummer, of the year and growth at its peak. Celebrate him at the height of his powers as the great tide of fire reaches its climax. You may wish to create a special form of words to use. Do this with focused intent, and visualise the god amongst you. You may sense his presence. Sit by the fire and meditate on the lord of the sun, fire and light.

The person chosen should then call upon the goddess as Ceridwen, mistress of the cauldron, mother of mystery, shapeshifter, lady of magic, vision and inspiration, lady of herb craft and mother of Taliesin. Again, you may create your own form of words for this; use whatever inspires you. Welcome her to your circle and sense her presence amongst you.

Ceridwen calls you to look into her cauldron in the west, to look within and see in its waters the reflected beauty of the earth, and then look beyond into the depths to see your own visions of goddess and god at Midsummer. Spend some time looking into the cauldron and meditating on the visions given to you.

Rap three times with a wand on the cauldron, then take the rose and dip it into the water in the cauldron. Sprinkle the water from Ceridwen's cauldron on the heads of everyone present, at the moment of Midsummer, when the sun god in his strength moves into the sign of the Waters of Life and the great tide turns once more. Receive the blessing of Ceridwen and the sun god.

Share the Midsummer feast, then thank the goddess and god and the spirits of the place, and close your circle.

A Spell for June: Storing the Warmth of the Sun

In June when the sun is at its strongest, our spell allows for a little of its warmth and power to be saved for the dark months of winter.

You will need

- Fresh flower petals
- A couple of vervain leaves (optional)
- A sheet of paper (newspaper or brown wrapping paper are ideal)
- Two squares of semi-transparent fabric (for example, muslin or organza), measured from the top to the bottom of your palm. You will make a charm bag, and as this is quite a visual spell, you want to be able to see the contents
- Needle and thread

Method

On a sunny morning in June, when the moon is waning, and after the dew has dried, gather fresh flower petals. Ask the permission of the plants and their blessing on your spell. Plants whose petals are starting to fall are ideal. Use whatever you like: wild flowers (but only plentiful ones; pick them gently and do not be greedy) and garden flowers, and choose bright colours. I like to include roses and marigolds. Use Saint John's wort if you have it. You will need enough to fill a small charm bag. As with all plant magic, do not allow the petals to touch the ground. Add a couple of vervain leaves if you wish.

Place the petals on the sheet of paper and put them somewhere out of direct light to dry. Spread them out thinly so they will dry easily. The drying process may take a few days or several weeks. Make sure the petals are completely dry and papery to the touch before you work the rest of the spell.

Cut out your fabric squares. With the wrong side of the fabric (if there is one) facing, place them together and sew them together on three sides. As you sew, concentrate your magical will. Picture the sun shining onto flowers in bloom. Turn the bag right side out.

Stuff the bag with the dried petals. As you do so, concentrate again on the warmth and power of the sun and ask the blessing of the sun on your magic. Then sew up the fourth side of the bag, sealing the petals and the magic in.

Place the bag on your altar to charge until the next new moon. Keep it safe and take it out on dark, winter days when you need to conjure up the midsummer sun, or give it as a witch gift to someone who finds winter difficult.

A Meditation for June: The Oak and The Holly

This meditation is about the moment when the year changes at Midsummer; when the rising tide of fire gives way to the ebbing tide of water, and the Holly King takes his place as the ruler of the waning half of the year.

Picture yourself in a green field in the evening of the Summer Solstice, when the sun stands still. At the western edge of the field, next to a hedgerow where wild roses bloom, is a lone oak tree. It is ancient, with wide spreading boughs, and it is flowering. The hedgerow is loud with the buzzing of bees, and with many birds singing. Behind the oak the huge golden sun is sinking low in the evening sky. You walk towards the oak tree. As you draw near you see that there is a man standing under the tree. He is tall, and stands very straight. He is dressed in a long green robe of emerald green embroidered in gold with acorns and oak leaves, and holds a staff made of a living, flowering oak branch. A young white roebuck lies at his feet, a viper slides through the grass, and a robin perches on his staff. He wears a crown of oak leaves and in its midst is a gold circlet with a shining gold sun in its centre. He is the Oak King, lord of the growing half of the year. He smiles at you, and his smile is full of the warmth of summer.

As you come close you see that behind the oak tree, in its shadow, is a much smaller holly tree, with a grey trunk and very deep green, glossy evergreen leaves. Standing by the holly tree, in the shadow of the oak, is another man. Like the Oak King, he stands tall and straight. He wears a long robe that is a green so deep it is almost black, embroidered in silver with holly leaves and berries. He holds a staff made of deep grey, polished holly wood. A grey she-wolf crouches at his feet, an owl perches in the tree above him and a wren, the smallest of the birds, flutters around his head. He wears a crown of holly leaves and ivy and in its midst is a silver circlet with a shining silver moon disc at its centre. He smiles at you, and you feel for a moment the cold of winter; of frost and snow. He is the Holly King, the lord of the waning half of the year.

The two kings stand site by side and embrace. As they do so the Oak King melts away and disappears. The Holly King, now alone, steps forward. He seems to grow taller and more regal, and has his own power and beauty. He raises his staff toward the setting sun in a silent gesture of triumph. Then he too is gone. You understand that the hinge of the year has swung, and the year has turned once more, this time towards autumn and winter. You take a leaf from the oak tree and a leaf from the holly tree as a token. The setting sun slips behind the two trees; the light fades and the first stars awaken. Return, slowly and peacefully, with the oak leaf and the holly leaf, to continue your journey on into the second part of the Witch's Year.

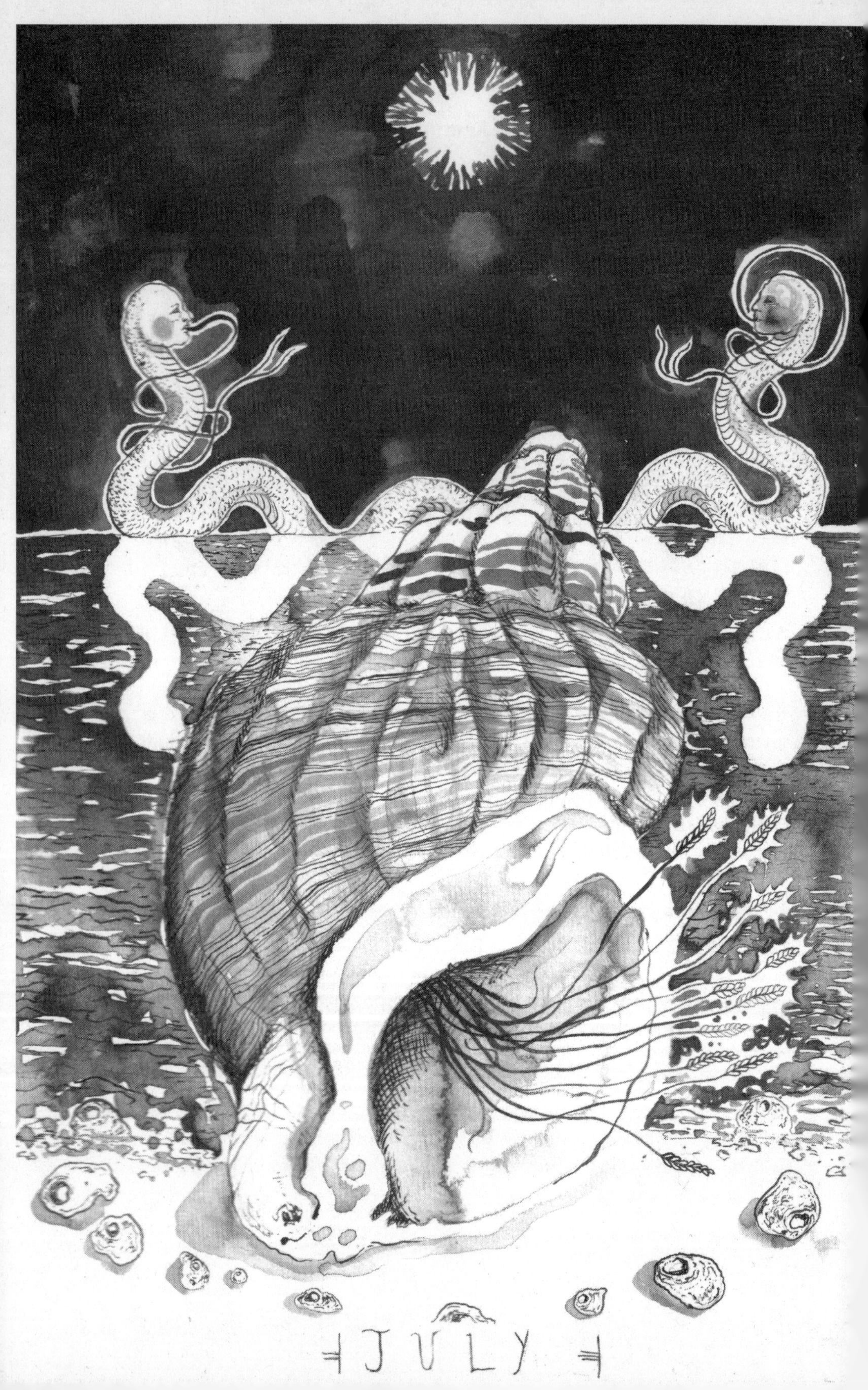
JULY

July

Reflection and Fullness

The Ripening Year

The big barley field is still and silent on a hot evening towards the end of July. The air is full of the sweet smell of barley just about to ferment. The combine harvester arrived soon after sunrise as the dew was drying, and roared up and down all day long in the blistering heat, cutting great swathes through the barley, spitting out bales of straw and generating clouds of dust that stung throats and made eyes water. Rabbits, hares and field mice scampered away, escaping just in time as the blades thundered on relentlessly. The barley is the first to go; the wheat fields will wait until August. Now the field rests peacefully in the evening heat. Only the stubble remains, with its dry, sharp stems, except at the edges where stray ears of barley lie flattened on the ground.

After they had finished combining, Reg, Jimmy and Mick left one sheaf uncut in the middle of the field. Everyone came out to watch, as they did every year. Each man took a small hand sickle and threw it at the sheaf, yelling as they did so. No one individual was responsible. Reg gathered up the remains of the sheaf and brandished it above his head, shouting, 'What have I? What have I?' and everyone shouted back, 'A neck, a neck'. Later the neck would be plaited and hung up in the barn until next year.

As the sun went down they arranged straw bales into a circle. The Boss brought out bottles of cider and we all sat and toasted the harvest, singing and joking, until the cider was all gone. Now, as it grows dark, I sit by my window watching the field as the last glow of the sunset fades and a fat waxing moon rises over the woods behind the farm. The silence deepens as the darkness grows, and the first stars come out. I have to keep very still. Then, as I watch, a line of shadowy grey shapes begins to move out from the woods and along the edge of the field. The gleaners; the roe deer who live in the woods, pick their way gracefully down the path

July Associations

Festivals: None

Figures: Thunder Gods (Zeus/ Taranis/ Thor, etc.), deities of springs, wells, rivers (Sul, Coventina, Tamara etc.)

More Than Human: Thunderstorms, the heliacal rising of Sirius, gifts of the sea (shells, pebbles, witch stones etc.), fossils, snakes/vipers

Totems and Symbols: Thunderbolt, serpent, sea shell (cowrie, conch, scallop)

by the hedge to eat the leftover corn. This is the only time that they are ever seen together out in the open. They know where to go, led by a beautiful antlered stag who sniffs delicately at the air, making sure it is safe. He stations two young bucks at either end of the herd and they stand, nervously watching, listening, sensing for danger as the others eat the precious barley grains that have been left just for them. Then suddenly they sense something, and are gone in an instant, running back along the field edge to the shelter of the woods, as the moon rises higher in the sky. The harvest time has begun.

The year has turned and with it the great tide. July brings peaceful reflection as we gaze deep into the waters of vision. We learn the magic of wells and rivers, of the seashore and its treasures, and of thunderstorms and serpents. Sirius appears as the dog days approach and hearts bring love and plenty. The harvest begins.

July can seem like a rather betwixt and between month; we have reached the second half of the Witch's Year and after the longest day at Midsummer the days will gradually grow shorter. Like January, which sits opposite July on the Wheel of the Year, this month follows a Solstice or solar standstill, one of the great hinges on which the year turns; and, like January, it is a time for reflection and taking stock before moving forward, this time towards autumn and winter. The mythic Oak King who ruled the growing first half of the year has been replaced by the Holly King, who will rule the waning half in his turn until Midwinter, and the wren, the bird of the waning year, has likewise replaced the robin.

There is a different energy now, because most growth has finished, and corn and fruits are starting to ripen before the harvest. This change is mirrored on an inner level; when July begins, it is time to pause and reflect on the first half of the Witch's Year; to look back and review what has been achieved and what has been learnt. There is a sense of calm, peacefulness and fulfilment, and the long summer days provide an ideal opportunity to stop for a while and think. Take time to do this; look back over your journal, the records of your spells and magic, and the things you have made. Review things honestly; this will give you a good sense of how you would like to move forward and what you would most like to discover and achieve next.

July is the time when Sirius, the Dog Star, and the brightest star in the sky, can be seen for the first time in the pre-dawn sky (the precise date varies from year to year). This first heliacal rising is considered to be of great magical importance. For the Egyptians, it was a sign that the Nile flood that made Egypt fertile would soon begin, and they thought of Sirius as a stellar form of the goddess Isis, called Sothis. I like to get up early and greet Sirius when it first appears. It signifies that the year has really turned, that the harvest season is about to begin and that a different kind of thinking and magic will be needed for the rest of the year. It is also a perfect moment to honour Isis and Osiris and ask their blessing. Spend some quiet time contemplating Sirius in the summer sky in the hour before sunrise, and communing with goddess and god.

THE ELEMENT OF WATER

At Midsummer the great tide of the year moved into the element of water and this month we will look deeper into the role water can play in witchcraft. Water is the element of vision, on many levels. It is the element of psychic vision, of inward sight; of looking, seeing and scrying. It is also associated with numerous goddesses; around the world goddesses are embodied in seas and rivers, and thought of as the source of life-giving water. Wells and springs have their own spirits and in most instances these are female.

In western magical practice, Undines are the elemental spirits of water, and usually appear in female form. Naiads are female Greek water nymphs who preside over wells, springs and rivers. They may take human shape and mate with mortals. The Welsh Gwragedd Annwn are otherworldly female water Faeries who live beneath lakes and rivers. They have their own herds of cattle and may walk out of lakes and appear to mortals. The well-known Welsh tale of the Lady of Llyn y Fan Fach tells of a beautiful otherworld woman who appeared from a lake with her Faerie cattle. A mortal man fell in love with her, and they married after he promised that he would never hit her. Inevitably, he did so three times, after her Otherworldly nature and failure to understand mortal customs led her to embarrass him in public. She returned to her home under the lake, taking the Faerie cattle with her, never to return, but passed on some of her magic to her mortal children who became renowned medical practitioners, the *Meddygon* (physicians) of Myddfai. This legend is attached to a very specific landscape, and if you wish to go on a quest for water spirits, the mountain lake of Llyn y Fan Fach, which has an overwhelming Otherworld atmosphere, and the nearby village of Myddfai can be visited.

Melusine, whose story is found throughout France and in the Low Countries, is a female well or river spirit and enchantress who is a fish or serpent from the waist down. Several noble medieval families, including members of the house of Anjou and also the English Plantagenet monarchs, were said to be descended from her, and to have inherited some of her magical powers. Like the Lady of Llyn y Fan Fach, she married a mortal, but on condition he promised never to watch her bathing. When he broke this taboo, she returned to her own element.

The kelpie is a dangerous Scottish river spirit, usually a male, who takes the form of a beautiful black horse and tempts humans, especially children, to climb on its back and ride. When they do so the kelpie plunges under the water, drowning them.

These tales warn of the potential dangers of water and its spirits, but also emphasise its otherness. Mortal lovers are passionately attracted to water beings and their magic because of their beauty and strangeness. They try, but ultimately fail, to understand and live with their Otherworld nature. Understanding the element of water and working with it are important in the practice of witchcraft, and this work can begin in July with encounters with holy wells, lakes and rivers that begin in the everyday world and take the witch on a journey inwards to deeper spiritual levels.

HOLY WELLS

Holy wells have played an important part in my witchcraft for many years; I visit them regularly to work with the spirits and seek visions, and use their water in rituals and spells. In the Celtic lands holy wells are often associated with eyes and some are said to cure blindness or improve vision. Spending time in meditation at one of these places deepens the witch's understanding of the element of water and all its magic, and will deepen the inner visual senses and abilities. If you find visualisation difficult, spend some time gazing into the water and meditating at one of the holy wells.

The old wells are liminal places too; doorways into the inner worlds, and places where spirits gather. They are places of mystery; crossing the threshold into a stone well house feels like entering a separate world; do it slowly and use all your senses. On a quiet July day, gazing into the still, dark water of a well pool brings not only reflection, but visions of the world within and the deep places of the world of spirit. If you can visit a well at night, look at the moon reflected in the water and travel deep into a world of vision and waking dreams. Anoint your forehead and hands with well water.

Take your witch's mirror to a holy well and dip it into the water, asking the goddess or well spirit to cleanse it and imbue it with the magic of vision. You can also do this with other witch's tools and special pieces of jewellery. Collect water for use at Sabbat rituals and in practical magic. Well water for ritual use should be stored in a blue glass bottle and can be left in the light of the full moon to receive the blessing of the moon goddess. It should then be stored out of the light until you use it.

The city of Bath is the site of Britain's only naturally occurring thermal waters and one of its most important, but often overlooked, Pagan sacred places. The Roman baths were built over the existing sanctuary of the goddess Sul, whose name is linked to old Celtic words for eyes and vision. The Romans called the city Aquae Sulis and identified Sul with their own goddess Minerva. Along with beautiful images of Sul and other deities, there is a wealth of evidence of how Romano-British people venerated the goddess and practised magic. The subterranean hot spring of the goddess, where the waters emerge wreathed in steam from the depths of the earth, is a sacred and mysterious place. It is still possible to honour Sul at Bath; at the spring and the Roman baths, and by taking the waters in the public spa there which explicitly reverences the goddess. Bathing in the hot waters of the goddess Sul, who has been honoured at Bath for over 2,000 years is a spiritual as well as a sensual experience.

Other ancient sacred springs that have been venerated down the centuries include those at Malvern in Worcestershire, which is home to several magical wells that spring from the base of the Malvern Hills, Buxton (Roman Aquae Arnemetiae) in the Derbyshire Peak District, and Harrogate in Yorkshire. At Carrowburgh on Hadrian's Wall there is a shrine to Coventina, goddess of the local springs. Chalice Well at Glastonbury is a place of contemplation set in quiet gardens, while the neighbouring White Spring has become a chthonic New Age sanctuary. The petrifying wells at Matlock Bath in Derbyshire and Knaresborough in Yorkshire are strange and magical places where limestone deposits in the water coat objects left in the wells in a stony substance. The well at Knaresborough is the site of Mother Shipton's Cave and was the place where a renowned medieval prophetess and magical practitioner worked.

Holy wells are especially venerated in the Celtic nations. Some are extremely ancient and associated with sites dating back to the Iron or Bronze Ages. In Wales, Ireland, Scotland

A Word About Clouties and Other Offerings

The centuries-old custom of leaving clouties at holy wells originated in Scotland and Ireland. It is a curing custom: small strips of cloth were torn from the clothing of a sick person and left at the well, usually tied to a hawthorn tree. As the cloth decayed away, so the illness would leave the afflicted person. In recent years the custom has become widespread and people now leave clouties at holy wells everywhere. The original clouties would have been made of organic materials (wool, linen and cotton) and would soon decay and do no damage. Clouties have become general-purpose offerings at wells and the majority of people leaving them do not know that the cloth should have come from the clothing of a sick person. Now people leave indestructible clouties made of artificial fabric that will not decay, and even strips torn from plastic carrier bags. This is doing damage and there have been instances of cows and other animals being hurt by ingesting plastic and nylon left at wells. These clouties will not 'work' magically because if the fabric cannot decay, the illness will not be cured.

Other 'offerings' left at wells, especially tealights, plastic jewellery and even flowers can also be harmful. Paraffin wax and metal tealight holders can poison aquatic creatures or be ingested by animals. Wax drips onto stones and kills lichens that have taken many years to grow. Large flowers quickly rot and pollute well water. A witch who is the guardian of a holy well in Dorset regularly removes refuse sacks full of plastic bags, nylon, tealight holders, plastic beads, rotting vegetation and other harmful stuff, and has had angry encounters with people who think it is their right to leave whatever they choose. Of course, these practices are well-meant and the impulse to leave something for the spirits at these liminal places is a powerful one.

Please think about this; if you must leave clouties, plan ahead and take a natural fabric with you (cut up an old cotton T shirt). I prefer to leave mental thanks and blessings. The holy wells are very special places and precious eco-systems; please cherish them rather than accidentally harming them.

and Cornwall, wells named after Celtic saints from the early Christian period may have already been sacred places when the saints arrived. Catholicism in Ireland has ensured the survival of the wells, but following the Reformation, many in Wales and Scotland fell into ruin. Some are now beyond rescue, but others that were lost or destroyed have been saved from oblivion and rebuilt; they are sacred places once again. I like to honour the goddess and the spirits at the many holy wells in Cornwall, amongst them Saint Clether (the most beautiful well chapel I know, with an extraordinary aura of peace and sanctity), Chapel Euny, Madron, Mylor, St Ruan, Whitstone (where an ancient carved stone head watches over the water), Sancreed, Laneast and Holywell Bay (where the spring flows into a sea cave that can only be reached at low tide). The wells of my native Ynys Môn are very special too; amongst them Ffynnon Seiriol at Penmon, Ffynnon Gwenfaen on the clifftop at Rhoscolyn, where two tiny white pebbles were the preferred offering to the saint, and the recently restored Fynnon Eilian, at the foot of cliffs just yards from the sea. Sadly, the twin wells of the saints Seiriol and Cybi at Clorach at the centre of Ynys Môn, the site of a local legend with strong Pagan overtones, are almost lost. In Cornwall, local Pagans have played a central role in restoring the old wells, and in some places they own wells or act as guardians. Most holy wells, apart from the most well-known ones, are peaceful places that are seldom visited and where it is possible to spend quiet time with the spirits and the goddess of the waters. A well that has become neglected or ignored will welcome your attention and its spirits will find a way of thanking you. Research your local holy wells and make time to visit them in July.

SACRED LAKES AND RIVERS

For our distant ancestors, water was a boundary between two worlds, and what archaeologists term 'ritual deposits' of precious objects, often of deliberately broken weapons, were placed in pools, lakes and rivers as offerings to the gods and spirits in the Bronze and Iron Ages. The story of the return of Arthur's sword Excalibur to the Lady of the Lake feels like a memory of these practices. The small lake of Llyn Cerrig Bach in Ynys Môn, close to the village where I grew up, was the site of one of the largest of these ritual deposits yet found. Objects found there included weapons, a chariot, ritual staffs, musical instruments and many other items. It was used for over 400 years in the Iron Age. When I was a young woman I sat by the side of the Llyn Cerrig Bach on a perfectly still July night, looking and looking at the full moon reflected in its waters until a vision of the spirits of the lake and the goddess who presided over it and the offerings made there long ago came to me and changed the course of my life. I began the journey into deep witchcraft that continues to this day.

Rivers have been understood as both sacred and powerful since the earliest times. The Severn, Wharfe and Tamar in Britain are the goddesses Sabrina, Verbeia and Tamar respectively, and the name of the river Dee is derived from the Latin *Dea* (goddess). The holy river Braint on Ynys Môn is named after Bride, and in Ireland the goddesses Boann and Sinann are the rivers Boyne and Shannon. Father Thames is an old river god. Linguists consider that river names are the oldest words in any given language. Rivers are deities and ancient boundaries and are held in awe; invaders and conquerors do not change their names, so it likely that the names we use for our rivers are those which have been used for thousands of years. Rivers must be respected and feared; riverbanks are betwixt and between, and dangerous places where the threat of drowning is always present. Folklore tells us that some rivers demand human lives; the Dart and the Wharfe are thought to claim a life every year and Dartmoor folklore avers that the Dart can sometimes be heard moaning and calling for its due.

A traditional Devon wishing spell requires you to tie a knot in a thin willow branch or similar vegetation hanging down over a river. (Be careful; this is a difficult and dangerous thing to attempt, and I cannot recommend that you try it!) As you tie the knot, you should speak your desire, and as the river flows away to the sea, your wish will be granted. Cecil Williamson once showed me a place on the River Exe where this spell had been carried out; a series of knots in willow fronds hung low over the river, some almost brushing the deep, fast-flowing water. Alternatively, to banish unhappiness or illness, stand on a bridge over a fast -flowing river. Cut a lock of your hair and throw it into the river while making your wish, let the river carry it away, and the unhappiness or illness will flow away from you with the water.

THE MONTH OF STORMS

July is the time for thunderstorms. In Pagan pantheons storms are presided over by gods who hurl thunderbolts across the sky including, amongst many: Zeus or Jupiter (the father of the Greek and Roman gods), Thor from the Northern pantheon, Celtic Taranis, Marduk in Babylon, Indra (India), Baal (the Old Testament of the Bible), Shango (Yoruba) and the dark Egyptian deity Set, lord of chaos and the desert.

Simply experiencing a thunderstorm late at night in July will bring the witch into contact with the three elements of fire, water and air combined into a unique force that flows through body, mind and spirit and invigorates and inspires. (A word on safety: do this from a safe place; do not risk being struck by lightning.) During a storm the air is full of teeming, dancing spirits that can be sensed strongly.

I use the power of a thunderstorm and call upon its spirits to charge objects, witch's tools and sometimes spells. These are left outside during the storm and not allowed to touch the ground. A piece of lightning-struck wood is a rare find that can be used as an altar to work with the deities and spirits of the storm. Rain water from a thunderstorm will be highly charged and can be used for spells or in rituals to invoke the thunder gods and spirits. Collect it in a glass or ceramic container (again, do not allow this to touch the ground). The water will be full of the power of the storm and can be used where quick, very direct results are needed, and in weather magic.

Protection against lightning strike is important for people who work outdoors. The traditional charm to ward off lightning is an acorn, carried in the pocket. The oak tree, the 'king' of the woods, is the tree of Zeus, Thor, Taranis and all thunder gods, so an acorn brings the blessing and protection of the god, and will keep the bearer safe from lightning. Silver acorn pendants fulfilled the same function. The strength and power of the oak was also used to protect homes. Oak lintels, doors and beams were not only strong, but also guarded against lightning. Doorways and windows needed special protection. Antique 'treen' carved or turned acorns made from oak wood and used as blind and curtain pulls, can be found in antique shops, and new ones are still made. Carved acorns placed on beams or rafters would prevent lightning from striking roofs and starting fires.

The pointed, bullet-shaped belemnite fossils, that were sometimes believed to be elf or Faerie arrows, were known as thunderstones and could be carried to ward off lightning. The fossil sea urchins known as shepherds crowns or Faerie loaves, and marked with a five-pointed star, provided similar protection.

SEASHORE MAGIC

July is the time for seashore magic. As we have already seen, the lunar and tidal rhythms are at the heart of the Witch's Year and we have been working in harmony with them since it began. Sea Witchcraft is a detailed magical practice in its own right; it is explained in depth in my book *A Sea Witch's Companion*. Experiencing the ebb and flow of the tides at the coast in July will bring you into closer harmony with the goddess of the moon, the sea gods and the spirits of the sea and shore, and will help you understand the physical as well as spiritual effects of the tidal rhythm on your body and mind.

The constantly changing liminal space between the high and low tidelines, that belongs to the spirits of the sea, is an ideal place for spell work. To work some simple sea magic, write a spell on the sand at low tide and as the tide rises, watch the sea wash over it and take the words away. The power of the tides will take your spell to where it needs to go. Asking the sea is a good old folk custom. The sea spirits have a habit of providing what is needed, even if it is not quite what you expected or wanted. Soon after taking over the Museum of Witchcraft in Boscastle from Cecil Williamson, Graham King needed some large stones to build a stone circle for a new display. These would have been too expensive to buy and transport. A few days later there was a massive storm and the sea delivered exactly the right amount of stones right outside the door of the Museum.

Years ago, sad after losing my favourite watch, but not really thinking about getting another one, I walked along the edge of the sea on a remote beach. Something glinted in the water at my feet; I picked it up. It was a watch. I shook it, thinking it could not possibly work after being in the salt water. It started ticking; I have used it for many years and still have it today. A wise witch learns to trust the sea and work with its gifts; to take what is offered and work with it creatively.

Ending the dumping of human rubbish in the sea and trying to remove existing pollution is becoming more and more urgent as our waste is causing terrible harm to the ocean and its creatures, so I take a refuse sack and begin any work at the shore with a beach clean. Practical action is backed up by magic, so I also recycle plastic and other rubbish washed up by the tide for magical purposes. Bits of old fishing nets, hooks and weights that do terrible damage to seabirds and marine creatures; rope, fishing floats, broken toys and all manner of things can be made into charms dedicated to ending marine pollution. Make a witch's ladder using seagull feathers from the beach or bits of discarded plastic, knotted into a piece of net or rope found at the tideline. I consecrate and use these in rituals on the shore before recycling them, or hang them up in my garden to work.

The treasure of the sea finds its way into rituals and spell work. Sea water for ritual use, especially where moon or sea goddesses will be invoked, can be bottled and taken home. Fishers at a coastal village near me dump discarded scallop shells on the beach. With a little sand added, they make ideal incense burners. Driftwood, left for several months to dry, is burnt on ritual fires or used for wands (*see* March). Sometimes the waves and rain wash fossils and crystals for charms and spells out of the soft clay cliffs of East Devon. (A word about fossils and crystals: I will gladly accept these when the sea washes them up at my feet, but mass chiselling and hammering them out of the cliffs is an increasing problem; please don't do it. Gifts from the sea are full of magic and far more precious than something hacked out of the earth.)

Pebbles picked up on the beach in the liminal place between the high and low tidelines become gateways to the magic of deep time. A pebble kept on my altar and found on an Ynys Môn beach is made of blue pillow lava that was spewed out of a marine volcano in a massive underwater explosion 400 million years ago, and is more than twice as old as the dinosaurs. Another piece of deep red jasper, polished smooth by the sea and found on the same beach, was once sand and has been transformed by the earth's own alchemy. A round grey pebble found at the edge of the waves in East Devon is hollow and filled with small white crystals. Another bears a red mark like a crescent moon. Pebbles on the beach attract and enchant us, and demand that we pick them up and look at them. As a witch and an animist, I understand that the rock on which we stand has its own life and its own indwelling spirits. Holding such a pebble in the hand is to feel the life of the earth itself, and to experience something of its great age, but also a sense of timelessness at the same time. Meditating with these and other beach pebbles is for me a way of working with the most ancient earth spirits imaginable. There is no formula for this; it has to be done instinctively just by feeling and sensing.

Witch stones, also known as hag stones, bride stones, or even just as holey stones, are stones with naturally occurring holes, found on the seashore. They are common around the southern Channel coast of England. They are mostly composed of flint, chert or limestone, and sometimes formed from the remains of fossilised sponges and come in all shapes and sizes. Throughout Britain they are used as protective charms. In folk magic they were used to protect farm buildings, animals and crops. They were hung up outside stables to stop horses from being hag ridden in the night by the monstrous night mare; placed on a cowshed or dairy they prevented the Faeries from stealing milk or butter. Very large witch stones can be found built into the walls of old houses and gardens in East Devon and Dorset. You may still see them hung up around farms. In contemporary witchcraft they are used as magical protection in many different ways and may be attached to wands and staffs and made into necklaces.

Nine large witch stones hung on an old piece of rope found on the seashore protect my vegetable garden; a tiny witch stone hangs from the rear-view mirror of my car, and a circle of witch stones threaded onto wire hangs in the fireplace. A witch stone is always hung on a thread or wire which is knotted or twisted to form a closed circle, and its protective magic starts working when the circle is closed. Hang a witch stone inside the front door of your house or thread one onto a keyring. There are plenty of examples of witch stone charms in local museums. Witch stones must be found or given, but never bought. Search for them on the shore and be inspired by the old charms to create your own protective magic with them.

The association between sea shells and goddesses is a strong and ancient one and as symbols they signify beauty and fertility. The scallop shell was the symbol of Aphrodite, the Greek goddess of love. She was born from the foam of the sea and floated to land on a scallop shell. She is depicted with a scallop shell covering her genitals, so the shell came to symbolise the sexuality of the goddess. Conch shells and other shells whose shape suggests a vagina were also sacred to Aphrodite and were left as offerings to her at her temple in Cyprus.

One genus of shell in particular, the cowrie, is associated with goddesses in many parts of the world and has been used in magical practice since prehistoric times. The collection of the Ashmolean Museum in Oxford contains a human skull from the Near Eastern city of Jericho that is 9,000 years old. It is plastered with clay and has cowrie shells placed in its eye sockets. Small cowrie shell beads, with holes drilled through them to take threads, have been found at Mesolithic occupation sites (6000–7000BCE) all around the Western and Northern coasts of Britain and Ireland. Cowrie shells were found in the graves of young girls in the very early pre-dynastic period in Egypt, circa 6200BCE, and later in Egypt were used as offerings to the goddess Isis and as money. In Bronze Age Europe they were funerary goods in the graves of women and children. The priestesses of Aphrodite used cowries in divination ceremonies. Cowries were used in rituals by the Mayans and Aztecs in Central America and in more recent times have been used as money in China, in Oceania and across Africa. In India they are used in the worship of the Hindu goddess Lakshmi and in Brazil in the practice of Candomble and Santeria to consult the Orishas.

Small cowries (*trivia monacha*/the spotted cowrie and *trivia arctica*/the Arctic cowrie) are found around the Western and Northern shores of Britain and Ireland. These are the same species as those found at the Mesolithic sites mentioned above, so if you can find cowries and use them in your witchcraft, you will be part of a practice that dates back 9,000 years. Cowries are special to Ynys Môn people. In my childhood I was taught that they brought good luck, and a large decanter full of cowries that my brother and I painstakingly collected has become a family heirloom. I still hunt for them on the shore and use them in my witchcraft. They are used in charms, to decorate mirrors for magical use, in rituals to invoke certain spirits, to honour the goddess, and as gifts for fellow witches. Find them if you can and make them part of your magic.

SNAKES AND SERPENTS

Thanks to human persecution and habitat destruction, snakes that were once common are now a rare sight. It is in July, at the height of summer, that we are most likely to encounter them basking in the sun or slithering away from a footpath.

The snake, or serpent, has been important in magic since the earliest times and was central to ancient Paganisms. In Middle Eastern mythologies the first deity was the primordial serpent mother, Tiamat or Tehom or Leviathan, that signified an archaic time before the gods existed. The image of the serpent biting its own tail is found in ancient Egypt in the tomb of Tutankhamun. For the Greeks, this was the Ourobouros serpent encircling the world, and its Norse equivalent is the Midgard Serpent. The Ourobouros is also found in alchemy. The serpent biting its own tail symbolises an endless cycle of life, death and rebirth, and in alchemical practice it signifies the world soul.

Cretan images from the Bronze Age show goddesses and their priestesses holding snakes and the veneration of snakes was widespread across the ancient Mediterranean world. Snakes were kept at the great oracular shrine of Apollo at Delphi and the priestess who gave the oracle was called the Pythoness. For the Egyptians Apep, or Apophis, was the chaos serpent that tried to destroy the Sun God Ra's boat as it sailed through the darkness each night. Wadjet, also called Buto, was the Egyptian serpent goddess who protected Lower Egypt and whose priestesses may have used snake venom in rituals. She also protected women in childbirth. Wadjet's symbol was the *uraeus*, a winged cobra surmounting the sun disk, depicted on the crown of Lower Egypt. The staff twined with snakes, or *caduceus,* which would later become the symbol of Hermes/Mercury and of physicians, originally belonged to Wadjet. Cleopatra was a priestess of the goddess as well as queen, and even in the late Roman era the snake and priestess were closely linked in Egypt. The snake was both feared, because of its venom, and respected.

It is a symbol of regeneration, renewal and transformation, because it sheds its own skin. It is also a symbol of wisdom and knowledge and was an oracular creature in many ancient cultures. In Sumer and Babylon the wise serpent was depicted guarding the moon tree of the goddesses Inanna and Ishtar, which bore the fruit of wisdom. The snake was at the heart of women's mysteries, being closely linked with menstruation, the moon, and endless, cyclical renewal. Our words Sabbath and Sabbat derive from the Babylonian *subbutu,* the time of Ishtar's menstrual period.

The Judaeo-Christian Garden of Eden myth can be thought of as a distorted variant of these Near Eastern myths; for the patriarchal monotheisms, the snake represented evil instead of wisdom. Christian saints did battle with serpents as symbols of temptation and wickedness. Saint Patrick was said to have expelled all the snakes from Ireland and as late as the nineteenth century in Ynys Môn a famous Methodist preacher was famous for killing vipers. For witches, the snake remains a potent symbol of the hidden wisdom associated with the ancient goddesses and with female sexuality. In some traditions it represents the energy of the earth herself. Snake deities and spirits may be invoked in ritual. In past centuries some witches kept snakes and other reptiles as working partners and some have an affinity with them now.

Snakes are still widely feared and have been hunted almost to extinction in some places. The adder or viper is the most common venomous snake in Europe and the only one native to Britain. Vipers were common during my childhood and can still be found in the sand dunes and wild places. Just after my periods started, I found a shed viper skin, truly a gift of Ishtar that connected me to ancient snake goddesses, and it has become one of my most precious magical belongings. It is used in goddess rituals, to contact snake spirits and in spell work.

In July, honour the ancient snake goddesses with your own rituals and, if you can visit heathland, grassland, dunes and uplands in July, especially in Wales and southern England, you may be rewarded with the sight of an adder or possibly the smaller grass snake. Connecting with these most ancient of creatures is a precious experience, full of its own magic.

Heart Charms and Talismans

The heart in witchcraft signifies not just love, but also of abundance, prosperity and good fortune. It is used in different religions (including Christianity and Hinduism) and magical systems and practices around the world as a charm or talisman. We have already seen its apotropaic function when used as a hearth charm (*see* February). A fabric heart charm can be made as a witch gift.

In July a fabric heart stuffed with dried yarrow, meadowsweet and a little vervain will aid peaceful magical contemplation. A heart stuffed with dried mugwort and rose petals can be placed under the pillow to increase dream recall. To repel moths, stuff a fabric heart with southernwood and rue, and gift a heart stuffed with fragrant lemon verbena to help someone who is feeling jaded and weary. Create your own variations. Every part of these processes requires your magical concentration, from the gathering and drying of the herbs to the sewing and filling of the fabric. A red heart pincushion is an old Devon tradition and they were often made by sailors for their sweethearts as love charms. They can also be made for a household to attract happiness and good fortune. Names and symbols were picked out on the heart in pins.

You will need

- Paper for a template
- Marker pen
- Scissors
- Red fabric; velvet is ideal
- Red thread
- Short pins (1cm long if you can get them)
- Kapok or unspun wool or other natural stuffing
- A pinch of dried vervain

Method

As with all spellcraft, do this with concentrated magical intent throughout.

Draw a heart shape on the paper (the size is up to you).

Place the template on the fabric; draw round it. Repeat this so that you have two heart shapes.

Cut out the heart shapes. Sew them together with the thread with the wrong side of the fabric outwards, leaving a gap of about two centimetres unsewn.

Turn the heart inside out and stuff it with the kapok or wool. The heart should be very tightly stuffed. Pack as much stuffing into it as you possibly can.

Add a pinch of vervain for enchantment.

Sew up the gap and use the thread to make a hanging loop if you wish.

Decorate your pincushion with pins. You can use words or initials or symbols; the choice is yours. Draw the design on paper first. Then make the design on the pincushion with the pins. Push each pin down into the pincushion as far as it will go, leaving only the head on the surface of the fabric. The finished pincushion should be placed on your altar to charge until the next new moon, when it can be gifted to its new home.

If you enjoy sewing, beaded or embroidered fabric heart charms can be made. If sewing is not your thing, heart charms can be made with modelling clay or dough, or cut from wood, or burned or painted onto wood.

A Spell for July: A Witch Stone Talisman

This spell consists of a witch stone and an old key, tied together with black ribbon. It is given as a gift to someone moving into a new home and brings prosperity and protects the home and its inhabitants. It can also be given to a couple at their wedding.

You will need

- A witch stone. You must find this yourself at the seashore; the finding is part of the magic
- An old key (these can be bought very cheaply at antique and junk shops)
- A length of black ribbon at least 1cm thick, measuring from the tip of your middle finger to your elbow
- Optional: a large 'bodkin' needle (the kind used to thread elastic)

Method

When you first find your witch stone, take it and hold it up to your eye and look at the world through the hole in it. This is an important part of the magical process. As you look through the hole in the stone, concentrate on your magical purpose; on the new home and the people that the spell is destined for.

Ensure the key is clean and free from any past associations. Wash it and then ritually cleanse it by placing it in salt water for seven days (a lunar quarter).

Thread the ribbon through the hole in the witch stone (use a bodkin if you need to), then thread the ribbon through the hole in the key, so that the witch stone and the key sit together on the ribbon.

Focusing your magical will, tie the two ends of the ribbon together, sealing the magic into the spell.

Put the spell on your altar until the next full moon, then give it to its new owner, wishing them love, luck and happiness in their new home. .

A Meditation for July: The Queen of the Year

This meditation offers you a chance to pause after the peak of Midsummer and look back and reflect on the achievements of the first half of your Witch's Year. You do not need to wait until the end of July to do this meditation; it can be done at any time during the month.

It's noon on a bright sunny July day, and you are standing in front of a large gateway. There is an iron gate and tall stone gateposts topped with granite spheres that gleam in the sun. Open the gate and go through it. Walk under an archway covered in red and white roses in full bloom. Their perfume is intense. You are in a garden in which all the flowers of summer are blooming. There are roses of every colour – lilies, irises, peonies. Every flower that you love is there. In the centre of the garden a woman sits on a throne. She wears a long white dress, embroidered with roses, lilies and bunches of grapes, and wears a necklace of large pearls. In her right hand she holds a golden sceptre tipped with a gold orb like the sun. On her head is a gold crown bearing twelve stars, one for each month of the year and each sign of the zodiac. On the side of her throne is carved the symbol of Venus – a circle with a downward pointing cross. The arms of the throne are carved with rams' heads and the back with flowers and fruits. This is the Queen of the Year. Behind her are an oak and a holly tree growing close together, and behind them is a grove of tall, almost black cypress trees. In the far distance you glimpse blue mountains. A stream flows from a spring under the cypress trees and over a small waterfall into a clear, stone-lined pool at the Queen's feet. You are filled with a sense of utter calm and peace. The Queen asks you to come close and look into the pool by her feet. As you look into the clear water, the Queen guides your vision and images form in the pool of all the witchcraft you have worked since the beginning of the year, month by month. As the visions form and rise within the water, you watch and ponder what you have learnt; the knowledge and wisdom you have gained from your craft. Take your time; with the Queen's guidance, work your way through the months until you reach the present point and are filled with a new understanding of what you have achieved and what you are becoming.

Renewed, and ready for the coming months, thank the Queen of the Year, bid her farewell and leave her garden, closing the gate behind you.

AUGUST

August

Reaping and Gathering

The Great Harvest

It is Lammas; the first day of August and a hot summer evening in Plymouth. There will be a full moon tonight and the high spring tide is rising; as we gather at the landing stage for the Cremyll Ferry in Stonehouse, small waves are overtopping the slipway already and the tide is bringing an intense feeling of brimming excitement. The River Tamar is the ancient border between Devon and Cornwall. Its tidal shores are liminal places, ideal for the honouring of goddess and god. The ferryboat comes slowly towards us, its engine echoing quietly on the still evening air. The tide is already so high that we have to scramble up a ladder on the side of the boat. The boat takes us west across Plymouth Sound; the sun is already beginning to sink towards the hills of Cornwall ahead of us. Someone points: a dolphin is following close behind the boat. It follows us all the way across to the Cornish side of the Sound, breaking the water with its snout and enjoying the game. As we land the tide is still rising; climbing down from the boat is difficult.

The evening is perfectly still as we walk along the shore through ornamental gardens until we find our place; a small deserted stony beach facing the city across the Sound. Behind us the sun is low in the west now, just above the oak and pine trees, and the sky is a deep gold. We make the Lammas fire and celebrate our ritual, honouring the sacrificed god as the corn harvest; cut down for us to eat and drink, he will sustain us through the coming months. Honouring too the goddess as both our mother the earth and as Tamara, the great life-giving Tamar river, flowing down from Dartmoor and merging with the sea right here. We eat cakes of barley, the body of our god, made with honey. Then, just after the huge tide peaks, we bring our offerings of corn from the fields; wheat, barley and oats, plaited together with August flowers and herbs – late roses, cornflowers, red flax, vervain and love-in-a-mist, and red rowan berries. We place them on the water. The high tide has passed and the river has started to

August Associations

Festivals: Lammas (1st)

Figures: Ceres/Demeter, Ceridwen, Lugh/Lleu, John Barleycorn

More Than Human: Meteors/shooting stars (Perseids), rowan berries, herbs at their peak

Totems and Symbols: Ear of corn, scythe

run out rapidly now on the ebb tide. We watch our Lammas offerings float lazily away to sea as the dusk grows. In the East, over Plymouth, a huge full moon rises over the dockyards and wharves, casting a glow of golden magic and a Lammas blessing over the city. No one speaks. We douse the fire with sea water, silently thank our goddess and god and the spirits of the place, and embrace. We walk slowly back along the Cornish shore to the landing place and in the gathering darkness the ferry boat carries us back over the Sound.

Everything is still and at peace, and moonlight, turning from gold to silver as the moon rises higher, glints on the water.

The grain harvest is at its peak and we celebrate the festival of Lammas with fairs and games and fires on the hilltops, and the god of the grain becomes bread and beer. Offerings are made to the mother of the corn and we make the Bride of the new harvest. In the harvest month, witchcraft is very practical; there are lots of things to be made and stored for later. Herbs are gathered for spells and sharp thorns for protection. We learn the magic of incense and of rowan berries.

August is the harvest month and it begins with Lammas. The energy of growth is over now; replaced with the peaceful ripening of seeds, fruits and berries. In the fields, the grain harvest that began in July is in full swing. Archaeological evidence shows that some kind of harvest festival has been celebrated at this time of year since farming first began, and our everyday calendar still reflects the old agricultural pattern of the year, with school and work holidays taking place in August. Lammas means 'loaf mass' and it was the time when the Anglo-Saxons offered the first bread of the new season to god. In Ireland it is

Harvest Customs

In our own times, witches and Pagans have claimed Lammas as their own special celebration of harvest. J.G. Fraser's widely-read work *The Golden Bough* (first published in 1890), which proposed a universal ancient Pagan religion centred on the sacrifice of the corn king in the fields at harvest time, provided the basis for many of the Pagan rituals that grew up during the twentieth century, but over the years our practice has grown and deepened, and at Lammas we find veneration of mother goddesses of the corn derived from ancient Paganisms, and elements drawn from the old Celtic and other harvest customs.

Now at Lammas, we give thanks to goddesses and gods for many different harvests, but the sacrificed corn god, often personified as John Barleycorn, who dies so that we can have bread, beer and whisky, is still at the heart of Lammas. It is a wonderful moment in the Witch's Year when we celebrate all the riches of the harvest and the gifts that mother earth gives us.

called Lugnasadh in honour of the god Lugh, who is associated with the sun and with fire, as well as with this time of year. In Scotland its Gaelic name is Lunasdal, and in Wales it is simply called Gwyl Awst (August festival). Lugh's Welsh equivalent is Lleu Llaw Gyffes.

Versions of a ballad celebrating the barley harvest and the brewing of beer, in which John Barleycorn is brutally murdered in the fields, date back to the sixteenth century, with Robert Burns contributing his own Scots version in honour of whisky in 1782, and are popular with witches, folksingers and beer drinkers alike:

There were three men came out of the west their fortunes for to try
And these three men made a solemn vow John Barleycorn must die
They ploughed, they sowed, they harrowed him in, throwed clods upon his head
And these three men made a solemn vow, John Barley corn was dead...

...They hired men with scythes so sharp to cut him off at the knee,
They rolled him and tied him round the waist, served him most barbarously...

...Here's little Sir John in the nut-brown bowl and brandy in the glass,
And little Sir John in the nut-brown bowl proved the stronger man at last

For the huntsman he can't hunt the fox, nor so loudly blow his horn
And the tinker he can't mend kettles or pots without a little of John Barleycorn.'

FOLK CUSTOMS

There is a wealth of Lammas folk customs. Marking harvest time with gatherings and fairs probably dates back to the beginnings of agriculture and Lammas is celebrated with fires and feasts on hilltops and high places, and with fairs and markets throughout the Celtic nations, and also in the West of England. In Ireland it was known as Big Sunday; people still celebrate on hilltops with fires, feasts and dancing. It is also known as Domnach Crom Dubh (Crom Dubh Sunday) after Crom Dubh (the dark, stooped one)/Crom Cruaich; an elder Pagan god to whom offerings and sacrifices were made on mountaintops, and as Garland Sunday because the holy wells are decorated with garlands of flowers. The ancient Aonach Tailteann was an assembly held at Lugnasadh consisting of the Tailteann games and a great fair that was held at the beginning of August in County Meath until the late nineteenth century. Irish legend states that it was founded by the god Lugh to commemorate the death of his foster mother Tailtiu. The riotous Puck Fair at Killorglin in County Kerry, in which a goat is crowned king, takes place at this time and is associated with Lugh. The Ould Lammas Fair at Ballycastle in County Antrim happens at the end of August. The annual Christian pilgrimage up the holy mountain of Croagh Patrick also takes place at Lugnasadh and may be an echo of an older festival of Crom Cruaich/Crom Dubh; gatherings took place in his honour there and the mountain is the centre of a ritual landscape dating back to the Bronze Age. In recent years, new Lugnasadh fairs have been springing up in Ireland, as have Gwyl Awst celebrations in Wales, as people once more take pride in their old gods and reclaim and reinvigorate the old customs.

Pagans in Devon and Cornwall have reinstated the old tradition of Lammas hilltop picnics; these now take place annually on Dartmoor and Bodmin Moor. The Tan Hill Fair in Wiltshire was a hilltop fair and gathering with games and prizes (given a royal charter in 1499) that took place until the 1930s; in recent years attempts have been made to revive it. A huge white leather glove, garlanded with flowers, was paraded through Exeter in Devon to mark the opening of the Lammas Fair. The parade still takes place, but sadly the local council has moved the fair to early July, thus divorcing it from Lammas and its traditional meanings. Honiton in East Devon still celebrates its Lammas Fair at the proper time with its garlanded glove and the bizarre and rather cruel Hot Pennies ceremony in which local children scrabble for hot pennies thrown from a balcony. In Scotland Lammas Fairs take place at St Andrews and Inverkeithing and at Kirkwall in Orkney; and the strange but unmissable custom of the Burryman at South Queensferry near Edinburgh, in which a man completely covered in sharp, itchy burrs parades through town all day, also happens close to Lammas. Fishing communities in Shetland celebrated the end of the white fishing season at Lammas with feasts and dancing. Why not start your own Lammas custom and celebrate the season with a Witches' Picnic on the summit of a high hill?

In Scotland and Ireland, Lammas fairs were also the time when trial marriages or handfastings (after which modern Pagan wedding ceremonies are named) could be celebrated. They did not require a church ceremony and lasted for a year and a day, after which the couple could either marry permanently or walk away without needing a divorce. These Lammas weddings were still occurring as late as the nineteenth century at Tailteann and elsewhere in Ireland, at Eskdale in the Scottish borders, and at Stenness in Orkney where Sir Walter Scott recorded that the couple would clasp hands through the holed stone called the Stone of Odin (sadly since destroyed by a farmer) before cutting a silver sixpence in half and keeping half each. They could divorce by going to Stenness church, where they turned their backs on each other and walked away out of opposite doors to signify the end of the arrangement.

The harvest itself is surrounded by traditional customs that honour the gods and spirits and are designed to ensure plenty, health and happiness. Experiencing the grain harvest in person brings a sense of connectedness, both to our mother the earth, and also to our ancestors who first farmed this land over 6,000 years ago. I once stood on the causewayed camp at Windmill Hill above the great henge and stones of Avebury as wheat was being harvested there, mindful that corn had been grown there since Neolithic times, and was probably grown as the henge builders worked. Until recent centuries, harvest was a pivotal moment in the year. Those of us who live in industrialised western countries are mostly divorced from the business of food production, but in former times our lives would have depended on the success of the local harvest. Until the mechanisation of farming, harvesting meant backbreaking labour under intense pressure. It is small wonder that rituals were needed to ensure a successful harvest, and to celebrate once it was gathered in. In Scotland the last sheaf of corn to be cut was called the Lammas Sheaf. It was not allowed to touch the ground and would be ritually presented to the farmer's wife at the farmhouse door before being hung up over the fireplace or the door, where it would remain until next year.

A widespread harvest custom called Crying the Neck in Cornwall and Devon and the Gaseg Fedi (Harvest Mare) or Y Wrach (the Hag or Witch) in Wales is still observed. In Cornwall and Devon, the final sheaf of corn is cut by hand with a scythe and held aloft. The person who cuts it then shouts, 'What have I?' and all present answer, 'A neck, a neck'. The neck is taken to the village church or a barn or farmhouse and corn dollies may be made from it. In Cornwall, Crying the Neck has become an important part of the local culture and ceremonies, some of them in the Cornish language, can be attended in a number of places. In Wales the harvesters would all stand back from the last sheaf and throw their scythes at it. The person whose scythe cut the sheaf would have the honour of carrying it back to the farm. The sheaf would often be garlanded with ribbons.

In many places, especially in Scotland, Wales and the north of England, the last sheaf is specifically identified as female, and may be given a beautiful dress to wear before being hung in a place of honour until the following year. In Scotland the last sheaf or kirn (corn) was sometimes cut by a young girl and bound with rowan berries to keep away malefic witchcraft. It was then made into a doll and given a child's dress to wear. In the West Highlands and Hebrides, the goddess Bride would be thanked for the harvest and the last sheaf was cut in her honour. The last sheaf would be kept until the following Candlemas (the Feast of Bride) when it would be fed to the horses before ploughing began. Some of these customs now find a place in witches' Lammas Sabbat celebrations.

Lammas sits opposite Candlemas on the Wheel of the Year and the two Sabbats are closely linked. My Lammas begins with the creation of the Bride for the next Candlemas. I am allowed by a friendly farmer to cut my own small sheaf of wheat at Lammas. He understands that witchcraft is good for his harvest and I will make gifts of charms for him in return. I cut the corn with a sickle, and wrap it in a white sheet so that it does not touch the ground. The corn is divided into one large bunch and two smaller ones and then I make a crosspiece of wood. I like to use rowan for this because it is associated with Bride. The upright piece is a little shorter than the large bunch of corn and the horizontal piece is about half that length. The two pieces of wood are securely tied together. Then the large bunch of corn is tied to the upright and smaller bunches are used for the arms and tied to the horizontal piece. The ears of corn form Bride's head and hands.

The old Bride is taken down from her place in the house and thanked. Her white dress is removed and put on the new Bride, whose waist is bound with ivy and rowan berries, and then with red and gold ribbons. The old Bride is dismantled; any remaining ears of corn are given to the birds (the crows and jackdaws love them), and the straw is burned on the fire at the Lammas Sabbat. The new Bride is carried into the house, welcomed, and hung up over the altar. She will be presented to the goddess and god at the Lammas ritual. I have witch friends who grow a small patch of wheat to make their own Bride and harvest bread at Lammas. If you don't have access to cornfields, you can easily buy bunches of corn for flower arranging from a florist. It is good to bring even a small bunch of corn into the house at Lammas to decorate your altar if you can; however distant most of our lives may be from food production, it will make the harvest very real and present.

Corn dollies are made in many places as harvest decorations. Traditions and designs vary from region to region; some symbolise the corn mother or harvest lord and there are horns of plenty, spirals and intricate knots. The old craft of corn dolly making is thriving and has spread to cities as well as the countryside; if you want to try your hand at it there are many workshops and classes on offer. Increasingly, witches and Pagans are making corn dollies too, to give as harvest gifts and to decorate altars.

Making a simple little corn figure in thanks for the harvest does not require specialist skills. Take a small bunch of corn and tie it round the middle to make a waist and you have your basic corn dolly. This can be a lovely activity for small children at Lammas. If this inspires you, you can add ribbons and rowan berries to the waist, make arms (like I do with my Bride), decorate it with charms and talismans, or give the dolly clothes to wear. Hang the dolly somewhere special until the next year, or keep it on your altar. Alternatively, simply plait a few stems of corn together and tie them with red thread at both ends to make a Lammas charm.

Bread should be offered to the goddess and god in thanks at Lammas. In Scotland the Lammas bannock (oatbread) was made in honour of the Virgin Mary with the grain that had just been harvested and cooked over a fire of rowan wood. Beautiful harvest loaves made in the form of wheatsheaves are still made in many places and are sometimes included in Pagan Lammas rituals. Baking and eating homemade bread at Lammas is an important experiential part of the Sabbat. Wheatsheaf breads and harvest loaves call for specialist skills, but soda bread, made without yeast and with just flour, milk and a little salt, is simple to make. You will find a recipe later in this chapter. It may be possible to find locally milled flour, perhaps ground in a watermill or windmill, or spelt or other ancient grains can be used. Add your own magical will to the process and make some for your Lammas Sabbat if you can.

Practice: The Lammas Ritual

At Lammas the goddess is envisaged as the mother of the corn; the goddess who brings agriculture and presides over the harvest. There are many harvest goddesses to choose from: Demeter or Ceres, Gaia (the earth herself), Inanna or Ishtar, and Apuleius in his novel *The Golden Ass* (from the third century CE) describes a beautiful vision of her as Isis, whose worship spread from Egypt throughout the Mediterranean world. Then there are Ceridwen (Wales), Banbha (Ireland), Sif of the golden hair (Norse), Parvati (India), Huichi (Japan), Inna (Nigeria) and the Inca corn mother, Pachamama. Greek and Roman images of the harvest goddess depict her with serpents, poppies, and the moon. For the sacrificed god of the harvest you could choose Lugh, Lleu, Babylonian Tammuz/Dumuzi (lover of Ishtar/Inanna), Egyptian Osiris (husband of Isis), Attis, Frey (Norse) or John Barleycorn himself. Of course, you can create your own personal vision of the harvest deities.

Preparation

The Lammas ritual should be celebrated outdoors if at all possible, and can be a glorious experience on a hot August evening as the sun sets. Celebrating on a hilltop fits perfectly with the traditions of Lammas, and working by a river or the sea will allow you to make offerings on the water, as in the Lammas ritual I described at the beginning of this chapter, or you could work in your own garden, where your personal harvest is taking place. Choose somewhere that inspires you for this profound ritual with its beautiful layers of meaning. A fire is an important element of the Lammas ritual, but please take extra care with it at this time of year and avoid any damage to fragile landscapes and wildlife (*see* 'Working Safely' in the Introduction to this book).

The ritual calls for a small bunch of corn and either a sickle or a knife. If you have a dedicated ritual knife, that can be used, or use whatever feels right to you. You will need the new Bride, if you have made one, or whatever corn dollies and harvest tokens you have made. Think about your own personal harvest that you will present to the deities at the Sabbat. This may be something that you have grown or made, or it may be something intellectual or creative, or your inner spiritual harvest. I also bring enough stems of corn for each person present to make a small plait, rowan berries, and whatever summer flowers I can find in the garden.

The Lammas feast should include bread and anything made with barley, oats and grains. Add other seasonal harvest foods that seem appropriate. If you want to have alcohol, beer is the obvious choice. If you are working with others, try to ensure that everyone brings something for the feast, as sharing is an important part of Lammas.

Before the Lammas Sabbat, spend some time meditating and visualising your chosen forms of goddess and god; let images of them fill your mind. At the working place the new Bride, corn dollies and the stems of corn and flowers are placed on the altar if there is one, or otherwise placed at the centre.

The ritual

The fire is lit and the circle cast. The spirits of the working place are welcomed. The goddess is invoked as mother of the harvest and the god as the harvest lord.

The new Bride is presented to the goddess and god and she is blessed and consecrated in their names.

The harvest is then presented to the goddess and god. Present the feast of bread, summer fruits and drink that you have brought, and whatever else you have made. Then present your personal harvest (physical, creative or spiritual), and ask the deities to bless it.

The sacrifice of the harvest is made. If you are working with others, one person representing the goddess takes the sickle or knife and another person representing the god holds up the bunch of corn. The bunch of corn is cut in two in a solemn manner. You can also carry out the entire ritual alone. The killing of the corn god can be ritually enacted if you wish. The aim is to express the deeper meanings of Lammas through simple ritual actions.

Following this I give everyone three stems of corn and these are plaited together with the flowers and rowan berries to make Lammas offerings. If working by the sea or a river, the offerings placed on the water to float away, or they can be left at the working place or offered up on the Lammas fire. The ritual concludes with the sharing of the Lammas feast. Thank the goddess and god and bid them farewell, and thank the spirits of the land who have been with you. Close the circle and remember to take home any residues and rubbish. The new Bride and the corn dollies should be taken home. Place Bride in her home; she will watch over your witchcraft until her time comes at the next Candlemas. The corn dollies can be placed on the altar; you can use them as charms and decorations or give them as witch gifts. Dispose of them by returning them to the earth (I feed the corn to the birds and compost the rest) before you make new ones at Lammas next year.

Lammas Soda Bread

If you are new to bread-making, soda bread is an easy place to start. It is made without yeast and does not require complicated processes or specialist baking skills. You can use any flour, but to honour the god of the harvest, I like to use spelt or an organic flour, and a visit to a traditional mill where flour is still made using wind or water power to get the flour for a Lammas loaf is a great way to connect with the harvest. This recipe will make one big loaf, suitable for a Lammas feast.

You will need

Equipment

- Mixing bowl
- Baking tray, greased with a little butter or oil (to stop your loaf from sticking to the tray)
- Spatula
- Knife

Ingredients

500g/2¼ cups flour

10g/2 teaspoons salt (if using sea or rock salt, grind it to a fine powder)

20g/4 teaspoons baking powder (bicarbonate of soda)

300ml/⅓ cup milk or plain yoghurt. I prefer to use yoghurt. (For a vegan alternative, use water or oatmilk)

A little extra flour for dusting

Method

Preheat your oven to 225°C (200°c fan)/gas mark 6. Lightly grease the baking tray.

Mix all the dry ingredients together in the bowl (use your hands or the spatula). Add the liquid and mix it well with the spatula until it has formed a dough.

Coat your hands lightly with flour (to stop the dough sticking to them), knead the dough briefly, form it into a ball, and flatten it slightly (it should be about 8–10 cm/3–4in tall). Place it on the baking tray.

Cut a cross into the loaf, so that it is almost cut into quarters.

Bake the loaf for between 20–25 minutes in the oven. It should form a good crust. Remove the loaf from the baking tray and let it cool (use a wire tray of you have one). When the loaf is cool, dust it lightly with a little flour.

The loaf can be torn into chunks and shared as part of your Lammas feast. Don't forget to consecrate your Lammas loaf to the goddess and god of the harvest, and leave a little for the Faeries and the birds.

HERBCRAFT IN AUGUST

Most of the herbs I use in my witchcraft are harvested during August and dried and stored for use throughout the rest of the year. When harvesting my aim is to be self-sufficient as I want to use only herbs I have grown myself; the gifts my plant allies give me in my witchcraft. Growing and harvesting in this way, if you can do it, will increase the effectiveness of your herbcraft because your plant allies will want to help you by lending their own magic to your spells, charms and incenses. As we saw in June, herbs for drying and storing should be gathered when the moon is waning, on dry sunny mornings when the concentration of essential oils and enzymes will be at its height. Never gather herbs when they are damp as they will rot. You may wish, like me, to keep a special blade solely for herbcraft. Remember, too, that magical herbs should not be allowed to fall onto the earth when you harvest them. They came from the earth, so dropping them onto the ground is disrespectful, and their magical virtue will dissipate into the earth. Gather them into a basket or a piece of cloth. Before cutting herbs, I sit with the plant for a while and ask its permission, before cutting the stems cleanly so that the plant is not damaged.

Once gathered, the herbs are tied into bundles with twine and hung up in a dry place, out of direct sunlight and where there is good air circulation, to dry. Paper bags can be placed over drying bundles to catch loose seeds and flowers. As soon as they are completely dry (that is, when the leaves crumble easily between my fingers), the leaves are stripped from the stems and are stored safely in airtight jars, ready to use. In August I will harvest the gifts of my plant allies mugwort and vervain. Some of the mugwort will be dried and put into jars, and some will be made into smudge bundles.

To make a mugwort smudge bundle, cut five or seven fresh mugwort stems and tie them together securely with twine at the base. Then bind a length of twine quite tightly in a spiral around the leaves. When the bundle is dry it can be burned as smudge in rituals. Mugwort is a very good psychic cleanser, and as it is the great herb of vision, using it as smudge will aid visualisation.

Vervain and mugwort stems that have been stripped of their leaves will be used to make small brooms to sweep the circle and ritually cleanse working spaces. Vervain brooms will attract spirits and increase enchantment.

Witch Bottles

Witch bottles are a centuries old form of forceful, no-nonsense protection that repels harmful magic. They are often found hidden away in the chimneys of old houses and examples can sometimes be seen in museum collections. The old witch bottles were meant to be noxious and revolting because they were intended to turn malefic magic back on itself and return bad intent to the sender. A bewitched person would fill a bottle with nasty, sharp things: thorns, pins and rusty nails, and top the bottle up with their own urine. The bottle would typically be placed in a chimney where the heat from the fire would warm the bottle and its contents. The hot nails and pins would cause pain to the sender, who would call off the magic. Alternatively, witch bottles would be hidden high up in chimneys, lofts or wall cavities and left to work their protective magic undisturbed. If you discover a witch bottle in an old house, the best advice is to leave it where it is, so that its magic can continue working.

Witch bottles are still made and used by witches. They are a very powerful form of protection and will repel not only malefic magic but also unwanted energies and attentions. They can be made using the traditional recipe but if you do not wish to use your urine, the bottle can be topped up with red wine or wine vinegar instead. Make this kind of witch bottle on the last day of the moon's cycle, and focus your magical will on protection as you do it. Stopper the bottle tightly and seal it with black wax. It should then be placed somewhere where it can do its work quietly and without being observed. A chimney is ideal, or a cellar or roof space, or the back of a dark cupboard. If you move house, the witch bottle should be left where it is as its magic belongs to the place it was made for. You can always make another.

I have evolved a new way of making witch bottles in response to requests for magical help and sometimes to give as as witch gifts. I mostly make them with positive and intentions and to attract rather than repel. They contain dried plant materials and so August is the best time to harvest the materials and make them. In my witch bottles layers of dried plant materials alternate with layers of rock or sea salt crystals. Salt is used in magic to purify, and it will also ensure that the contents of the bottle stay dry. Unlike the old witch bottles, these can be placed in plain sight, as looking at them increases their magical effectiveness.

A witch bottle that harnesses the power of the sun will make a home feel warm and happy, and promote wellbeing. It will contain marigold flowers, and other dried red or orange flowers, rowan berries and red chillies. A witch bottle made with rose petals, lavender flowers and mugwort will create a peaceful, contemplative atmosphere and assist with visualisation and dreaming. A witch bottle containing vervain, yarrow and rosemary will attract enchantment to the home. Once you grasp the principle of this, you can create your own recipes for witch bottles.

You will need

- Small bottles with stoppers. The bottles should have necks wide enough to take your plant materials
- A wooden spoon
- Sea salt or rock salt
- Dried plant materials of your choice
- Wax to seal the bottles (a candle is easy to use)

Method

Before you start, make sure your bottles, salt and plant materials are completely dry as damp will ruin your bottles. Use the plant materials in separate layers rather than mixing them together. Concentrate on your magical intention throughout the making of the bottle.

Place a layer of your first plant material at least 1cm deep in the bottle, and ram it down tightly with the handle of the wooden spoon. When finished, the bottle should be as tightly packed as possible, so that the contents cannot move about.

Next, place a layer of salt in the bottle and pack this down tightly. Then place a layer of another plant material in the bottle and pack it down.

Repeat this process, alternating layers of plant material and salt, until the bottle is completely full. There should be no space left at the top.

Stopper the bottle and seal it with wax. The easiest way to do this is to drip wax from a candle.

Choose a colour of wax that reflects your magical purpose.

A Witch Axe

The witch axe is another form of protection that will repel anything that is not wanted. It should be made in August. It is a tiny, powerful form of concentrated magical protection that really packs a punch. It is made from a rose stem with a thorn, and blackthorn spikes can be added if you wish. If possible, harvest these from your garden, or places where you work with the Faeries or spirits, as they will be asked to help with the magic.

You will need

- A very small bottle with a stopper. The ones I use are 5cm tall and can be obtained from craft suppliers. The neck should be wide enough for a rose thorn to pass through
- A sharp blade or secateurs
- A piece of rose stem with a thorn
- Blackthorn spikes (optional)

Method

Make the witch axe when the moon is waning. In your garden or other working place, find a rose bush with thorns. Sit quietly with the rose bush for a while and ask its spirit and the Faeries to lend their power to your magic. Find a piece of rose stem that bears just one thorn. You may have to search for this, as the stems often bear two or three thorns in the same place.

When you have found a single thorn, ask permission of the rose, then carefully cut the stem just above it, and then below it. The piece of stem should be 3–4cm long, and the cuts should be clean, with no ragged edges. This can be a difficult operation and requires persistence. The stem and thorn should look like a tiny axe.

Put the axe on your altar and leave it to dry thoroughly. This should take a couple of weeks.

Put the witch axe in the bottle and seal it.

If you feel the need, you can add two or three dried blackthorn spikes. A well-made witch axe will be a feisty magical object that bristles with an edgy energy.

Incense

Making your own incense for use in rituals is a very satisfying part of witchcraft, especially if you make it with the help of your plant allies. Many of the ingredients can be found in the witch's garden. It is easy to do, as it essentially means mixing dried plant materials together into incense blends. The skill lies in choosing the materials both for their magical meanings and their aromatic qualities. Effective magic involves all the senses and incense plays an important role in ritual and also in operative magic. It is used to honour deities, summon spirits and aid magical work. As we have already seen, the incense used in rituals is loose blended incense burned on a charcoal block rather than ready made joss sticks. Complex incense blends made for the Sabbats and to honour various deities can be bought from magical suppliers, but I prefer to make my own using mostly things I have grown or gathered.

If incense-making attracts you, it is a subject than can be studied in great depth, and you can bring together complex chains of symbolism, referred to by magical practitioners as correspondences, linking the properties of plants to the elements, deities, planets, colours and much more. This is also a very creative practice if you are attracted to perfumes and like working with your sense of smell; good incense is very welcome at all rituals and celebrations.

In August, try making some simple incenses using basic ingredients and equipment. A good incense blend should consist of dried plant materials (flowers, leaves, stems, seeds, berries or roots). These can be used alone, but are often combined with a gum or resin which will bind the incense mixture and help it to burn slowly on the charcoal and produce aromatic smoke. Good gums and resins include gum arabic, gum benzoin, frankincense, myrrh and sandarac, and they will all add their own perfume to the mix. Unlike most of the things I use in my witchcraft, these must be bought from specialist magical suppliers or herbalists but you will only need small quantities of them. Essential oils can also be added to incense blends but should be used very sparingly (only one or two drops at most) as a damp, oily incense mix will not burn well. A pestle and mortar is a very useful item and recommended if you want to specialise in making incense, and can also be used for grinding dried herbs and seeds.

You will need

- Dried plant materials, gums and resins. Optional: essential oils
- A large mixing bowl

- Optional: a pestle and mortar. Alternatively, you can use a rolling pin and kitchen paper
- Small, lidded airtight jars

Method

Cut or tear the plant materials into small pieces (they should fit easily onto a charcoal block). Large lumps of gum or resin should be crushed with the pestle and mortar. If you do not have one, use a rolling pin and a board, but place the gum or resin between two sheets of kitchen paper to stop the rolling pin and board being impregnated, as gum or resin can be difficult to remove.

Put all the materials into the mixing bowl and blend them together with your hands. As you do so, concentrate on your magical purpose. If the incense is for a Sabbat ritual, concentrate on the meanings of the Sabbat; if the incense will be used to honour a deity, visualise the deity as you blend the incense and ask their blessing.

Put the incense into clean, dry, jars and store it out of direct sunlight. It is ready to use immediately.

Start with the following very simple recipes, then experiment and create your own; the possibilities are endless.

Altar incense

Two parts frankincense

One part dried rose petals

One part dried vervain (leaves and stems)

Vision incense

One part dried mugwort (leaves and stems)

One part dried vervain (leaves and stems)

One part dried lavender flowers

Purification incense

One part dried bay leaves

One part dried rosemary leaves

A pinch of gum benzoin

A pinch of gum Arabic

Midsummer incense

Two parts dried marigold flowers

Two parts dried oak leaves

One part frankincense

WITCHES' BREW

Witches' brew is a herb tea I have used for many years to aid visualisation, divination, and scrying. It also facilitates dreaming. Mix together equal parts of dried mugwort, vervain, yarrow, rose petals, and lavender flowers to make witches' brew. Use one teaspoon of this mixture per person as a herbal tea.

In August the rowan trees are covered with bright red berries and on the moors and hilltops they are a glorious sight. Once on a walk to Wistman's Wood on Dartmoor in August as a storm approached, I saw a rowan tree covered in berries. The berries shone so brightly against the black storm clouds that it looked as if they were fairy lights. As we saw in March, rowan is the great protective tree and is associated with Bride. The red berries are the colour of blood and bring strength and energy. A delicious jelly that has a smokey-sweet taste all of its own can be made from rowan berries, and makes a great addition to Sabbat feasts.

In Poland the berries are used to flavour vodka. This is easy to make and the method is identical to the one you learnt in May to make plant tinctures: put some rowan berries in a jar, top the jar up with vodka and leave it for several weeks, shaking the jar every few days. Rowan vodka makes a good witch gift for friends at Yule.

The Lammas Sabbat and the harvest retain their influence over my witchcraft throughout August. I delight in harvesting herbs and flowers, and the first blackberries, and in collecting feathers and other finds. There is a pervasive sense of everything coming to fruition, and enjoyment of all the gifts of the earth, but at the same time an awareness that autumn is coming. The swifts are the first of the summer birds to leave on their long migrations south, departing from my village just after Lammas. The days are growing noticeably shorter too. In mid-August the annual Perseids meteor shower takes place. This is a spectacular sight, especially if it happens when the moon is waning and the sky is dark. Hundreds of tiny shooting stars can be seen late at night. The Perseids signal that summer is slowly ending, and that it is time to complete the harvest and gather in everything, in a magical sense as well as literally.

A Spell for August: A Circle of Rowan Berries

This month's spell harnesses the power of brilliant red rowan berries to protect your home and special places. The rowan has a unique magical energy that you will soon learn to recognise. The spell complements the rowan cross that we made in March but while that charm is carried about the person, the rowan berry circle does its work in the home. It can be made to help a friend whose home needs protection if you wish. It should be placed where it can do its work quietly and without becoming the object of attention.

You will need

- 28 rowan berries, picked at the beginning of August when they are at their brightest and ripest. Welsh and West Country tradition dictates that these should be picked from a tree you have not worked with before. To keep taking berries from the same tree would be an insult to its spirit. As rowans are so plentiful on the moors and mountains, it is always easy to find a new tree.
- A length of red embroidery thread, measured with your arm outstretched from the tip of your middle finger to your nose
- A sharp needle

Method

As you make this spell, concentrate throughout on protecting your home (or the place the spell is intended for). Visualise protection, safety and security throughout the working.

Thread the needle with the red thread. Leaving a length as long as your middle finger at the end, tie a knot in the thread, concentrating your magical will as you do so.

Carefully pierce a berry with the needle and gently pull it onto the thread next to the knot. Tie another knot next to the berry. Then place a second berry next to the second knot. Continue in this manner until all the berries are threaded. There should be a knot between each berry.

Tie the two ends of the thread together with a triple knot to seal the magic in. Leave the rowan circle on your altar until the next new moon, then hang it somewhere in your home where it can do its protective work, or give it to its new owner.

Meditation: The Mystery of the Harvest

This month we meet the ancient goddess of the corn, who has been honoured in many guises for thousands of years.

You are standing in a field of barley on a hot August night. In the east, beyond the field, behind a line of old oak trees you watch a huge full moon rising, glowing almost golden. The barley has been harvested, except for one small stand in the centre of the field. There is a strong smell of barley and hot earth. As you watch the moon, a figure takes shape in front of it, seeming to rise up out of the earth until she stands tall before you. It is the goddess of the harvest: Demeter, Ceres, Inanna, Isis. She has had many names in many places and at many times.

She is crowned with a round, golden full moon, that shines like a mirror and either side of the moon are ripe, golden ears of corn. Amongst the corn are red poppy flowers and poppy seed heads, and vipers nestle around them and twine in her hair. She is clothed in a robe of pale, gleaming rainbow colours with a deep blue indigo hem like the night sky with stars glittering along its edge. In one hand she holds a gold bowl, shaped like a boat, and from her belt hangs a bronze sickle.

Greet the goddess by whatever name you know her, and honour her, bowing your head before her. When you raise your head again the goddess has placed her bronze sickle at your feet. She motions to you and you understand what you must do. Pick up the sickle and calmly and deliberately cut the last remaining stand of barley. As you do so, it seems as if the barley and the field itself cry out to you. You feel the pain of the barley as it dies and a pang of sadness and your eyes fill with tears.

The goddess holds out to you her boat-shaped bowl. In it is a liquid, with herbs, poppy seeds, grain and other things you cannot recognise, that smells of barley. This is the *kykeon*, the sacred drink of the mysteries of the goddess. She motions to you to drink from the bowl. The liquid tastes bitter. As you swallow it you see a vision of the seeds of grain, lying inert in the earth. As you watch the seeds sprout and grow green and tall until they become a ripe crop of barley. You see visions of all the seeds of everything that is, germinating, growing to fullness, dying down and germinating again, and you understand the mystery and the beauty of the harvest – that all life is a circle; that everything that is born grows, dies, and grows again, just as the corn does in the field.

Then you are standing with the goddess once more in the moonlit field. The goddess holds out her hand to you. In her hand are three ears of golden barley which she gives to you. In return for this gift from the goddess, you dedicate your own harvest to her, whatever it may be. As you watch, the vision of goddess fades and you are alone in the moonlight in the harvested field. Return gently, bringing the mystery of the harvest and the gift of the goddess with you.

SEPTEMBER

September

Balance and Serenity

The Sunset of the Year

On a misty, drizzly morning I am approaching Cenarth and a crowd of people are standing on the riverbank, staring silently and intently at the water. The River Teifi is broad here and flows over a series of shallow waterfalls. Intrigued, I stop to look and join the crowd in the soft rain, gazing at the water rushing over the falls. Then someone points: a big, silvery salmon is trying to jump up over the rocks to the quiet water above the falls. It fails and falls back. It tries again, and again. Cenarth is a salmon leap, one of the biggest and best, and famous since ancient times. The medieval poets and chroniclers wrote about it and the Mabinogion *tells of places of deep enchantment close by. The salmon is the fish of knowledge, and the oldest of all the animals.*

The salmon must journey up the river, overcoming rapids, waterfalls and rocks, to reach their spawning grounds. Across the breadth of the falls, more salmon are hurling themselves upward through the white water and falling back again, exhausted. Their struggle against the power of the river seems like an impossible task and I think that surely they must be dashed to pieces against the rocks, but they keep on instinctively, leaping upwards and falling back. Eventually one fish makes it up to the calm water and a cheer goes up from the crowd. The rain grows heavier. I watch the salmon battling against the water, leaping, falling, leaping, falling back again.

The sound of the rushing water becomes a hypnotic roaring in my ears. I don't realise until much later, but I have become entranced. A connection happens and my mind is in the white water with the salmon; without knowing, I become the salmon. There is no sense of a struggle, just a calm, all-consuming instinct; an all-powerful will that drives it/me forwards and up through the translucent falls in a never-ending moment until with one great leap I/we arrive in the still pool above the weir.

September Associations

Festivals: Autumn Equinox (21st)

Figures: Arthur of Albion, the Lady of the Lake

More Than Human: Apples, berries (sloes, hawthorns, blackberries, etc.), hazelnuts, salmon leaping, owls at night, Equinox high tides

Totems and Symbols: Apple, salmon, hazel

The salmon gives a flick of its tail and releases me. It swims on upstream on its quest and suddenly I am standing on the riverbank again, soaked and shivering in the heavy rain, but glowing golden with a new kind of understanding. It is an embodied magic; an instinctual knowledge of autumn, river, tide, moon and an endless circular journey of life and water. I can feel it flowing within me like the river. Three hours have passed in a few seconds.

September is the ninth month and the last when the light will be greater than the dark. We learn of the wisdom of the hazel and the salmon, and the magic of apples. At the Autumn Equinox towards the end of the month, the god of growing things will leave on his journey through the dark months, and we journey with him into the inner worlds of dreams, and visions will begin. It is the month when the wild harvest begins in earnest; everything is gathering itself in for winter. Summer has gone; September is a time of harvesting, both physically and spiritually; storing the gifts of summer for the months to come.

At the Equinox the great tide of the year turns again. The ebbing tide of water ends, and the tide of air begins to rise. It will peak at Midwinter. We have already seen that the biggest sea tides of the year occur around the Equinoxes when the gravitational pulls of the moon and sun combine, so a new or full moon close to Autumn Equinox will bring spectacularly high tides. Coastal and rural wisdom also holds that the weather changes at Autumn Equinox, which is often accompanied by major storms and rain.

At the beginning of the month, swallows and other migrant birds leave on their long journeys across the world, and many animals prepare for hibernation or store food for hard times to come. As our eco-systems grow ever more fragile, the approach of winter is an especially difficult time for our fellow creatures. I begin September by working everyday protection spells and charms for the wild animals and birds around me, and provide practical help such as food, materials for hibernation and resting places. The nine knots spell, which we learnt in January, is very effective for this purpose. During the month, as the nights draw in, I will hear owls and foxes calling in the darkness for the first time.

Herbs can still be picked for drying on sunny days and seeds collected and saved to use next year. Seeds of your magical plants can be stored in paper bags or envelopes, or simply left on the plants. Some will fall to the ground and be nurtured by the earth until they germinate next spring, and others will provide welcome food for birds and animals. Continue the process of transferring dried herbs to airtight jars for use throughout the winter. Ideally, these should be stored out of direct light. Stems of mugwort and vervain can be used to make brooms or cut up to use as incense, so that none of the plant is wasted.

Fruits, berries, seeds and nuts are everywhere, and are at the centre of magical work this month. Practical magic in September means collecting some of the wild harvest for use in spells and charms and also perhaps using some of the earth's gifts to create delicious things to eat and drink. Made with magical intent, these can be shared at Sabbats and rituals and given as witch gifts. This is the month when the witch's kitchen really comes into its own. When wild harvesting, please always take only what you need and leave plenty for the creatures that will depend on the harvest to see them through the winter.

The month begins with an ancient folk custom. The Abbots Bromley Horn Dance, which takes place in Staffordshire on or around September 9, is England's oldest danced tradition and was first recorded in 1225. Its origins and meanings are lost in the mists of time, but for witches who venerate a horned god it is of real interest and a great day out, and visitors are welcomed. Six Deer-Men wearing huge reindeer antlers, and accompanied by a Fool, a Hobby Horse, a Bowman and Maid Marian, dance around the village of Abbots Bromley all day. Radiocarbon dating has established that the horns, which are kept in the church when not in use, are at least 1,000 years old.

THE POWER OF NINE, THE HAZEL AND THE SALMON

> *The weird sisters, hand in hand,*
> *Posters of the sea and land,*
> *Thus do go about, about,*
> *Thrice to thine and thrice to mine,*
> *And thrice again to make it nine.*
> *Peace, the charm's wound up.*
> Shakespeare: *Macbeth*, Act I, Scene iii (the three Weird Sisters work their spell)

Nine, being three times three, is a consummate magical number; the number of completeness. It features in many magical systems, is used extensively in spells and charms, and is closely associated with witchcraft, as Shakespeare knew. The power of three, multiplied three times, gives a spell immense power; you have already used it in the first spell you made at the beginning of the year. Multiples of nine, however you add them up, will always make a total of nine (for example: $3 \times 9 = 27$; $2 + 7 = 9$, or $9 \times 15 = 135$; $1 + 3 + 5 = 9$); try it and see. This gives nine a special place in the magic of numbers. The ninth month shares in this special completeness and magic made in September benefits from the power of nine.

Blodeuwedd (*see* June) was created from nine flowers by Math, and magical charms feature nine flowers and nine herbs. There are nine classical Muses who preside over the arts. The Norse mythos describes nine worlds connected by the world tree, Yggdrasil, where the god Odin hung in agony for nine days and nights to gain the wisdom of the runes. The old Irish gods, the Tuatha de Danaan, sent nine waves to repel the invading Milesians, and in Irish myth the mystical ninth wave separates this world from the Otherworld across the western ocean. Tennyson in his *Idylls of the King* pictured the ninth wave washing the infant Arthur ashore at Merlin's feet. At the Autumn Equinox Arthur will be given into the care of the nine Ladies of the Lake; sisters or priestesses of Avalon. The number nine recurs many times in the Welsh Arthurian stories; the cauldron in the Otherworld to which Arthur and his companions journey in the poem *Preiddeu Annwm* (The Spoils of Annwm) is warmed by the breath of nine maidens, and the tale of Peredur, son of Efrawg in the *Mabinogion* features the terrifying nine witches of Caer Lloyw (Gloucester).

Hazel is the tree of the ninth month. It is the tree of wisdom and a great aid to magic-making. It is central to Celtic practices. The druids used hazel staffs or wands and a forked hazel stick is still the tool of choice for water diviners. In an Irish legend that parallels the Welsh story of Ceridwen and Taliesin and the cauldron of inspiration, nine hazel trees grew around the well of Segais. Their nuts, which contained all knowledge and wisdom, fell into the water where a salmon fed on them. This salmon was accidentally eaten by the hero Fionn macCumhaill, who, like Taliesin, gained all knowledge, wisdom and foresight as a result.

In both Welsh and Irish myth, the salmon is the oldest and wisest of all creatures, and can confer magical knowledge and wisdom. The water from the well of Segais was sacred to the goddess Boann. She caused the well to boil up and overflow and together she and the water became the River Boyne that flows past the great megalithic and sacred site of Newgrange in County Meath. In medieval Ireland the penalty for felling a hazel tree was death, and this also applied to apple trees (*see* below). In Greek and Roman belief, the hazel was the tree of Hermes/Mercury who bestowed gifts of wisdom, creativity and eloquence and was the patron deity of physicians. Hazel is associated with poetry, and with vision, intuition and divination. There is archaeological evidence that hazel has been used in magic since very early times and the nuts eaten at ritual feasts, so eating hazel nuts in September is a simple magical but very effective act that connects the witch with all the qualities of hazel, the tales of the cauldron, the well, the salmon of wisdom and the number nine. Seeing a salmon leap is a rare experience these days, as human folly has led to the decline of wild Atlantic salmon, but it is still possible to witness this extraordinary sight in a few wild places.

Weave this intuitive web of ninth month images and connections in September to find creative inspiration and wisdom and deepen your magical skills.

FINISHING THE WAND

It is time now to finish and polish the wand you cut in March. Do this early in September so that it will be ready to use at the Equinox. It should be dry and easy to work by now. If you removed the bark in March, you can trim and sand the wand smooth if necessary. I prefer to use sandpaper rather than power tools for this task; I am not an accomplished woodworker so if I can do it, anyone can. Working by hand focuses my magical will and increases my personal connection with the wand. If you decided to leave the bark on the wand, just trim any rough edges with a craft knife or sandpaper. I have two wands: the spiral ash wand that I described in March was finished with beeswax (warmed slightly and applied with a soft cloth) and I renew this every year in September before the Equinox. My other wand is made of blackthorn, cut from a hedge next to a cromlech in Ynys Môn, a special place for me since early childhood. It is in its natural state, with red-black bark. The tip of the wand can be carved if you wish, or a piece of deer horn or a stone fixed to it. In some traditions, a phallus is carved at the tip of the wand; other witches may carve something that represents the tree or its spirit. I avoid commercially bought crystals in my witchcraft, because they are frequently mined in destructive and damaging ways, and the workers who mine them are subject to exploitation. Of course, this is a matter of personal choice. I prefer to find what I need, because something you have found yourself is a gift from the spirits of the land and will add to the magical power of the wand. Crystals and other precious stones (jasper and agate, for example) can be found at the coast or on a countryside walk, and if you ask the spirits and let them lead you, you will surely be given what you need. My blackthorn wand is tipped with a gleaming red and black serpentine pebble from the Lizard in Cornwall.

I choose not to paint or varnish my wands, but this is another personal choice and symbols or images can be painted or burnt onto the wand using a pyrography tool. Find a suitable piece of cloth to wrap the wand when it is not in use, or make a bag for it.

When the wand is ready, return with it to the tree it was cut from. Show the wand to the tree, ask its blessing, and ask the spirit of the tree to be with you when you use the wand and to aid you in your magic. You may seek a vision of a Dryad or tree spirit when you do this. Your wand will be used for the first time in a ritual at the Equinox Sabbat, and as a final stage in its preparation, conduct a simple ritual of consecration. Try to do this at least a week before the Equinox Sabbat. You will consecrate the wand with each of the four elements. Place your wand on your altar for two or three days prior to the ritual.

Practice: The Threefold Consecration of a Wand or Similar

You will need

- Water from your favourite holy well
- Dried mugwort herb
- Mugwort anointing oil if you have made it, otherwise use another anointing oil of your choice
- A charcoal block and your incense burner (*see* August for incense-making)
- A candle for your altar

Method

Cast a circle around yourself and your altar. Respectfully ask the tree spirit in your new wand to be with you, and call upon goddess and god (in whatever form seems appropriate to you) to be with you and bless the work. Light the charcoal block in your incense burner. When it is glowing, place a little dried mugwort on the charcoal. Pass the wand through the smoke three times, asking the elements of air to bless the wand. Next pass the wand through the flame of the altar candle three times, asking the element of fire to bless it. Then sprinkle well water on the wand three times, asking the element of water to bless it. Next anoint the wand three times with the anointing oil and ask the element of earth to bless it. Hold the wand aloft before the altar and dedicate it to goddess and god and the spirits, vowing as you do so that it will be used to make magic in their names. Thank the goddess and god and the spirits and close your circle as usual.

The wand should be wrapped and left on the altar until the Equinox Sabbat. Always remember that your wand is a living, consecrated magical tool with its own indwelling spirit; look after it carefully and keep it safe and covered and away from prying eyes when not in use. After the Equinox, you can use your wand in all your rituals and in operative magic to add focus and strength to your charms and spells.

THE WILD HARVEST

Blackberries are the archetypal hedgerow harvest. Collect them to make blackberry and apple pies or crumbles for Equinox feasts, or use them to make flavoured vodka or vinegar. If you want to try your hand at jam making, blackberry and apple is the easiest place to start. Blackberries should not be picked be picked after the Equinox because local traditions throughout Britain state that the Devil spits on them (or worse) then. Alternatively, after Equinox, the Faeries claim them and will be angry with you if you steal them. They definitely taste past their best in late September, and should be left for the birds as well as the Faeries.

Be creative with the wild harvest of September. When the earth presents you with unexpected gifts of nuts, fruits and berries, find ways of using them to make magic. Acorns can be used to decorate the altar at Equinox or threaded onto a necklace in honour of the god, although it is necessary to use very fresh ones as the outer shells can be very tough and split easily. Make a circle of horse chestnuts (conkers) by threading them onto wire and hang them up at Equinox. They are soft when fresh and can easily be pieced with a nail or knitting needle.

Hawthorn Vinegar

Hawthorn berries are everywhere in September. The hawthorn trees, laden with deep red berries that provide a feast for the birds, are one of the glories of autumn and remind us again that hawthorn is the great Faerie tree. The berries have magical uses. They should be picked on a dry, sunny September morning when the moon is waning and, like most magical plant ingredients, should not be allowed to touch the ground, so catch them in a basket or a cloth. The dried berries can be used in incense and in charms and spells, especially in Faerie magic.

Fresh hawthorn berries can also be used to make a delicious and very magical vinegar, which takes on the berries' bright red colour and can be used, mixed fifty-fifty with olive or sunflower oil, to flavour salads and other foods at the Equinox feast. It can also be used in your Faerie magic. Hawthorn vinegar is made in a similar way to the plant tinctures that we made earlier in the year.

You will need

- Fresh hawthorn berries
- Cider vinegar (ideally organic, with the 'mother')
- A glass jar with an airtight, non-corrosive lid
- A fine mesh sieve
- Bottles to decant the vinegar into

Method

Gather enough hawthorn berries to half fill the glass jar (ensure they are clean before putting them into the jar).

Fill the jar with cider vinegar.

Leave the berries and vinegar to steep for up to two weeks, shaking the jar gently every few days. The vinegar will soon take on the bright red colour of the berries.

When the vinegar is ready, strain it through the sieve, discarding the berries (mine go on the compost heap) and decant the vinegar into clean glass bottles. It is ready to use immediately.

A Faerie Bottle

A Faerie bottle is a September variation on the witch bottles that we made last month. It is an aid to contact with the Others and makes a great witch gift. The method is the same: the dried ingredients are placed in a small glass bottle, which is then sealed and tied with thread, and all of this is done with focused magical intent. The ingredients for the Faerie bottle are:

- Dried hawthorn berries: if possible use a small bunch of berries still on the twig and with a few leaves and thorns attached
- Dried vervain leaves or stems

The finished Faerie bottle should be wrapped and tied with green thread as this is the Faerie colour.

Sloe Gin

Sloe gin is a traditional delicacy with great magical as well as alcoholic power; if you wish to use alcohol in your magic, then sloe gin is the ideal choice and it also makes a superb Yule or Midwinter gift for witch friends. It is very easy to make. Sloes are the fruit of the blackthorn tree, and carry all the magical meanings of the blackthorn. They are commonly found in hedgerows throughout the West Country and Wales, and on clifftops and other coastal places. When picking sloes, do not be tempted to snack on them as they are extremely astringent and bitter; this bitterness means that the recipe requires the addition of a little sugar. Sloe gin is made in a very similar way to Hawthorn vinegar.

You will need

- Sloes (enough to half fill your jar)
- An airtight jar
- Sugar
- Gin (use basic unflavoured gin)
- A fine mesh sieve
- Bottles to decant the gin into

Method

Pick enough sloes to half fill your jar.

The old-style method required the sloes to be pricked all over to puncture the skin and release their juice, but this can be avoided by placing the sloes in a freezer for at least a week. This breaks their skins.

Allow the sloes to thaw out, then place the sloes in the jar and add two tablespoonfuls of sugar (more if you want your gin to be sweeter). Cover the sloes with gin, seal the jar tightly and leave it somewhere out of direct light for about six weeks, shaking it gently every few days so that all the juice is released from the fruit.

When the gin is ready, strain it through the sieve, discard the sloes (gin-soaked sloes left on my compost heap have led on occasions to slightly tipsy jackdaws, magpies and crows) and decant the gin into bottles. Sloe gin needs to age and should not be drunk before Yule. It can be kept for years (if you have the will power) and vintage sloe gin is delicious.

THE AUTUMN EQUINOX

The Autumn Equinox is the moment when light and darkness must be reconciled within ourselves. We are leaving summer and the light behind for the inner journey into night and the world of sleep, dreams and visions, when growing things will lie dormant and seeds rest within the earth, sleeping peacefully until the light will free them again in spring.

The modern Pagan custom of naming this festival 'Mabon' does not work for me. As someone who grew up with Welsh traditions, it simply does not fit with the Welsh mythos and customs. Mabon ap Modron/Son of the Mother (or Maponus as the Romano-British knew him) would more logically be associated with spring than autumn. Alban Elfed, used by modern druids, makes more sense, but I am sticking with Equinox because it reminds me that this is a time of balance that heralds the coming of darkness and winter. Like the Spring Equinox, Autumn Equinox is both a moment of balance and a time of transition and must be negotiated with care. It is a time full of profound meaning. It is the absolute opposite of the edgy, energetic Spring Equinox and is a time of peaceful melancholy and reverie, when the inner world of dream and vision beckons. The seasons must turn and carry us with them; summer must pass but it will come again in its turn. It is the time when the witches' god, the lord of all growing things, journeys into the Otherworld, to rest and renew himself while the earth sleeps and until winter passes, but he does not leave us alone, for soon in October we shall see his image in the night sky.

The goddess at this time is the dark lady who presides over the god's Otherworld journey and likewise guides us, as the tide of the year enters the element of air, into our own inner worlds. Sadness at the passing of summer is a natural thing, and the Equinox shows us how to understand this and accept and love it. The usual meaning of 'melancholy' is sadness or depression, but it has another more magical meaning; that of a deep and very peaceful creative reverie in which visions and ideas are revealed to us, and through which we can accept and understand the mysteries of the turning seasons on an instinctual level that is beyond words.

The withdrawal of the god into the inner realms at the Equinox is expressed beautifully in the medieval Arthurian mythos, which has become an important part of the contemporary witchcraft that we weave together. Arthur is the god of the year; after being mortally wounded at the battle of Camlann, his last battle, he is taken by the Lady of the Lake by boat to the Isle of Avalon, there to find rest and be refreshed, before he can return again. Visiting the earthly locations of this story in September can bring a deep connection with its meanings, and with the Equinox. Slaughterbridge near Camelford and close to Tintagel in North Cornwall (an area full of Arthurian associations) is the reputed site of the battle of Camlann, and Tennyson wrote about it in his *Idylls of the King*. A short walk along the bank of the River Camel leads to a sixth-century CE stone, inscribed in Ogham and Latin, which is known locally as the Arthur stone (although it actually reads 'Here lies the son of Macarius'). It is one of the most haunted places I know.

THE LADY OF THE LAKE

Glastonbury (*see* April) is the earthly gateway to Avalon ('Land of Apples'). The Arthurian mythos is a complex mix of old Welsh/British legend, medieval Christianity and modern Paganism that continues to be refreshed and grow, and all these things come together in Glastonbury to form a living tradition full of spiritual meaning. Witches take what they find meaningful from the mix. The magical power of Glastonbury, in the low-lying landscape of the Somerset levels, surrounded by ancient apple orchards, has always seemed to me to be at its height in the time between the Autumn Equinox and Samhain, when the god journeys to the Otherworld Avalon and enters into his time of repose through the gates of earth. On autumn days this can be felt physically as well as psychically and emotionally.

Before celebrating the Equinox Sabbat, I visit a lake or pool to seek a vision of the Lady of the Lake, the autumnal goddess who bears Arthur away to Avalon, give thanks to the spirits of the place and to the Lady, and meditate on the meaning of the season. There are a number of locations in Cornwall, the West Country and Wales associated with the Lady of the Lake. One such is Dozmary Pool on Bodmin Moor in Cornwall, where it is said that Arthur's sword, Excalibur, was returned to the Lady after Arthur's last battle at Camlann. As we saw in July, for our ancestors, lakes and pools were liminal place; entrances to the Otherworld where deities were honoured and propitiated. The lake of Llyn Cerrig Bach in Ynys Môn, close to where I grew up, and where a great 'hoard' of Iron Age objects were thrown into the water as votive offerings, is a very special place of liminal magic. A meditation at one of these places in September can be a profound experience. The goddess can be honoured at any lake or pool that holds meaning for you and by practising your witchcraft in this way, you are helping to re-enchant the land.

APPLES

The association of the apple with goddesses is a profound one in many cultures. If you cut an apple in half widthways (not vertically), you will see that its seeds make a five-pointed star, or pentagram, one of the most important symbols of witchcraft that has many layers of meaning. It signifies the four elements plus spirit, and the five stations of life (birth, initiation, marriage, death and rebirth). It is the symbol of the planet Venus, so the apple is sacred to Venus and Aphrodite and many other goddesses, especially those associated with love and sexuality. In many mythologies apples of immortality grew in a paradise garden presided over by a goddess. These included the Near Eastern goddesses Astarte, Inanna and Ishtar, whose sacred moon tree was guarded by a serpent; the Judaeo-Christian myth of the temptation of Eve would seem to be a patriarchal, misogynist distortion of these stories, which identifies women as the source of evil. Golden apples of immortality were bestowed on the gods by the Norse goddess Idunn, and in ancient Greece Hercules tried to steal the golden apples of the goddess Hera from the garden of the Hesperides (the nymphs of the sunset). These were also guarded by a serpent. The sea god Manannan mac Lir was the guardian of the silver branch of Irish mythology, from which hung nine golden apples of immortality, and which played music that could lull mortals into a deep sleep or trance. The branch could enable the living to visit Tir na nOg, the Land of Youth. In the Welsh mythos the apple is sacred to Ceridwen, the goddess of the cauldron and of plant magic, and also to Olwen. Pomona was the Roman goddess of orchards and apple trees.

Apples were the fruit of Faerie; for a mortal to accept and eat an apple in Faerie was disastrous and would mean that they would never be able to leave. For both Scandinavian and Celtic Pagans, the apple was the passport to the next world, or Isles of the Blessed in British myth, and corpses were buried with apples. In one medieval Arthurian story, Merlin kept an apple orchard at Glastonbury. Avalon may thus be understood as the land beyond death to which Arthur is taken by the goddess to find rest until it is time for him to return again.

The apple season begins in September and will continue until Samhain or Hallowe'en at the end of October. Mark its beginning this month with a small personal ritual. On a Friday, the day of the week named for Venus and Freya, cut an apple in half widthways, look at the five-pointed star, and meditate on all its meanings and symbolism. Commune with the apple deity of your choice before eating the apple. In the West Country, apples are everywhere in September, and the season is celebrated not only with cider, but also with apple juice, apple cake, apple jams and jellies, apple pies, baked apples and every other form of apple produce you can think of. Cored apples can be cut into rings and dried for use in winter and to make decorations for Yule. Celebrate the goddesses of love and sensuality in September by eating apple produce and trying apple recipes, and make sure that apples are included in your feast at the Equinox.

Practice: The Autumn Equinox Ritual

The Equinox ritual is the culmination of all the magical work of September, and many of the things you have made this month will be used in the celebration. The mood of this Sabbat is one of calm, loving acceptance of change; of peaceful melancholy and reverie as we turn away from summer; of quiet dreaming with the god as he journeys inwards, and with the dark goddess who guides him. It is also a time when witches consider our own magical and spiritual harvest and meditate on what has been achieved at the end of the growing season. As with Spring Equinox it is a point of balance; a moment of equilibrium between light and dark, but at this Equinox it is the dark that will grow and which must be welcomed. The great tide of the year has now reached its halfway point and we are about to enter the tide of Air with all its virtues and qualities. At Autumn Equinox the sun enters Libra, the cardinal sign of Air. Air is the element of the mind and the intellect, and it is both a time when new ideas begin to form, and a time to review how the great tide has worked in our lives since the Spring Equinox; to examine how we have used the gifts of fire and water before the year leads us deeper into the airy world of cold starry skies, frost and ice. We may see beyond the immediate season and glimpse the pattern of the great tides moving ceaselessly behind our lives.

Preparation

Decorate the altar with all the fruits of September: hazel nuts, apples, hawthorn berries, acorns, pine cones, autumn leaves. Be creative and use whatever you can find that embodies the season for you. I like to place an apple bough with its fruit on my altar to represent the silver bough; the passport to the Otherworld of Celtic tradition. I may add circles of horse chestnuts or thread red and golden autumn leaves onto a string and hang them over the altar. A deep midnight blue altar candle symbolises the Lady of the Lake and the god's Otherworld journey. The altar should feel peaceful and harmonious and help to create a contemplative mood in keeping with the quiet but profound nature of the Equinox. You will need your new wand.

Food for the Equinox can include anything made from the seasonal harvest of September: apples, blackberries, hazelnuts, and whatever else is in season. In Scotland, it is customary to bake the Struan Micheil or Michaelmas cake or bannock (unleavened bread) made from barley, oats and wheat grown during the year. Combining fresh fruits and nuts and the sweet jams and jellies that are traditional in September with some form of home-made bread and cider or apple juice to drink makes a simple feast that reflects perfectly the meanings of this Sabbat.

The ritual

Cast the circle using your newly consecrated wand for the first time. You should really feel the power of the wand as you do this; it will amplify your magical will and lend a new strength to your witchcraft. Its link with you will grow every time you use it.

Light the candle on your altar. Call upon the dark goddess as Lady of the Lake and the god as Arthur of Albion to be present. Move around the circle with your wand and, beginning in the east, bid a ritual farewell to summer, to the light and to their elemental gifts. Visualise these gifts as you move round the circle. In the east bid farewell to the gifts of air: the sounds and scents of summer carried on the air. In the south bid farewell to the gifts of fire: the warmth and light of the summer season. In the west bid farewell to the gifts of water: warm seas and gentle flowing streams; and in the north bid farewell to the gifts of earth: the flowers, leaves and fruits. Acknowledge that the season of light is over and welcome the coming darkness.

Honour the goddess as mistress of the silver wheel of the zodiac, as the power behind the stars, and as the dark lady of the great tides behind death and birth, who presides over all the lives we have lived and will live. This part of the ritual is very much about understanding and accepting that we are mortal beings and that our lives are finite. The dark lady destroys what we need to leave behind as we journey onwards. The goddess can be invoked using the web of symbols we have worked with during September: the hazel that signifies embodied magical knowledge and wisdom; the apple with its five-pointed star, the passport to Avalon or the Land of Youth; the salmon, oldest and wisest of the animals, who swims from the well at the source of all rivers across the oceans of the world, and the well itself. Sharing hazelnuts and apples amongst those present can create an instinctive understanding; these fruits of the season and its spiritual meanings are not separate, but are parts of one continuum.

Then the god's journey into the Otherworld is visualised, or if you are working with others, it can be enacted. I once had the profoundly moving experience of celebrating the Equinox at a small lake with an island in its centre; a witch representing the god was rowed in a small boat on his journey to Avalon. However you choose to do this, envisage the silent journey of the sleeping god to Avalon, and his passing from the outward world. Use images of the sunset, autumn leaves, bare trees, mist, seeds, acorns and pinecones to invoke him. As he leaves this world, there should be a last vision of him transformed; his body made of stars and crowned with antlers.

Then it is time to meditate, firstly on the summer that is ending and what has been achieved and harvested, and then on the coming of darkness and winter. This process should not be rushed; when it is complete, the transformation of the Equinox will be accomplished and will bring an acceptance that we are ourselves part of the endless turning of the seasons, and that rest and night must follow growth and light. This meditation may lead to extraordinary visions and insights.

After the circle is closed, share the Equinox feast. Make sure that there is a little left over that can be given not just to the Faeries and spirits, but also to wild animals and birds. Giving to the wild creatures is especially important at this Sabbat, because the coming winter will be a hungry time for them. I put the Sabbat gifts in special places in the garden and work a protection spell as I do so. This is complemented on a practical level by providing safe places for hibernation and food for birds during the lean months.

A Spell for September: The Blackthorn and Hawthorn Charm

This charm embodies the moment of balance between light and darkness at Equinox. It will help you achieve balance between the light and dark parts of the self and guide the passage into the dark part of the year.

You will need

- A hawthorn twig
- A blackthorn twig
- A length of black woollen yarn
- A length of white woollen yarn
- Scissors

Method

Cut a hawthorn twig and a blackthorn twig, making sure that there are plenty of thorns on each twig. The twigs should measure from the tip of your middle finger to the bottom of your palm. Remember that both hawthorn and blackthorn have Otherworld associations. Ask permission of the trees and spend some time in meditation with them, wishing them and their spirits good health and the blessings of the season.

Cut a length of black and a length of white yarn, each measuring from the tip of your middle left hand finger to the tip of your middle right hand finger when you stand with your arms outstretched. The yarns should then be twisted together to form a strong cord: tie one end of the two threads to a hook or door handle and hold the other end. Twist the two threads together until the entire length is tightly twisted. Focus your magical will on this as you are doing it.

Keeping a tight hold of the end of the cord, take it to the other end, put the two ends together and carefully let go of the end you are holding, so that you allow the two threads to spring together and twist around each other forming a strong cord.

As the threads twist themselves, they seem to take on a life of their own, and you will sense the spirit force in them. This is a very old witch's way of making powerful magic and the cord you have made will be full of your magical intent. The finished cord will be about half the original length.

Make a knot in each end of the cord to secure it and seal the magic in. Then carefully cut the cord in two, making a knot in each new end.

Bind the two twigs tightly together at each end with the cords you have made, concentrating on the unity of dark and light, of blackthorn and whitethorn, and the balance of the Equinox. Secure each binding with three knots to seal the magic in. The charm can be placed on your altar for the Equinox Sabbat ritual. It can be kept until Samhain, and then added to the ritual fire.

Meditation: The Inner Orchard

This meditation will create another inner working place, to complement the Magical Study that you visualised in January. The Inner Orchard will become an inner world landscape where you can work nature magic focused on the turning of the seasons. In this meditation it is visualised at the Autumn Equinox but it can be visited throughout the Witch's Year. Have a glass of water and an apple beside you for when you finish the meditation.

You are sitting under an apple tree in an ancient orchard at the foot of Glastonbury Tor. It is a still, silent, misty September morning; you cannot see the nearby lakes and marshes on the Somerset levels and only the top of the great conical hill with its ruined tower is visible above the wreaths of mist. All around you the apple trees of the orchard are laden with fruit and the rich, sweet scent of apples hangs on the air. Spend time here amongst the old, gnarled apple trees watching birds in the branches and insects feeding on fallen apples.

An older man, bearded and carrying a tall staff of hazel wood and a willow basket, is walking between the trees. He beckons to you and you see that his basket is full of ripe apples. He is the keeper of the orchard and there is a strong sense of wisdom and magic about him. In the distance in the mist, you hear a sound like the gentle lapping of water on wood. The orchard keeper walks towards the sound and you follow through the trees until you come to the edge of the orchard. In front of you a lake stretches away into the mist. It is perfectly calm and radiates stillness. The sound grows louder until you see, looming out of the mist, a boat; a black barque with a high prow. As it draws nearer you see that it is being rowed by eight women, dressed in deep blue like the midnight sky. There is no sound other than the water lapping against the oars and the boat, and a sense of complete peace and stillness surrounds you. As you stand with the orchard keeper, the barque comes to rest at the shore by your feet. On it lies a tall, regal figure on a bed made of red and gold autumn leaves. Perhaps he is a man, perhaps a god. He is sleeping an enchanted sleep from which he cannot wake. In the crook of his arm is a tall spear; its blade gleams with a golden light although no sun is visible through the mists. Beside him sits a veiled woman, dressed in the same midnight blue as the oarswomen; the Lady of the Lake with her sisters. She is guarding him, guiding him, holding him in a peaceful enchantment.

The Lady beckons to the orchard keeper. He steps onto the barque and you see that there are tears in his eyes. You sense that he has been here before, many times. He takes the most perfect, golden apple from his basket and places it in the sleeping man's hand. The Lady draws aside her veil for a moment and thanks the orchard keeper, and you see that she is smiling a smile that is beyond sadness or happiness. Then she draws her veil over her face once more. The orchard keeper steps back onto the shore and the boat moves silently on towards the west. Huge gates loom in front of it. Beyond them is a land that you cannot see; Avalon; the Otherworld. The gates swing open and as the barque passes silently through them you see that the sleeping man has been transformed; his body seems to be made of stars and on his head are huge antlers. The apple in his hand is made of golden light. Then the barque passes from view, and the great gates of Avalon swing shut behind it. You are once more alone with the orchard keeper amongst the apple trees. He tells you that this is the mystery of the Equinox.

The orchard keeper takes you to the centre of his orchard where nine hazel trees grow in a circle overhanging a well of clear water that flows into a stone pool in which a large, speckled salmon swims. The water flows away through the orchard to the lake. Nuts from the hazel trees fall into the water and, as you watch, the salmon eats them. The orchard keeper seems very familiar, as if he is someone that you have always known, and you recognise that he has the knowledge and wisdom of all times and all places. He holds out two gifts to you: a hazel nut from one of the trees by the well, and a golden apple from his basket. They embody the wisdom and the magic of autumn, of the Equinox. He tells you to keep them safe within yourself and learn from them. You may return to the orchard that grows by the gates of Avalon whenever you have need and learn from him. You thank him; he bids you farewell, turns away and disappears into the mist.

Gently, when you are ready, return to the everyday. To return yourself fully to the plane of earth, drink a little water and eat your apple.

OCTOBER

October

Twilight and Transition

The Spirit World Beckons

It is the first week of October, a cold, clear night, and very, very late. The days at this time are still warm, but at three o'clock in the morning the air is chilly and a heavy dew already carpets the ground, although it is still too early in the year for frost. Autumn Equinox has passed and the nights are growing longer; dawn is still some hours away. The scents of autumn are on the air: woodsmoke, damp leaves and earth, and the sweet, cloying smell of fallen apples in the orchard at the edge of the village. A dog fox barks somewhere across the fields and the sound carries on the still night air. A barn owl answers back from the orchard. The darkness is a deep, velvet blue and it is the end of the lunar month, so there is no moon.

We have kept our vigil long past bedtime. As our eyes grow used to the darkness, we see the line of old oak trees that straggles along the south-eastern horizon. This is the time. Just above the trees, tilted almost to the vertical, the three bright stars of Orion's belt hang, burning silver and bright, beginning their climb high into the late night sky. Orion the Hunter is visible once more, for the first time since he faded away and left us just before Beltane. He strides across the dark heavens, travelling on towards the west where he will eventually disappear into the daylight when dawn comes.

Wrapped up warm against the encroaching cold, we raise a glass of cider to him, greeting and honouring the lord of the dark half of the year, the night hunter, leader of the Wild Hunt, lord of the depths of earth and of the starry skies. We call the Horned Hunter of the night by his many names: Orion, Osiris, Herne, Cernunnos, Gwyn ap Nudd, Janicot or just Old Hornie. It is a joyous moment as we celebrate the return of the darkness, for we are children of the light and darkness equally. We hug each other and rejoice as the dark part of the year begins.

October Associations

Festivals: Samhain (31st), Calan Gaeaf
Figures: Orion, Hecate, Persephone, the Horned Lord, ancestors
More Than Human: First sight of Orion, spiders' webs, fungi
Totems and Symbols: Orion's belt, spider's web, skull (Mexico)

As October begins, summer is gone, but the Horned Hunter of the night is with us again and the Wild Hunt is coming. The tide of air flows through us and the journey into darkness gathers pace. We learn the trance-inducing magic of webs and threads and meet the Fates and goddesses who spin and measure. At the end of the month is the great Sabbat of Samhain, when we encounter ancient deities of witchcraft, honour our ancestors and the veil that separates the worlds of the living and the dead is thin.

The first sight of Orion in the pre-dawn sky at the beginning of October is always a profound and emotional experience. For witches, it is a sign that our god is still with us. The god of growing things left us at the Equinox, and disappeared into the depths of earth to find rest in Avalon, but now we see his sign in the heavens. He has become the Night Hunter, leading the Wild Hunt across the starry skies. It is time for us to follow him into the night; into our interior world of dreams and visions to gain wisdom that we can bring back into the everyday and use in our lives. To see the pre-dawn, or heliacal rising of Orion, you must get up before dawn, because this is when the Hunter will rise in the south-eastern sky and as it grows light, he will quickly disappear into the brightness of the daylight. He will be our guide through the dark months, and walk with us until spring returns, rising earlier and earlier every night, until in the depths of winter he will rise just after the sun sets.

THE WILD HUNT

The legend of the Wild Hunt that is found throughout Europe has been with us since medieval times, and has become a central element of our folklore. The Wild Hunt is a pack of spectral hounds, led by a fearsome huntsman, that hunts for souls on wild winter nights and may steal the living away to the Otherworld or Hell. Its approach is usually announced by the distant baying of unearthly hounds, heard on the wind. In the Christian form of the legend, the hounds are led by the Devil who will carry their victims off to Hell.

In Wales the hounds are white with red ears and eyes and are known as the Cwn Annwn (hounds of Annwn/the Otherworld). Their huntsman is the Otherworld figure, Gwyn ap Nudd, who rides out of Glastonbury Tor to go hunting on dark, stormy nights. On Dartmoor in Devon, the Wishounds are led by Dewer (the old local name for the Devil). In Somerset the dogs are the Gabriel Hounds or Gabriel's Ratchets; in Cornwall the huntsman Dando leads his pack of Dandy Dogs and in other parts of Britain they may be called the Yeth Hounds, Tell Hounds or just the Hounds of Hell. In old English, the hunt is the Herlathing, led by King Herla. Throughout northern Europe and Scandinavia it is Odin who leads the Wild Hunt. The story has become almost universal in European folklore and is found in France, Italy, Spain and across Eastern Europe.

Other folkloric figures said to lead the Wild Hunt include Sir Francis Drake (in Devon), Gwydion (in Wales), King Arthur, Herne the Hunter and Sigurd the Dragonslayer. Medieval chroniclers recorded terrifying appearances of the Hunt, led by the Devil: its rampaging presence was recorded at Peterborough and Stamford in Lincolnshire in 1127, where it menaced badly behaved monks and priests. Folklorist Jakob Grimm did much to popularise the story and there are numerous fictional accounts of the Wild Hunt. Alan Garner's 1969 children's novel *Moon of Gomrath* contains a marvellous portrayal of the Herlathing. It features in paintings, film and TV programmes, music and superhero comics.

In contemporary witchcraft ritual and practices, the Wild Hunt is not feared, but celebrated as the wild and untamed force of nature led by a Pagan deity. It has been invoked in eco-rituals to defend wild places threatened by development and destruction. In coven witchcraft, pursuit by the Wild Hunt may be enacted as part of initiation rituals. The traditional advice of the folk tales is very clear: if you hear the baying of hounds on a dark and stormy night, lock and bar the doors and windows and stay safe inside until the danger has passed. However, adventurous witches who wish to experience the power of nature in all its untamed wildness and meet the Horned Hunter and race across the wild night sky with his hounds may choose to ignore this at their own risk…

The great tide of Air that began at Autumn Equinox is rising. It leads us deep into the inner worlds and in October we begin the inner journey that will lead us to the spirit world at Samhain. Samhain lies opposite Beltane on the Wheel of the Year and both these Sabbats are times when the gates of the spirit world are open. Whereas at Beltane the Otherworld entices us to leave the safety of the everyday and enter the hollow hills, at Samhain it is the spirit world that find its way to us, and the dead walk with the living.

It is important now to spend as much time as possible with your familiar spirits as they will be your guides and helpers at Samhain and beyond. Make sure that spirit houses and any other things you use for spirit work are clean and in good condition. Remember to record your inner journeys, dreams and visions as the Otherworld comes close to our own and spirit presences are all around us.

THE MAGIC OF THREADS

On misty October mornings cobwebs hanging heavy with beads of dew remind us of the goddesses who spin and weave and cut the thread of each life. The image of the three Fates is a very ancient one. The Greek Moirae were usually depicted as elderly sisters. Clotho spun the thread of a life, Lachesis measured it, and Atropos cut the thread, determining the hour of a person's death. They are paralleled in the Northern tradition by the three Norns: Uld, Skald and Verdandi who sit by the well of Urdr at the roots of Yggdrasil, the World Tree, and work the threads of life. The concept of Wyrd, a web of fate and past, present and future, in which each life hangs, is fundamental to the Northern system of magic.

Working with threads is one of the most ancient of human activities. We have been knotting, sewing, braiding, weaving for many thousands of years, probably since our ancestors lived through the Ice Ages over 30,000 years ago. The first threads would have been animal sinews used with bone needles to sew hides into clothing, or to thread stones, shells and bones onto necklaces. The adoption of agriculture in the Neolithic brought with it wool and plant fibres such as cotton (in Egypt and other parts of Africa) and flax (in Northern Europe), and spinning and weaving. All these activities have always been done primarily by women, and have always been full of spiritual meanings and magical significance. I like to imagine a woman, one of my first witch ancestors, many thousands of years ago in a cave shelter at the edge of a glacier looking up at the full moon and knotting nine threads in a cord just as we did at the beginning of the Witch's Year.

Spinning wool, flax or cotton was an extremely labour intensive and time-consuming process. Spindle whorls and weights are common finds at archaeological sites from the Neolithic onwards and innumerable women spent large parts of their lives spinning thread down the ages. Spinning can also be a magical and meditative activity; concentrating your intent while watching a cloud of wool turn into a single thread is an effective method of spell casting, and it's not too difficult if you want to try. Drop spindles can obtained from craft shops and, in areas where sheep are kept, it is possible to gather wool from hedgerows and bushes and experiment with spinning.

Knitting and sewing are more complex and highly effective forms of operative magic and everyday witchcraft. They are repetitive activities which are trance-inducing and create a heightened state of awareness which is ideal for spell-making. I have been knitting for many years and it is one of my 'go to' magic methods. The majority of knitters make things for family and friends, without pay, and love and good luck are stitched into them, even when the knitter is not consciously aware of this. Knitting for a new baby is not just about providing baby clothes; the knitter works love and good wishes into the whole process.

Many thousands of women, my own grandmother included, knitted scarves and socks for their menfolk who were sent to fight in the First World War and their love and fervent good wishes for a safe return were knitted into every stitch. The Shetland Museum, which showcases many items of the islands' traditional knitwear, includes a very battered jumper that survived a Second World War prisoner of war camp; its owner understood the power of its making and knew that if he kept it safe with him, he would return home again.

Knitting with conscious intent is a powerful thing, and easy to incorporate into your witchcraft. Simply knit and repeat over and over what you wish to achieve as you do it. After a while, you will be in a 'knitting trance' and won't even be aware that you are doing it. I have used knitting very successfully for house magic. When someone needs a new place to live, I ask them to draw or describe the sort of house they want, then make a knitted picture of it for them. A friend undergoing radiotherapy needed warm socks knitted with love, not just to keep him warm, but to keep him safe through the treatment. A big shawl, made to look like waves breaking, was knitted to concentrate my magical will when I was writing my last book *A Sea Witch's Companion,* and was taken to a favourite beach and dunked in the sea there before the book was published.

Crochet and sewing, especially embroidery done by hand, will achieve similar results. Sewing is also used to make bags or covers for magical equipment (and becomes part of their magic) and altar cloths. I have special sewing needles that are only used for spellcraft so I sewed and embroidered a very simple needle case from a piece of felt and some old blanket to keep them safe. All these things are part of witchcraft at its best: simple every-day activities that are full of the most profound magical meaning.

Last month we learnt how to make two threads twist themselves into a cord. Very long twisted cords can be made by having two people stand some distance apart outdoors and twist threads between them. The resulting long cord will be approximately half the length of the two threads you twist together. These cords have many uses in witchcraft. They can be used to mark the perimeter of a working circle, or cut into shorter lengths and used to wrap or bind items, or as ties for charm bags or hangers for wands. In some craft traditions, witches wear a cord around their waist which is also used in group spell-making. Making such a cord yourself gives it added power and meaning. A cord for use in sea magic can be made on the shore; a cord for tree magic can be made in woodland and a cord can be made at special places such as a sacred site or stone circle. The colour of yarn used to make the cord should be chosen to reflect your magical intentions. Cord-making is often used to combine two magical principles or forces symbolised by different colours. To work with dark and light together, twist black and white cords; to work with the moon and sun, twist gold and silver, or to work with fire and water, twist together red and blue. Different combinations will suggest themselves to you.

Plaiting (also known as braiding) deploys the power of three, as three threads are plaited together to make one. A plait has a very different energy to a cord. The force in a twisted cord is created when the two ends of the twisted threads are brought together and they twist themselves around each other in a rapid burst of magical energy, and a twisted cord will always contain this force and have an edgy, energised feel. A plait is made slowly, as the three threads are passed over each other many times and a plait contains a force that is built up by slow repetition and that can be released slowly over a long period of time. A plait is ideally suited to the magic of curing, and for encouraging something unwanted to leave. The first step is to tie the threads together at the top while concentrating and focus-ing the magical intent. As the threads are plaited, the witch thinks constantly of their mag-ical purpose, and may repeat a simple spell. At the end the plait is secured with another knot, and the magic becomes active.

My coven works a curing spell known as the Big Red Plait. It is deceptively simple. A very large amount of red woollen yarn is cut into lengths about two metres long, usually about the height of the person we are working for. We agree on a simple verbal spell, usually 'somebody be well' or similar. The top of the plait is knotted and the threads divided into three big bunches. Then everyone takes turns plaiting the bunches of threads over each other, repeating the spell as they go, with every ounce of everybody's magical will, concentration and energy put into the task, until the entire length of yarn is plaited, which can take a long time. The bottom end of the plait is then knotted, and each person adds a charm, such as a witch stone. The coven sits in a circle, holding the plait, with one person holding both ends together, and with a final burst of magical concentration, the spell is activated. This is usually an exhausting procedure if done properly. The plait is given to the person it has been made for.

As plaiting uses the magical power of three, it is ideally suited to lunar magic and for making offerings to triple goddesses. Black, white and red threads (the colours that represent the new, full and old moon phases respectively) can be plaited together to make a lunar charm. This is done as a form of physical meditation to bring you closer to the moon goddess, or used as a form of magic to help with menstrual problems or to help bring your own body cycles into phase with the moon. A plaited moon charm, perhaps with a small piece of silver lunar jewellery added, makes a good gift for a young girl at her first period. Visualise the three phases repeatedly as you plait the threads. Plait an offering to the triple goddess (maiden, mother and crone, or the three Romano-British Matres) using whatever colours have meaning for you, or begin the magical work of Samhain by making plaited offerings for Demeter, Persephone and Hecate. For Faerie magic, plait green threads and tie them around a hawthorn twig. A plait made of three black threads at the old moon will have strong banishing properties if done with concentration.

Other materials can be used: leather threads can be plaited into a necklace or bracelet for ritual use. Plaiting is used in bread making and plaited loaves can be made for ritual feasts. We have plaited our hair since at least Egyptian times and plaiting the hair often has a magical context. In the nineteenth century, the hair of loved ones who had passed away would be plaited and kept, sometimes made into jewellery as a keepsake. If a 'ritual' haircut is used to mark a major life change, some locks can be plaited and kept. I still treasure and use a plait of my hair made after an important witchcraft initiation. Plaiting can be used in myriad ways; once you understand the magical principles, you will see that the possibilities are endless and create your own plaited magic whenever you need it. You can boost the power of your plaits by using nine threads instead of three to harness the qualities of nine that we explored in September. You can make a plait of the whole Witch's Year by choosing a thread to for each month, grouping them into three groups of four and plaiting them together. If young children want to help with magic for good luck and related purposes, making plaited charms is a good place to start as the process is a simple one that small hands can manage fairly easily.

October, when nights grow longer and the spirit world comes close, is the ideal time for all forms of thread magic. If you intend to give witch gifts at Yule/Midwinter, then things made with threads are ideal and can be made now. Just because the magic of threads has traditionally been a gendered activity doesn't mean it has to remain that way. It is a great autumnal magical activity for people of all genders and none.

FINDING MAGICAL ITEMS: CECIL WILLIAMSON AND THE SPIRIT KNIFE

October, when the spirit world comes close, is a very good time to forage for pre-loved witches' tools and magical items at antique fairs and similar events. I am always surprised at how frequently items that have clearly been used for magical purposes turn up in these places and my own finds have included wands and ritual knives, jewellery, bowls, chalices, witch bottles and all manner of things used in witchcraft. It is not unusual to find an item which has a spirit living in it, and to find that the spirit feels confused and sad because it has been abandoned by its previous owner. If you find such a 'lost' item, you will know immediately, because the indwelling spirit will communicate with you in some way. Usually, it will be so pleased to have found you that it will hold onto you, and not let you go. Unless the spirit tells you to go away, rescuing such an item is an act of kindness; you have acquired a new spirit friend and it will reward you.

This can sometimes be a complicated process. I once bought an odd knife with a deer horn handle at an antique fair. There was something not quite right about it and it was not something I wanted at all, but as soon as I picked it up it made a huge connection with me and would not let me put it down. It also radiated a feeling of deep unhappiness which intensified after I took it home. I left it downstairs on a table when I went to bed. In the middle of the night I was awakened by a loud crash. The knife was on the floor on the other side of the room from where I had left it. If it had fallen off the table, I couldn't work out how it could have travelled so far. I put it back on the table and went back to bed. Shortly afterwards, the same thing happened again; the knife was on the floor, several yards from where I had left it and the feeling of unhappiness was overwhelming. The doors to the room were closed and nothing living could have entered it. It was a disturbing experience, to say the least.

I asked Cecil Williamson (*see* February) what to do. His collection of witchcraft artefacts included many that had belonged to witches who had passed, and he was adept at working with their spirits. He explained that the knife had obviously chosen me, that it was unhappy, and that I would need to find out why and make a relationship with it. Walking away was not an option. He suggested I should sleep with the knife under my pillow.

I did so with some trepidation, and in a series of dreams (mostly nightmares) over the next few nights the knife revealed its history. It was unhappy because it had belonged to someone who had used it very badly. Its voice needed to be heard. I listened, and gradually the knife and I began to trust each other and formed a close bond. I told it my witch name, and after a while it rewarded me with the gift of its own name. We have worked together ever since. The knife is kept safe in its own 'house' and is never shown to anyone else.

If something with an indwelling spirit comes into your possession, respect its privacy and do not draw attention to it or show it off to friends. Let it get used to its new home and to you, and get to know it. In my experience the spirits in pre-loved items tend to be private creatures. If a spirit has chosen you, it will usually have chosen you alone, because when you met it recognised something in your witch nature, and it will not want to be paraded in front of everyone. Some aspects of witchcraft are solitary ones, even if you work rituals with other people, and spirit working is one of them.

You will sometimes be advised to 'cleanse' pre-loved items by expelling whatever spirit lives within them. I would never to do such a thing without first getting to know the spirit and exploring whether it wished to stay with me, as driving a spirit away and thus deliberately making it homeless without very good reason seems to me to be a dreadful thing to do. I also do not consecrate pre-loved items in the ways described elsewhere in this book unless their spirits ask me to. I just make sure they are cleaned, repaired if necessary, and generally loved. Spirits are not predictable and should not be expected to behave according to pre-ordained rules and do your bidding. They are independent creatures and must be respected as such, and finding out who they are and how they like to live is an essential part of working with them. Working with the spirits I encounter in this way is an important part of my witchcraft. Do not be fearful about getting to know spirits; approach them with a good mix of curiosity and caution and you will be rewarded with a special and unique friendship and magical help.

Witch's lore dictates that you should pay whatever the seller asks for magical items and not haggle. In this process you are being led by fate and the spirit world; to haggle would be damaging magically, and if the thing is meant to be with you, it will come to you. Do not force the issue, and if you do not like the price, or cannot afford to pay it, then walk away, because the item is not for you, or it is not the right time. Besides, the 'I want it/get it at all costs' mentality does not work on a magical level, and less is definitely more.

SAMHAIN

Samhain, known to the wider world as Hallowe'en, is the time that everyone associates with witches, but its true significance is little understood, and tends to be obscured; submerged under the hugely enjoyable and very lucrative festival of Hallowe'en with its trick-or-treating, horror films, fright nights, parades and parties that have spread around the world from the US. These originated in the Celtic and European Samhain customs that were taken across the Atlantic by colonists and merged with indigenous traditions. Behind all this lies a Sabbat of very profound meaning and significance for witches; a time when we go deep inside ourselves and reach beyond the world of the living.

A number of strands combine in the celebration of Samhain. At its heart is a recognition, seemingly fairly universal, that at this time of year the world of the dead draws close to that of the living; the living may meet the dead, and ghosts, the spirits of the dead and the discarnate, are everywhere. As witches say, the veil between the worlds is thin. At Samhain the living may meet those they have known and loved who have departed this life. Rituals can take the form of powerful enactments of Underworld myths, particularly the classical Greek mythos of Demeter, Persephone and Hecate, and the dark goddesses and rulers of the worlds of the dead may be invoked. For many, Samhain is also the time when ancestors are honoured.

DEMETER, PERSEPHONE, HECATE AND HADES

The mythos of the goddess Demeter and her daughter Persephone was at the heart of the great mystery religion celebrated at Eleusis in Greece in classical times. Many thousands of initiates underwent profound, personal experiences and visions there that convinced them that they would be reborn into eternal life. We do not know the exact nature of this experience, because it was considered so precious and sacred that it could not be spoken of. However, the myth of Demeter and Persephone is well-known.

The goddess Demeter was the mother of the grain who gave agriculture to humans. Barley was the crop most sacred to her. Her young daughter Persephone was abducted by Hades, lord of the Underworld where the dead lived, and taken there to be his queen. Wild with grief for the loss of her daughter, Demeter roamed the world searching for her. She neglected the earth and crops failed, the land became barren and people starved. The goddess Hecate helped Demeter discover where Persephone had been taken and she appealed to Zeus for the return of her daughter. Hades had to agree that Persephone could return to her mother, provided she had eaten nothing while she was in his dark kingdom. However, she had eaten six pomegranate seeds and so could only live with her mother for six months of each year. For the other six, she had to reign with Hades in the Underworld, and during that time winter occurred on earth. When it was time for Persephone to return to Demeter, Hecate guided her back through the Underworld. Samhain rituals may feature elements of this mythos: barley and pomegranates are offered and Demeter, Persephone and Hecate can be invoked.

HONOURING HECATE

Hecate is honoured by witches at Samhain. She is a dark and ancient goddess, older than the Olympian pantheon of the Greeks. She was a triple goddess, depicted on statues as a three in one figure with three faces, facing three ways, carrying a torch and often accompanied by dogs, who were sacred to her. She was a chthonic deity, and a psychopomp who guided the souls of the dead through the Underworld. She was often depicted with keys, because she could unlock the gates between the worlds of the living and the dead. Her rituals were celebrated during darkness and she was a goddess of liminal places and the protector of entrances and gateways, where her shrines protected against the unwanted attentions of the restless dead. She was closely associated with the moon, and the yew tree, the tree of death and rebirth that we still grow in graveyards, was sacred to her, as were poisonous plants including aconite, belladonna and mandrake. One of her titles was Apotropaia (she who averts evil) and she was also called Hecate Trivia (Hecate of the Three Ways).

In this guise she was worshipped by night at places where three roads met, and where cakes made with honey were offered to her at the new moon. She was the fearsome deity of witches; the rites of the famous witches of Thessaly were dedicated to her and she played a continuing role in Roman religion. Very unusually, Hecate survived down the Christian centuries, becoming renowned in the Middle Ages as the goddess of the dark moon, witches and necromancy. She was well known to Shakespeare; his audiences knew her as Hecat, and the Three Weird Sisters in *Macbeth* made offerings to her. She has continued to be associated with magic and with witchcraft ever since, and is revered by many witches as the goddess of their craft, so it is very appropriate to honour her at Samhain.

At the new moon before Samhain, I conduct a small personal ritual to Hecate: late at night at a deserted rural crossroads overhung with oak trees where three lanes meet, I offer red wine and honey cakes to her. Honouring Hecate in this way creates a deep connection with this ancient goddess and is a powerful prelude to the Samhain ritual. Find a place

Other Samhain Goddesses

If you do not wish to work with Persephone or Hecate in your Samhain rite, choose another of the dark goddesses associated with the Underworld who are appropriate to this time. Some witches work with the White Goddess described by Robert Graves; a deity who has lunar qualities as well as chthonic ones. Others honour Binah, the Dark Supernal Mother of the Qabalah, visualised as the dark ocean from which all things are born and to which all return after death, or the Egyptian goddesses Isis (in her dark, veiled aspect) and her sister Nepthys. You may wish to use your own unique concept of the dark goddess at Samhain.

where three roads meet and make it sacred to Hecate, goddess of witches. Other witches celebrate Hecate in rituals in caves or underground places. I once took part in a large scale Hecate ritual involving many witches, celebrated in the depths of the caves at Wookey Hole in Somerset where the sense of connection with the Underworld goddess and an ancient Pagan past was overwhelming.

HONOURING THE ANCESTORS

Who are our ancestors? I do not have wealthy or illustrious ancestors; I can't trace my family back through many generations to medieval forebears, and nor would I want to. Beside me as I write this is a round, black, almost translucent piece of flint. It is a Neolithic scraper that would have been used to clean animal hides. I found it in the middle of the village where I live, in the muddy bank of the stream where cows' feet had churned up the ground. It was left there at least 5,000 years ago. It was made with a lot of skill by someone who knew exactly what they were doing; it fits snugly into my hand, weighted so that it is easy to hold and use and the scraping edge is still sharp after all this time. The maker was someone who lived here by the stream; in some sense an ancestor, going about their everyday life just as we do here now. I place the flint on my altar at Samhain, to honour those who lived here long before me; the ancestors of this place.

Some of us know exactly who our direct ancestors are; others of us, like me haven't much idea, and the concept of 'ancestors' has changed. We might feel a strong attachment to a community where our family have lived for many generations, or to an ethnic, cultural or linguistic group. For most of us now, ancestors are the people we choose to identify with, rather than people from whom we are directly descended, and witches are no exception. Pagans may identify with the people who built the great megalithic henges, stone circles and passage graves, because, although we can't know with certainty, their spiritual practices seem to have much in common with our own. They may visit these places at Samhain to give thanks to the ancestors who built them and left them for us to marvel at.

As a witch, I choose as my ancestors witches from former times: Temperance Lloyd, Mary Edwardes and Susannah Trembles, three Devon women who were the last people in England to be judicially murdered for the crime of witchcraft in 1684, and Isobel Gowdie, the seventeenth-century Scottish witch, who bequeathed to us (in the record of her trial) details of her practice that are still used today. I have a strong emotional and spiritual kinship with these women and have met them in my dreams and visions. I also choose as my ancestors magical practitioners who built up the knowledge and ways of working that I use in my own craft, and, in more recent times, the artists and writers whose work inspires me, and the women who fought for education, the vote and other rights and freedoms that benefit me today. Choose as your ancestors those who you identify with, and those who have inspired you, and thank them and honour them in your Samhain ritual.

Apples and Samhain

The apple season that began in September continues until Samhain and at this time we think particularly of the apple as the passport to the Otherworld and to the land of the dead. The apple can be included in the Samhain feast, and old apple games such as bobbing for apples threaded on a string or ducking for apples, where apples have to be retrieved from a bowl of water using only the mouth and teeth, can also take place after the ritual.

Practice: The Samhain Ritual

As we have seen, the veil between the worlds is thin at this time, and at the Samhain Sabbat we commune with the dead and the ancestors. The central element of the Samhain ritual is a feast for the dead, to which the beloved dead and, if you wish, ancestors, may be invited. This requires some forethought and preparation. My feast for the dead has evolved over many years and is drawn from various mythologies, poetry and archaeological sources. The dead have their own plate and horn cup which are only ever used in this ritual. Horn cups other implements are used in traditional forms of witchcraft as they are believed to hold their own spirit force. The food for the dead comprises ears of barley, pomegranates (cut in half to reveal the seeds), apples, poppy seeds or flower heads, pure rock or sea salt, cakes made with barley and honey, and red wine mixed with honey to drink. This food is magical and spiritual sustenance for the dead. Red mullet was sacred to Hecate so I add some small metal fishes to the feast. You can include a few foods you know that your beloved dead enjoyed to strengthen the link with them.

One of my coven always invited the spirit of a much loved family dog to Samhain and chocolate raisins, his favourite treat, were provided for him. You can also create your own Samhain incense, using whatever herbs you consider fit the occasion.

Preparation

The Samhain ritual must be carried out during the hours of darkness. The tone is a solemn and serious one (at least at the beginning), as befits working with the spirit world. I like to spend some time before this ritual preparing mentally. I need to be in a calm and focused state of mind, with all intrusive everyday clutter banished from my mind. Some quiet time spent relaxing and meditating on the dark goddess and horned god helps me get to the right place.

The food for the living at Samhain should also include pomegranates and apples and dark coloured foods. Use your imagination and creativity. It is usual to drink red wine or pomegranate juice.

You will need candles for the quarters (I prefer to use simple white ones at Samhain), two black candles for the altar (one for the dark goddess, and one for the horned god), your broomstick (if you made a small broomstick with mugwort or vervain stems earlier in the year, you can use this) and your wand.

The ritual

Begin by sweeping around the perimeter of your working area with the broomstick, mentally clearing away all psychic dirt, bad thought and unpleasantness. Light your incense. Light the candles on your altar and at the quarters, then cast the circle with your wand. Welcome all the spirits who will be with you: your familiar spirits, spirits of the land, elemental spirits and all those who have come to join you. It is quite usual for the circle to feel crowded with spirit presences at Samhain.

Beginning in the east, go round the circle and snuff out the candles at the quarters (do not blow them out, use a snuffer), leaving only the altar candles lit. Call upon the horned god to be with you and visualise him. He journeyed before us into Avalon at the Equinox, and now at Samhain he is the keeper of the gate between the worlds of the living and the dead. Ask him to open the gate for you, so that the beloved dead and the ancestors may come and be with you at your feast.

Call upon the dark goddess at Samhain as Persephone, queen of the Underworld, or Hecate, guide of souls, or in whatever guise seems right to you. She is the eternal power behind birth, death and rebirth, the source from whom we all come and to whom we must all return.

The gate between the worlds is now open, and goddess and god are with you. Place the feast for the dead in the centre of your circle and invite your beloved dead and ancestors to join you. Speak their names aloud (this is important) and invite them to your feast. Send time with them, remembering them, thanking them in whatever way you wish. This can be joyous. You may hear spirit voices,, see visions or sense presences in other ways. This is normal at Samhain. After a while you will sense that the hour has passed and the feast is over. Bid the beloved dead and ancestors farewell, and you will sense them retreating back into their own place. Wait in silence for 20 heartbeats. Then re-affirm life by lighting the quarter candles once more. Sit quietly for a while and meditate on all that you have seen and experienced. Then share the feast for the living. This will help you return from the world of spirit, which can be a little difficult at Samhain.

Thank the horned god and the dark goddess and bid them farewell. Snuff out the altar candles. Close your circle, putting out the quarter candles as you go. After the ritual, leave the remains of the feast for the dead outdoors as a gift for the Faeries, spirits and more than human.

A Spell for October: Cecil's Knitting Spell

This spell comes from Cecil Williamson. It is intended to get rid of something that is not wanted. Like all of Cecil's magic, its effects are powerful and direct, so think carefully about how to use it. Be careful, as they say, what you wish for...

You will need

- Knitting needles
- Black knitting yarn
- An open fire. If you have a hearth where a fire can be lit, use that. Otherwise, light a small fire outdoors

Cecil Williamson used glass knitting needles for this spell. I have a pair of these, and they can be obtained if you intend to specialise in knitting magic, but ordinary knitting needles will work perfectly well.

Method

Decide what you wish to get rid of (you could, for example, rid yourself of negativity, or a bad head cold) and compose a simple verbal spell that you will be able to repeat over and over again. 'Bad thoughts go away' or 'Head cold be gone' would work well.

Take the needles and yarn and cast on a small number of stitches. The number is not important; you just need to produce a small piece of knitting.

Knit your stitches and keep on knitting them. As you do so, repeat the words of your spell over and over. Keep knitting and keep repeating the spell. The power of the spell will grow as you do this with a slow and powerful intensity. You will feel it gathering around you. Don't rush this; keep knitting and repeating the spell until you judge that the power of the spell is as great as you can make it.

Then do not cast off the knitting; rip it (unfinished) off the needles and immediately put it on the fire and watch it burn away to nothing. This activates the spell and you must now stop thinking about it. The smell of burning yarn is not very pleasant, but this is part of the magic.

Meditation: The Autumn Hunter

Samhain sits opposite Beltane on the Wheel of the Year, and this month we return to the forest that we visited then. Whereas in May we met the green lady and lord of growing things, now it is the horned one of autumn who awaits us.

It is autumn in the forest. The ground is carpeted with autumn leaves of many kinds and colours. Oak trees tower overhead and their leaves spiral lazily to the ground through the still air. The rich smell of autumn, of decaying leaves and fruit, is everywhere. Birds peck at the last of the hawthorn berries. Cobwebs are strung from ferns and brambles. Amongst the fallen leaves lie shiny horse chestnuts, acorns and chestnuts in their prickly cases. Red squirrels scrabble for them and cache them in the undergrowth. Fungi sprout from the forest floor, big parasol mushrooms and innumerable toadstools, and a shaft of sunlight lights on a group of bright red and white spotted fly agarics. On the largest of them a fat green toad blinks at you; a messenger from Faerie perhaps. The fly agarics grow beside a path that winds its way through tall trees and thick underbrush, as if they are pointing the way, and you follow the twisty path deeper and deeper into the trees.

You become aware of the sound soft footsteps padding along somewhere near you. They sound like human footsteps not animal ones, but you cannot see anyone. When you stop, the footsteps stop, and when you start walking again, they start too. Then, a little way ahead of you, the path twists sharply to your left and you glimpse a tall figure. It looks like a man, but much taller and on its head are huge antlers, like a deer's. The figure walks on down the path and you follow it. It stops, and you pause too, then it walks on, and you follow again. It is leading you on. Then you reach a clearing in the heart of the forest. The tall antlered figure stands before you in all his glory and you understand that he is neither man nor animal, but god. This is the god of the witches, the Horned Lord, called Cernunnos, Herne, Robin, Janicot and Old Hornie. You feel pure joy in his presence. In the centre of the clearing, the Horned Lord makes a huge, dark gate appear between two ancient oak trees. He motions with his hand and the gate swings open. Beyond it is darkness; you can see nothing but you know that this is the land of the dead, and you understand that the Horned Lord will guide you through this gate when the time comes. You feel no fear, just joy. The Horned Lord smiles, the gate closes, you look round and he has gone.

Return through the forest, taking in all of its autumn magic, past fly agarics, toads, and through the great trees until you reach home with the knowledge of the Horned Lord safe within you.

NOVEMBER

November

Scrying and Dreaming

Visions in the Darkness

On 5 November in Ottery Saint Mary the night air is thick with smoke and the acrid smell of burning wood and tar. Thousands of people throng the streets of the small Devon town for Bonfire Night and the annual Tar Barrelling. The crowd is so densely packed that any movement is difficult. A great shout goes up and a huge barrel, thickly coated with tar and with the top and bottom knocked out, is set ablaze. It burns from end to end, and the flames leap high into the still air. One of the men hoists it above his head and begins to run down the road with it, through the crowd, who desperately try to get out of the way. He has little protection from the flames; only thick felt gauntlet gloves and hat, and felt pads on his shoulders. He throws the barrel to another man and it progresses uncertainly through the crowd. People are terrified and excited at the same time, screaming and trying to get out of the way as the flaming barrel is thrown towards them. There is a faint but persistent and worrying smell of burning flesh. The barrel men just tough it out.

The barrel is thrown from man to man; to drop the barrel would be shameful and provoke ridicule or worse. No one can hold it for very long, and it starts to disintegrate in a mad shower of sparks. Somehow it keeps moving. Pieces of it begin to fall into the crowd and people are trying to brush bits of flaming wood from their clothing and hair. I am carried along in the throng; sometimes my feet do not touch the ground as the press of people surges onwards. I arrived with several other people but have lost them all somewhere in the crowd. I have no idea where I am or where I am going. Then suddenly a space opens up before me and as it does so the flaming barrel, now rapidly falling apart, flies straight towards me. I fling myself to the floor onto something hard and flat as the barrel shoots past my head, slightly singeing my hair and eyebrows as it passes. The barrel and the crowd go on their way, and I see that I am in the churchyard, lying face down on a gravestone.

Somewhere above me a gibbous moon is riding high in the sky. A little way down the road the last remains of the flaming barrel fall in pieces on

November Associations

Festivals: None
Figures: The Morrigan, the Cailleach, the Wild Hunt
More Than Human: Corvids
Totems and Symbols: Labyrinth, raven

the ground and burn away to nothing. People are cheering and clapping. The spirits of winter and darkness have been welcomed in the time-honoured fashion.

November is the month when we embrace the dark: after honouring the spirits of the dead and welcoming the darkness with fire at Samhain, in November we meet the goddesses of the winter months who preside over the inner worlds of magic and enchantment: the Morrigan, Morgan le Fay, Arianrhod and the Cailleach or Hag. We make friends with crows, ravens and other corvids, the messengers of the Morrigan. A journey to the heart of the labyrinth and the world of dreams, inner visions and scrying leads to a deeper practice of magic. We learn to scry and make a dark mirror. Death and the darkness are ever-present and we learn to respect them. The spirit world is always very close if we can acknowledge its presence.

November begins with fire festivals. In Britain these ostensibly commemorate the infamous Gunpowder Plot of 1605, when Guy Fawkes and others tried unsuccessfully to blow up the Houses of Parliament, but they have the more ancient and universal functions of both welcoming the darkness of winter with fire, and trying to scare it away; a last hurrah as the darkness gathers. The desire for wild festivities at this time, and for bonfires and fireworks, is hard to resist.

At the beginning of November too, the commemoration of the dead and honouring of the ancestors that began at Samhain continues. On 1 November Mexico celebrates the Dia de los Muertos or Day of the Dead, when people remember their beloved dead and feast with them in graveyards. There is an acceptance that death is always with us, and that the spirit world co-exists with this one. In Mexico, *memento mori*, especially brightly coloured skulls, are everywhere; skull candles light the windows and children feast on candy skulls and skull cakes and biscuits. Christianity celebrates its ancestor festivals with All Saints Day on 1 November, and All Souls Day, when the baptised dead are remembered, on the day after. An old folk tradition once widespread in England and Wales, was souling: the making of soul cakes that were offered as food to welcome the returning dead at this time. Children would go begging for these from door to door, and this custom, which mixes Christian and timeless Pagan elements, and was taken by emigrants to the Americas, is one of the origins of the trick or treating now practised at Halloween. Souling is still proudly practised in Cheshire by the Antrobus Soul Cakers, who perform a riotous mummers' play, complete with Dick the Wild Horse; a figure rather like Mari Llwyd whom we met in Wales at the beginning of the year, while begging for soul cakes. It takes place on the days around All Souls Day in the pubs of Antrobus and its neighbouring villages, and provides a lovely conclusion to the round of ancestor customs at Samhain.

After this, autumn fades into winter and the dark part of the year begins in earnest. There is a sense that a real threshold has been crossed. While everyone else may think of November as a dark and dreary month, or just part of the run up to Christmas, for witches this time of shorter days and long, dark nights ushers in a welcome change of direction. As the year travels ever closer to its darkest point, we turn away from the external world, and look inwards to the world of spirit, dreams, inner visions and intense magic. The darkness is something to be welcomed, not feared. Our winter rituals take place at night, and it is in the dark that our dreams and visions of the gods and spirits are revealed to us. November is the time to improve those magical skills that take us into the inner realms, such as visualisation, divination, scrying and working with our familiar spirits, and to learn new ones.

THE GODDESSES OF WINTER

Now is the time to welcome the goddesses of winter: the Morrigan, the Cailleach or Hag, Morgan le Fay, and other deities who preside over the darker aspects of life, including death. These deities may be unloved or feared by others, but witches welcome and honour them. As the long nights close in, we accept that the darkness is as important as the light, and also that death is a part of life. The Celts and Norse peoples, who live where winters are long and dark, have traditionally respected the goddesses of winter.

The Morrigan is an Irish goddess whose name means 'Great Queen'. She is very present in modern witchcraft and is a dark goddess who presides over death and the darker aspects of life, and whose symbol is the raven or crow. As a harbinger of death, she would appear as an old woman washing clothes at a ford to warriors before a battle. She appeared in this guise to the mythic hero Cuchulainn before his death in battle, and was described in the Irish tales as a raven who would fly out of the hollow hills or mounds of the dead and perch on standing stones, thirsting for blood. She was a triple goddess of fate, war and death whose three aspects were Anu, Badh and Macha. Anu represented fertility and plenty, Badh was a crow, and she presided over a cauldron, and Macha's name meant 'battle'. The Morrigan is also associated with the waning or dark moon and with the menstrual blood of women. She may be honoured especially in the last week of the lunar cycle, and women may feel a deep and instinctual link with her during their menstrual period. If she is welcomed and accepted, she becomes a deity of initiation and a bringer of visions who can reveal the deepest hidden aspects of the witch's being. She is associated with both earth and fire, and therefore with all that is volcanic. Altars and shrines may be decorated with corvid feathers and skulls and black stones and jasper or bloodstone and other volcanic minerals in her honour.

The Cailleach or Hag is another Celtic form of the winter goddess. The year itself can be thought of as a triple goddess, with Bride being the spring Maiden, Mother/

Queen goddesses being the summer aspect, and the Cailleach or old Hag ruling the winter months. In recent years the Hag or Crone goddess has become an increasingly important aspect of witchcraft. Our image of the historic witch is, of course, that of the excluded and persecuted elderly woman, so reclaiming and honouring the Cailleach has become a way not just of showing respect for older women, but also of honouring those who were persecuted as witches. She embodies the power of the witch.

The Cailleach is found throughout the folk traditions of Ireland, Scotland and the Isle of Man. The name 'Cailleach' means The Veiled One in Gaelic and Irish. She is a very ancient deity of the land, the mother of the old gods, referred to in the oldest songs and stories. She is also present in Wales, sometimes called Y Wrach (the Witch) or Y Gawres (the Giantess). Across the Celtic lands many landscape features are named after her; being the oldest of the old, she creates the landscape, especially mountains. As the Cailleach Bhearra she was the wife of the sea god, Manannan macLir and the Beara peninsular in West Cork is her domain. She is particularly associated with Neolithic tombs and ancient stones in both Ireland and Wales. She was said to have dropped the stones of the megalithic tombs on the hilltops called Slieve na Calliagh at Loughcrew in County Meath from her apron. The same legend is attached to the megalithic tomb of Barclodiad Y Gawres on Ynys Môn close to where I grew up; its name means the Giantess' Apronful. Similar stories are found elsewhere in Wales and Ireland. One of the largest stones at Loughcrew is called the Hag's Chair; the Cailleach will grant you any wish you make while sitting on it. She presides over the winter weather, especially storms and thunder. She is neither good nor evil, but the power of winter and a force of nature, and is both honoured and feared.

In Scotland she is associated with the fearsome Corryvreckan whirlpool between the islands of Jura and Scarba. The first storm of winter there is said to be the Cailleach washing her plaid. At Gleann Cailliche in Glen Lyon in Perthshire an age-old Pagan ritual is still enacted in her honour. A group of anthropomorphic stones are taken out of their little stone shelter, the Tighe nan Cailleach at Beltane. They watch over the glen until Samhain, when they are put back into their house for the winter months.

In Wales, Cyhiraeth, a skeletal old woman who appears to foretell a death, is also a form of the Cailleach. In November I make a very simple small image from pebbles in my garden to welcome Y Gawres/the Cailleach and honour her during storms and wild weather.

The winter goddess is also honoured as Morgan le Fay, the dark enchantress of Arthurian legend. The Welsh deity Arianrhod's name means Silver Wheel, and her story is found in the *Mabinogion*. She is a star goddess who gives her name to the Corona Borealis, the constellation that circles the northern pole star, whose stars never set, and is associated with the night sky in winter. You may find your own, personal form of the winter goddess. Learning to welcome the goddess in winter and understanding her ways and customs is an important part of witchcraft that makes the season of cold and darkness something to be celebrated and enjoyed rather than endured.

Practice: A Rite of Dedication to the Morrigan

This rite should be conducted at your altar at the dark of the moon during the hours of darkness, preferably late at night. Use it together with the meditation for November to learn the ways of the lady of darkness and winter.

You will need

- One black candle
- One red candle
- Your witch's mirror
- Corvid feathers
- A black pebble
- A red pebble (please find the pebbles for yourself; searching for them is part of the magic)
- A charcoal block and incense burner
- Morrigan incense (recipe below)

Ritual

Decorate your altar with the corvid feathers and black and red pebbles. If the Morrigan inspires you, add other items of your own choosing. Place the candles on either side of your altar. Stand your mirror upright on the altar so that it will reflect the light of the candles. The room should be dimly lit; use only what you need to see by.

Light the charcoal and when it is glowing place a good pinch of your Morrigan incense on it. Light the candles. Let the everyday world fade away and concentrate your magical will on the candlelight.

Call silently on the Morrigan, saying inwardly whatever words come into your mind. Dedicate yourself to the Morrigan, again using whatever words come to mind. Offer your incense to the Morrigan. Allow images of the Morrigan to grow in your mind, experiencing whatever comes without trying to analyse it.

When you sense that enough time has passed, thank the Morrigan and snuff out the candles.

When the charcoal has cooled, bury it and any remains of the incense in earth. Leave the feathers and pebbles on the altar until the new moon. After that, you may use them in spells if you wish.

An Incense to Honour the Morrigan

Ingredients

- Dragon's blood
- Cypress
- Black poppy seeds
- Essential oil of patchouli
- Women may wish to add a drop of their menstrual blood.

Method

Mix the dragon's blood, cypress and poppy seeds together.

Add just three drops of patchouli oil.

INTO THE LABYRINTH

The labyrinth is a perfect symbol for the magic of November. It is emblematic of all the inner magical arts and the journey to the heart of magical knowledge. The labyrinth is not a maze. A maze consists of many pathways and dead-ends designed to entertain and confuse, while a labyrinth describes a mythic or spiritual journey. There is only one way into a labyrinth and one way out; to enter a labyrinth is to embark on a journey to its centre, where knowledge, wisdom or power may be gained, and then taken back out of the labyrinth, along the only pathway, into the world.

Minoan labyrinth. (Original drawing by Jeff Saward, final graphic by Vicki Keiser/The Labyrinth Society)

The labyrinth image dates back at least to the Bronze Age Minoan civilisation of Crete, and may be even older. It is found all over the world: on Greek coins, jewellery and vases, and as mosaic pavements, and paintings and graffiti at Roman sites including at Pompeii. Labyrinths are carved on Pagan standing stones from the Viking era in Scandinavia. Labyrinth pavements are found in Christian buildings from the sixth century CE Basilica of San Vitale at Ravenna to medieval cathedrals in Italy and France; the best known is at Chartres. Landscape labyrinths, carved into turf or laid out in stones, are found all over Europe and Scandinavia and new ones are still being created. In the city of Bath in the West of England (*see* July and the goddess Sul), a beautiful labyrinth created in 1984 is situated in a public garden next to the famous Pulteney Bridge. Landscape labyrinths were once common throughout England but many were destroyed by farming in the eighteenth and nineteenth centuries. Some survive, and discovering these can be a delight. Well worth a visit are the stone labyrinth on St Agnes in the Isles of Scilly (reputedly created by a bored lighthouse keeper), the Mizmaze at Breamore in Hampshire, the Turf Maze at Wing in Rutland, Julian's Bower at Alkborough in Lincolnshire and the City of Troy at Dalby in North Yorkshire. There are two small labyrinths carved onto the wall of a ruined building at Rocky Valley near Tintagel in Cornwall. This place has a strong magical atmosphere and is much loved by witches and Pagans.

The labyrinth is at the heart of one of the best-known Greek myths. It describes how the Greek hero Theseus slew the Minotaur, a terrifying monster, half man and half bull, that lived at the heart of the first labyrinth built by Daedalus for Minos, king of Crete. Theseus did this with the aid of Ariadne, who provided a ball of thread to guide him through the labyrinth. Witches recognise her as an archetypal spinning and weaving goddess.

To journey into the labyrinth is to leave the external world behind and make an interior journey to seek what is at the centre. This journey can be made for various magical purposes: to seek initiation or knowledge, or to encounter the goddess or god, to meet a spirit, to gain a new skill, or to seek answers. Walking a large landscape or floor labyrinth creates a sense of calm concentration, and of leaving the everyday world behind. Visualising the labyrinthine journey by following a small labyrinth (on paper or cloth) can produce the same effect. When you reach the centre, you will experience a sense of profound peace and be ready to meet the object of your quest. Entering the labyrinth can also be done as a visualisation in ritual at this time of year, and we will return to this in our meditation.

Set yourself the task of making a labyrinth in November. This is a powerful magical and creative act. If you want to do this on a large scale, go to the seashore and trace one in the sand at low tide. This is an activity that really needs several people. Walking a labyrinth by the sea is a marvellous and elemental experience. It can be used to encounter the goddess of the moon and tides, one of the sea gods such as Dylan Eil Ton or Manannan MacLir, or simply to summon the spirits of the sea. After walking your seashore labyrinth, give thanks to the sea deities and spirits and leave your labyrinth as an offering to them for the incoming tide to take.

At a witch friend's house in Brittany some years ago, a friend and I found a large heap of white quartz stones (left by the Faeries or other kindly spirits, we thought) and we made a very large labyrinth in the woods there. Carting loads of stones was hard but inspiring work that took several days. Walking inwards to its centre and out again under the trees at night, lit by countless candles, was a transformative experience for the witches present, and it is still used in rituals to this day.

I save some ashes from the Samhain ritual fire and make a small November labyrinth with them in my garden, just big enough to walk to honour the spirits of winter and the dark nights. After use, it is dispersed by the wind and rain. A labyrinth made of birdseed can be given as a witch gift to the birds.

A small-scale labyrinth is just as effective. The design may look difficult but is actually quite easy to create for yourself with a little practice. If you are unsure about this, try tracing one first. It can be drawn or traced onto paper or embroidered onto cloth. An embroidered labyrinth makes a beautiful altar cloth for ritual work. It can be worked onto a charm or spell bag, or can be used to great magical effect to decorate a bag for tarot cards, runes, ogham sticks, a dark mirror, or other divination tools. Its magical meanings align perfectly with divination work. Items decorated with the labyrinth make good Yule gifts for witch friends, and a friend once made labyrinth biscuits with the design piped in icing for a celebration. A labyrinth can be painted, carved or burnt onto a wooden box or other object. I made one with small silver sea shells collected from a favourite beach and glued onto a piece of board. A Cornish witch made me an altar from a big piece of yew wood carved with a labyrinth. As yew is the tree of death and rebirth (which is why it is planted in ancient churchyards), I use it for working with the spirits of the departed. The possibilities for labyrinth-making are almost limitless; let these ideas inspire you to create your own.

SCRYING: LOOKING INTO THE MIRROR

Scrying is an old word that means 'looking, and in witchcraft it carries the sense of looking into the spirit world. It is a form of deep meditation that is practised by looking into a reflective surface such as a mirror and training the eyes and mind to see beyond reflections and into the world of spirit until visions are received. Scrying is quite different from visualisations or path workings where an inward journey is made or a sequence of narrative visions is followed. In scrying there is no sense of a journey; the scryer waits for visions to appear or answers to be given. It requires practice and concentration and is one of the oldest magical arts that has been practised since the earliest times.

The first scrying mirrors were still, reflective pools of water, and stories of seeing visions in sacred waters are found in many cultures and mythologies. In ancient Greece nymphs presided over sacred pools where divination took place, and pools of still dark water were venerated in the Bronze and Iron Ages as the abodes of gods and spirits. Some of the holy wells and springs that we venerate today (*see* July) may have originated as sacred divination places in ancient times.

Burnished bronze mirrors were used by the Egyptians and have been found in the graves of Bronze Age women, thought to be priestesses, in Europe.

In more recent times crystal balls or shewstones and glass mirrors and surfaces have been used to scry. A large piece of black obsidian (volcanic glass) that was used as a scrying mirror by the Elizabethan magus Dr John Dee can be seen in the British Museum. Any reflecting surface can be used to scry, but a dark surface that allows you to focus on the spirit world works best.

My first scrying 'mirror', which I still visit regularly, was a very still and clear circular rock pool at a remote place on the coast of Ynys Môn. It was shown to me by my father when I was a small child and I have used it to speak with the spirits ever since. At the pool, which is scoured by the tides twice each day and which can only be reached at low tide, I make an offering of a tiny white quartz pebble to the spirits, then gaze at the surface of the water until the world goes away and the spirits manifest in the patterns of light and water. I also scry with a dark or black mirror and sometimes a large earthenware bowl with a glossy black interior surface, filled with water. If you are new to scrying, a bowl of water is the simplest way to begin. If you can't find a bowl with a dark interior surface, simply put some black ink into the water to lessen shine and reflection. I prefer not to use crystal balls. Like other crystals, they are often mined in a very destructive way, and contributing to harm done to mother earth in the name of witchcraft or magic is not something I want to do.

Scrying is deep magic that must always be done with serious intent and never be treated lightly or done to impress people. It is a very quiet, intense activity that can be practised alone or with other witches. Do not rush into scrying; wait until you feel ready to do it and are confident in your magical abilities. It is always done during the hours of darkness and is most effective in the winter months between Samhain and Candlemas. Close contact with the spirit world began at in October Samhain, when we feasted with our ancestors or beloved dead. At this time of gathering darkness, the skills of scrying, of looking and listening, can be developed and become a central part of witchcraft.

To begin scrying, you will need your scrying bowl or mirror (*see* below). Scrying is a slow business that will take as long as it takes; make sure there are no restrictions on your time before you begin because human time is an irrelevance to the spirit world. Scrying is best done only for serious magical purposes; when you need the guidance of the spirits.

Do not use it too often, or for minor, trivial things; if you do not take the spirits seriously, they will not take you seriously either. Always approach spirits respectfully and ask them politely to join you; never command them. Treat them as you would expect to be treated yourself.

The space where you work should be quiet and dark; use only enough light to see by, ideally just one or two candles. I use two candles. I prefer black candles as light-coloured ones can be distracting, but this is a personal choice. These candles are only used for scrying and are put away safely when not in use. They are placed on either side of the bowl or mirror and lit before the work commences. Always cast a circle round yourself before scrying: this is to make sure that you will be safe at all times, because contact with the spirit world can be a little unpredictable, especially when you are new to it. When you have cast your circle, call on your familiar spirit to watch over you and keep you safe.

When scrying, you should have confidence in your magical abilities and should not be afraid, because the spirit world can sense fear, but you should be very alert, keep your wits about you and trust your instincts. If anything unexpected that you do not like makes its presence known, with the aid of your familiar spirit, tell it to be gone in no uncertain terms.

The actual scrying process is a simple one. There are no complicated ritual words and formulae, but you may find it takes practice before you succeed at it. Do not expect to succeed with scrying straight away; perseverance is required, because this is a deep magical skill that will not manifest itself instantly.

When you have lit your candles, cast your circle and summoned your familiar spirit, put yourself into a light trance state. Use deep breathing to first relax your body and switch off all extraneous everyday thoughts. Then focus on your magical will. You should be physically relaxed but with your will finely focused on your magical purpose. Gaze into your scrying bowl or mirror. Do this slowly and keep doing it for as long as it takes. At first you may see or sense nothing, but after a while you will find that you go beyond the reflective surface in your mind's eye and into the inner worlds of spirit. Let this inner vision develop slowly; do not attempt to force it or rush it. Keep gazing into the inner world to the exclusion of everything else. You will find that gradually visions emanating from that world will manifest from the darkness. If you have asked questions, answers will come, but not necessarily in the way you expect.

Scrying is about looking, so you are most likely to see visions, but you may also be spoken to by spirits. You will find that spirit visions and voices will stay in your mind very vividly, like recordings, and you should be able to recall them clearly. Do not try to analyse them while they are happening; just let your mind take them in. You will be able to ponder them later. Sometimes you may sense while scrying that something has manifested with you. If this happens, do not be afraid. Ask your familiar spirit to protect you. Keep looking into the mirror or bowl and do not be tempted to look behind you because whatever has manifested must stay within the liminal reflecting surface. Then, with the help of your familiar spirit, ask respectfully but firmly that whatever has manifested should depart.

Once you sense that visions and answers have been received, do not prolong the scrying process. You may feel slightly tired at this point, or your concentration may waver for a moment. This means it is time to end the session. Thank the spirits and bid them farewell. You will sense that they are withdrawing. Once this is done, thank your familiar spirit and bid them farewell too. You will now be alone once more in your circle. Close the circle and snuff out the candles. As scrying does not happen in human time and can be a very intense process, it is quite usual afterwards to think that just a few minutes have elapsed, and then to find that several hours have passed by. As with all intensive magical work, eat and drink something to earth yourself. Then rest and reflect on the experience. Take some time to do this; it is important not to rush back to everyday activities after scrying.

Making a Dark Mirror for Scrying

The dark or scrying mirror must be made by the witch who will use it, otherwise it will not work for them. It should never be bought because the act of making it is an essential part of the magic of scrying. A dark mirror can be made very simply using a picture frame and black paint. This does not require any specialist making skills and pre-loved frames can be obtained cheaply from charity shops and recycling centres. Some witches like to use a clock glass rather than a picture frame because the concave surface is said to work best, but clock glasses can be difficult to obtain and this method will require you to make your own frame. Whatever you choose, make sure that the glass is free from damage, scratches and chips. If the frame you choose does not already have a back, you will need to make one. I have suggested using cardboard for this, but if you have carpentry skills, you may wish to make something more permanent from a wooden board. The size of the frame is entirely up to you; choose whatever you think will work best. The finished dark mirror must be kept out of daylight and away from prying eyes when not in use, so a piece of cloth is therefore required to wrap it. Find a fabric that feels right to you. My dark mirror is wrapped in black velvet tied with ribbon. The dark mirror is one of the most private and personal of the witch's tools. It may be used in a circle with other witches, but otherwise should not be displayed or shown to other people.

You will need

- A picture frame with glass in it
- Black acrylic/water-based paint
- A paintbrush with soft bristles (a large watercolour or similar artist's brush works best)
- Cardboard and masking tape (only if your frame has no back)
- A piece of cloth large enough to wrap the mirror in

Method

Carefully remove the glass from the frame. Ensure that the frame and the glass are completely clean and dry.

Paint the back of the glass with the black paint. Apply the paint in a thick, even coat, making sure that the glass is completely covered. Leave the paint to dry, then apply a second coat. Further coats may be necessary; it should be impossible to see through the paint as any little gaps that let light through will distract you when you scry.

When you are sure the glass is covered, and once the paint is completely dry, fix the glass into the frame with the painted surface at the back. The back of the frame will protect the glass from scratches.

If the frame has no back, cut a piece of thick cardboard to make a backing, and fix it to the frame with masking tape.

Wrap the mirror securely.

Your mirror is now ready. Before using the mirror, cleanse and consecrate it. To cleanse the mirror, use the method for the witch's tools described in January. To consecrate it, use mugwort and vervain, being herbs of vision and enchantment respectively. Dried mugwort and vervain should be rubbed thoroughly over the surface of the mirror, or it can be sprinkled with a few drops of the tincture of each herb.

THE MORRIGAN'S MESSENGERS: MAKING FRIENDS WITH CORVIDS

In November corvids – the crows, jackdaws, magpies and rooks that scavenge and feed on carrion – are everywhere; in cities as well as the countryside they make their presence felt now. People feared these birds and associated them with death because ravens (now rarely seen outside wild places) and crows fed on corpses left on battlefields. Traditionally corvids have also been associated with witchcraft. In some witchcraft trials there were accusations that witches shape shifted into crows, or had familiar spirits in the form of crows or ravens. If treated kindly and fed, corvids may form friendships with humans, and it is easy to see how old women who fed scraps of food to friendly crows or magpies could become targets for fear and suspicion.

Crows were not just associated with the Morrigan; the story of the giant Welsh god Bran/ Bendigeid Fran whose name means Blessed Crow or Raven is told in the *Mabinogion*, and he and his daughter Branwen (shining or white crow) are closely associated with Ynys Môn where you can visit Bedd Branwen (Branwen's grave), a Bronze Age grave on the banks of the river Alaw, and other places associated with their story. After many exploits and adventures, when Bran died, his head was cut off and eventually buried beneath the White Mount, the sacred hill on which the Tower of London now stands. This is the origin of the Ravens of the Tower, the mythical totem beasts of London. Tradition holds that if ever the ravens were to leave the Tower, Britain would fall, and urban legend recounts that Winston Churchill deliberately had the wings of the ravens clipped to prevent this from happening during World War Two.

Corvids are famously intelligent. I observed a team of jackdaws working together on a cold November day to uproot the large, heavy pole holding my garden bird feeders so they could share the contents. It took a lot of perseverance, but they knew exactly what they were doing and worked for 20 minutes to get what they wanted. I began to provide a special food supply for the corvids, so as not to deprive other birds of their food, and they quickly learnt where it was and came to expect it. Corvids make great friends and allies for a witch if you can cultivate a relationship with them.

In Indian astrology crows are very important and are sacred to the planet Saturn, which has its own complex set of meanings and correspondences, but which at its simplest symbolises mortality. Its colour is black. In India, crows are therefore fed on Saturn's Day (Saturday), so I started to make special rice balls for them on Saturdays, working with a traditional Indian recipe. Corvids can be welcomed in November with a labyrinth laid out in bird food, left on a flat surface, but make sure it is safe from cats and other predators.

I am regularly rewarded with scavenged gifts brought by the crows, usually ring-pulls, bottle tops and bits of shiny foil wrapping, and beautiful stray feathers. I use these in my spells and ask the corvids to add their blessing to the magic. When I awake on winter mornings there are large numbers of crows and jackdaws sitting in the trees behind my garden. I used to think they were just hanging about until I realised that they were making sure that I was properly awake and that all was well; as soon as I go to the window and wave, they make a lot of noise and come down for something to eat before getting on with their day.

Some years ago, I was privileged to experience the winter raven roost in the forest at Newborough in Ynys Môn. There are fewer ravens now, but at the beginning of this century up to 2,000 birds roosted there. On a cold November evening, I watched from the nearby saltmarsh as innumerable black ravens, the biggest corvids I had ever seen, flew into the pine forest. They wheeled overhead, cawing, circling, landing and taking off again and again as the darkness grew. For a timeless moment I became part of the sound they made, and the onrush of their wings. For that short while it seemed I was no longer human and knew how it felt to be a bird; the strangest and most beautiful thing. Then they settled into the trees and became invisible and silence fell.

This link with the corvids is an example of lived, experiential witchcraft; of magic made and experienced through contact with these beautiful creatures who allow me to work with them and learn from them. A willingness to step outside the purely human, anthropocentric view of the world has always been a characteristic of witchcraft which recognises the spirit within all living things. Think of the traditional affinities between witches and their cats, or of witches who worked their magic with the help of toads or snakes. In former centuries this was something that was feared, but at a time when we need to learn from the more than human, perhaps it can become a positive recognition that humans are not the centre of the universe, and that we have much to learn from the beings who share this world with us.

A Spell for November: For Magical Dreams

This spell is designed to improve dream recall and to bring magical dreams. It can also help to improve visualisation and scrying skills. This spell should be made during the hours of darkness when the moon is waxing. Throughout the making of this spell, your magical will should be concentrated on magical dreaming. Visualise yourself lying asleep and dreaming beautiful dreams (or if the spell is intended for someone else, visualise them).

You will need

- A piece of black cloth about 6in (25cm) square
- Black thread
- 1 tbs dried mugwort herb
- A pinch of dried rose petals

- A pinch of lavender
- Mugwort anointing oil or essential oil (optional)

Method

Lay the cloth square flat. Then place the mugwort in the centre of the cloth.

Add a small pinch of rose petals and one of lavender, concentrating your will ever stronger as you do so. If you made mugwort anointing oil in the summer months, add three drops to the mixture if you wish. Alternatively, you can use essential oil of mugwort. (This last step is optional.)

Twist the edges of the cloth together into a bag, so that the ingredients are secure inside.

Take the thread and, concentrating intensely, wrap it three times tightly round the neck of the bag.

Secure the thread with three knots. As you make each knot say inwardly 'Come, dreams!' The spell bag should then be left on your altar until the full moon. On the day after the full moon it should be placed under the pillow.

As an alternative, you can sew the cloth into a small bag as the first stage of making this spell. This should be done by hand, concentrating the magical will as you sew.

A Meditation for November: Journey to the Heart of the Labyrinth

For this meditation you will need an image of a labyrinth. If possible, use one that you made earlier in the month. Before you begin the meditation, study the labyrinth carefully and trace the path in to its centre and out again with your finger several times. Keep doing this until you feel very familiar with the path of the labyrinth. You should be able to visualise it in your mind's eye. Then when you are ready, close your eyes and begin.

It is a dark November night. There are no stars and the thin crescent of the new moon is setting in the west. Follow a path that winds across a field towards the setting moon until you come to a rock face that towers above you. There is an opening in the rock, just big enough for you to enter, lit by a reddish glow. Squeeze through the opening in the rock. You are standing in a large cavern. The darkness is lit only by the red glow of flaming torches around the rocky walls. The space is warm, comfortable and nurturing. You look down and see at your feet a lantern that gives a gentle, silvery light. There is deep silence and peace. Pick up the lantern and carry it with you. On the ground ahead of you there is a labyrinth made of dark stones. As you step up to its entrance, the pathway through the labyrinth is illuminated by the light of your lantern. The path ahead is mysterious but inviting. A woman's voice inside your head calls to you and bids you to follow the path into the labyrinth. You hesitate, fearing the darkness ahead. The voice keeps calling to you. It is strong and insistent, and you sense this is a threshold between worlds that must be crossed. Without looking behind you, enter the labyrinth very deliberately, leaving the outside world behind, and walk its path slowly and with magical intent, circling, doubling back on yourself, walking and walking with a calm sense of anticipation, led by the silvery light, seeking the path to the centre. The voice that called to you is gone, time seems to cease operating, and you feel that you have been walking this path in the silent darkness forever. There is nothing but the path, leading you on. You persevere, banishing any doubts and fears that may come, following the dimly lit path in the cavernous darkness. At last, when all sense of time and the outside world have gone, the path ends in a small circular space. You have reached the centre, and you wait, calmly and peacefully.

You hold up your lantern and see before you the stooped figure of an old woman, cloaked and veiled. Around her are many black birds: ravens and crows. You cannot see her face. She welcomes you and you realise her voice is the one you heard that invited you to enter the labyrinth. She asks you if you know who she is, and you reply yes, she is the Morrigan, dark, veiled and ancient goddess of winter and the old year. She asks your name. You tell her, and she speaks your name back to you. It echoes in the silence. She asks you why you have entered her labyrinth, and you reply that you wish to know her, the dark goddess at the centre. You ask what you must do to serve her, and she replies that you must learn to love the darkness and winter, when all of nature seems dead, as much as the light and warmth of summer. You promise that you will. The Morrigan lifts her veil, just a little, and you catch a glimpse of a face that is more ancient than anything you have ever seen, but at the same time has no age at all. The Morrigan offers you three gifts; one for each aspect of her triple nature. Her skeletal hand touches your forehead; you look for a moment into her deep, black glittering eyes, and she gives you a fleeting vision of the year that has been: the green growth of spring, the bright warmth of summer, and the rich harvest of autumn; the year that will come again. Then one of her ravens flies onto your outstretched hand and gives you one of its glossy blue-black iridescent feathers. Then the Morrigan holds out her hand to you and gives you a deep red pebble of ancient jasper that gleams in the darkness. You sense the dark, glowing volcanic heart of the earth that lies beneath all things and you begin to understand the Morrigan. Keep these gifts safe inside yourself.

Thank the Morrigan. There is a fluttering of dark wings, the veiled figure is gone, and you are alone once more at the centre of the labyrinth. There is only one way you can go. Hold up your lantern and with renewed energy and intent, follow the twisting, turning path back through the labyrinth until you reach the exit. Set down the lantern; walk back through the rocky cavern with its flaming torches and back through the gap in the rock into the November night. In the east, Orion, the Horned Lord of winter, and the Seven Sisters have risen to greet you. You have walked the labyrinth and come to know the Morrigan, ancient goddess of winter and the dark.

DECEMBER

December

Joy and Peace

The End is the Beginning

As Midwinter Day approaches, storms have taken the very last autumn leaves from the trees and only holly and one isolated pine tree show green. The hedgerows' bare hawthorn branches and brambles are grey with Old Man's Beard. Heavy rain is falling. The road is an old ridgeway and an ancient boundary between the low-lying wetlands and the hills of the south-west. It has been a road for thousands of years. In summer it is deep in woodland; now, at the year's dying, the bare bones of the trees reveal the landscape beyond. To the far north-west of the road, by Brean Down and Brent Knoll, lies the grey-green Severn Sea with the mountains of Wales rising beyond, and to the north Glastonbury Tor and the orchards of Avalon rise above wisps of mist that swirl just above the ground on the Somerset Levels. In the east, Arthurian Cadbury is lost in more mist, and to the south, orchards, green pastures and meandering streams edged with pollarded willow trees stretch away to the Blackdown Hills and Dorset. The earth is deep in its midwinter sleep.

Travelling towards the west along the ridge road, suddenly the heavy rain is replaced by fitful sunshine. The Midwinter sun remains low in the sky even at noon; its golden light is in my eyes turning everything in my line of vision to gold and reflecting more gold off the wet road. It changes everything and suddenly, along the highest stretch of the ridge, mistletoe is everywhere. This is known as good mistletoe country, but I have never seen so much of it, or so many berries on its leaves. It hangs in huge, fat balls from the trees and in places masses of it trail down towards the road. In the blinding sunlight its leaves shine more gold than green. I have to stop and wonder beneath a stand of birch trees full of great masses of mistletoe, lost in a world of gold and green and pale white berries. I have never gathered mistletoe myself before,

December Associations

Festivals: Yule/Midwinter/Mothernight (21st), Saturnalia (25th)
Figures: The Unconquered Sun, the Child of Promise, the Great Mother, Holda, the Snow Queen, Odin, Thoth
More Than Human: Wren, mistletoe, evergreens (holly, ivy, bay)
Totems and Symbols: Triple spiral (as at Newgrange), wren

but finding a couple of footholds I surprise myself, scramble high enough to grab a large, branching spray and almost fall back to the ground triumphant and hailing the gods of Midwinter, my hands and face sticky with the viscous crushed berries.

The next day the Romanis come selling holly and mistletoe, as they do every year, and bring me a huge ball of Somerset mistletoe for the Midwinter ritual. It is hung in pride of place, and the little spray I gathered adorns the statue of the horned god on my altar. The shortest day dawns; the sun will return and the endless round of the year will begin again.

The Witch's Year enters its last month as the darkness reaches its peak with the shortest day and the festival of Yule. On the Mothernight (the old Saxon name for the Winter Solstice – *see* below) the infant sun is reborn as the year's journey nears its end, and gold and green shine in the darkness. It is time to enjoy all the customs of Midwinter: guising, mumming, hunting the wren and order displaced by Misrule. We bring evergreens into the home, make the Yule log and give witch gifts.

THE WINTER SOLSTICE

In December the year reaches the Winter Solstice and the Sabbat of Yule, when once again the year turns. Everything in December looks forward to Yule, and is focused on it. The moment when the days reach their shortest point, and the sun begins its slow return from the darkness, has been marked everywhere for thousands of years, and we have inherited a medley of customs and traditions, both ancient and modern that can be difficult to disentangle. At Midwinter, much of the world likes to celebrate a hugely expensive festival of conspicuous consumption; a splurge of shopping and feasting that can be hard to resist. As a witch, my approach to midwinter is a little different. The Yule ritual, and its attendant customs and celebrations, is a joyous time for witches as the great dance of the year comes full circle, but in a way that is distinctive as well as meaningful.

Yule sits opposite Midsummer on the wheel of the year and like Midsummer it is one of the two Solstices or solar standstills; the hinges on which the year turns. At the Winter Solstice, the waning half of the year will end and growth will return, imperceptibly at first. In the folk magic traditions, the Holly King, who has ruled the year since Midsummer, will give way to the Oak King once more, and the robin redbreast will replace the wren. The great tide of the year will turn again too; the flowing tide of air will become the ebb tide of earth, that will be with us until the next Spring Equinox. For a few days the sun will seem to stand still before the days lengthen again. The earth tide is a nurturing one; earth protects the seeds of life that slumber within it, keeping them safe until the light and warmth return and growth can begin again.

The winter Solstice was the most important point of the year for the first farmers, our Neolithic forebears. The great ritual sites at Newgrange and Dowth in Ireland and the complex at Maes Howe in Orkney are all aligned to the Midwinter Solstice sunrise. They were both womb and tomb; the birth places of the sun and the houses of the ancestors. When the solar year was reborn, so too the spirits of the ancestors, embodied in stone and sunlight, lived on and guided the living. Watching a line of sunlight entering the passage grave at Newgrange at the winter Solstice and illuminating its chamber with rose golden light is an unforgettable and overwhelmingly moving sight which I have been privileged to witness. Seeing and feeling the light reflected on the stones and on the bodies of those watching is a visual and physical experience of renewal that works on what can only be described as a very deep magical level as well as a spiritual one. Although in our own times Stonehenge is used for Midsummer celebrations, it was also originally intended to mark the Winter Solstice sunset, and there is archaeological evidence that huge midwinter gatherings and feasts took place at Durrington Walls close by. Marking the shortest day and the return of the sun has always had many layers of spiritual significance.

The ancient calendars used lunar months, and reconciling the solar year with the shorter lunar year and the movements of the stars has always been problematic. Today we manage the problem by having a leap year once every four years. The ancient Egyptians solved the issue by having a calendar with twelve fixed months plus five extra 'intercalary' days that were added when needed around the Winter Solstice. These days were also the birthdays of the gods. Thoth, god of wisdom, magic, writing and all the sciences amongst other things, also had something of the trickster about him. At first the year was only 360 days long and the sky goddess, Nuit, mother of the great gods, could not give birth to them within these days. Thoth gambled and won five extra days from the moon in a game of dice (some versions of the story say he cheated) and thereby allowed Nuit to give birth to the great timeless gods (Isis, Osiris, Nepthys and Set) and the calendar to come into being. These five days were special magical days that were somehow outside time, and this sense of being outside normal time at the winter Solstice was handed down to the Greeks and the Romans, for whom the Midwinter festival of Saturnalia took place on extra days that were outside the normal calendar, and something of this timeless sense still survives in our own Yule celebrations too.

The reconciling of the solar and lunar years is also the origin of the Christian feast of the Twelve Days of Christmas; which shares the sense of being outside the ongoing calendar of months and weeks. For everyone, it seems, irrespective of their beliefs, this is the time when the year stands still, and normal patterns of work have to stop until the solar standstill ends. Wherever the Winter Solstice is marked, it is recognised as a time of feasting and celebration, and also as a time for giving and sharing. It seems that many of the older customs continued to find a place in medieval Christmas celebrations. By the fifteenth century,

Christmas had become a very social festival, celebrated by whole communities. It had also become a time of wild celebrations and over-indulgence in feasting and alcohol, and other ungodly forms of enjoyment, so much so that in the seventeenth century, the Puritan regimes in England and Scotland banned the celebration of Christmas, and many of the older customs were probably lost at this time. As Christmas was gradually reinstated, it became more centred on the family rather than the community, until by the mid-nineteenth century many of the old social customs and seasonal celebrations had withered away entirely. Happily, in our own times, determined attempts are being made to reinstate the old Yuletide customs. It has become something of a truism, and also perhaps an irrelevance, to say that Christianity 'stole' or took over old Pagan customs *en masse*. The rebirth of the sun at the Winter Solstice is a joyous thing, and it seems to me that we have a universal and timeless desire to celebrate the return of the light as a birth at midwinter, with evergreens and light amidst the darkness and with feasting and the sharing of gifts.

The Roman Midwinter celebration of Saturnalia was marked by a week of feasting when the usual social order was overturned. Masters were expected to serve food to their slaves, and a Lord of Misrule presided over the festivities. Homes were decorated with evergreens and gifts were exchanged. The cult of the Persian solar god Mithras, which was popular with the soldiers of the Roman army and spread throughout the empire, celebrated the rebirth of Sol Invictus/the Unconquered Sun at the Winter Solstice. By the fourth century CE, the Christian church had decided to fix the date of Christmas Day as 25 December. Although the biblical record gives no clue as to what time of year Jesus was born, this made perfect sense as it was the time when the birth of the sun child was universally celebrated.

In the Northern Pagan traditions, Yule belonged to Odin, the All-Father. Odin rode his eight-legged horse, Sleipnir, across the sky at Midwinter and delivered blessings and curses, and Norse tradition identifies this as the source of gift-giving at Yule. Odin is also venerated as a 'shamanic' deity and identified with the use of the fly agaric fungus, both as an entheogen and an aid to warriors in battle. The fly agaric is called 'raven's bread' in the Norse sagas. Ravens were the birds of Odin; two ravens called Hugin and Muninn (Thought and Memory respectively) flew around the world every day and brought information back to Odin. The red and white fly agaric finds its way into Pagan iconography at Yule.

The historian Bede wrote in the eighth century CE that the Saxon Pagans had called Midwinter *Modranicht*, meaning the Night of the Mothers, but does not relate how it was celebrated. It is possible that this was a memory of the widespread worship of the Matres or Matronae; the triple mother goddesses who were venerated throughout Britain and Northern Europe in Roman and post-Roman times and whose shrines and altars can be seen in many museums. The name Modranicht has inspired witches in our own times, and so the longest night is celebrated as the Mothernight. In witchcraft Yule rituals, the goddess may be simply be referred to as the Great Mother, from whom the sun is born. Alternatively, she may be honoured as the icy, snowy goddess of the cold; the Lady of Midwinter called in Northern Europe Holda, Holle, Perchta or Old Mother Frost; who is found in folklore and featured in the fairy tales of Jacob Grimm. Holda was associated with spinning and weaving flax, and with all the work that women did in the home and kitchen, and she rewarded hard work and punished laziness. In medieval times it was believed that she led great processions of women who would ride in spirit with her through the sky at night while their husbands slept. They would fly on distaffs or broomsticks to Holda's mountain and feast with her, and sometimes take part in battles, and here we probably have the origin of the image of the witch riding a broomstick. The ninth century CE *Canon Episcopi* condemned women who rode with 'the witch Holda' and the medieval church authorities explicitly associated her with old Pagan goddesses such as Diana. She was also identified in some parts of Germany as a leader of the Wild Hunt. She took the souls of children who died unbaptised and they joined her night rides. She presided over storms and winter weather; snowflakes are said to be Holda plucking her geese or shaking out her feather pillows. In alpine areas of Germany, Switzerland and Austria, Holda and the Wild Hunt still feature in masked midwinter or Christmas processions. She has continued to grow, over the centuries, into a witches' goddess. As the goddess who personifies winter weather, she has hair as black as the raven, lips as red as blood and skin or clothes as white as snow (like Snow White and other fairytale women). As befits a winter goddess of ice, frost and the cold, she can also be cruel; the terrifying Snow Queen of Hans Christian Andersen's fairy tale, whose kiss will turn your heart to ice, can be identified as a form of Holda. I celebrate Holda at Yule as the lady of all the aspects of midwinter; as both Frost and Fire, the spinner and the weaver, and above all as the goddess of witches.

The god at Yule is celebrated as the Unconquered Sun reborn, or as Odin, the All-Father. In the Northern Pagan traditions, Yule is Odin's feast, and he may be one of the origins of the modern Father Christmas figure. Norse Yule traditions, including the Yule log (*see* below) are linked with Odin.

EVERGREENS AND MISTLETOE

The custom of bringing evergreen leaves and boughs into the house at Midwinter dates back to at least Roman times. The desire to celebrate with living, green plants when the rest of nature is locked in its winter sleep and the year is at its darkest is universal. The traditional Yule evergreens are holly, ivy, bay and pine or fir, and branches were used to decorate rooms and doorways, with particular attention paid to the area around the hearth. Holly is, of course, the king of the waning half of the year, who will be replaced in his turn by the Oak King at Yule. The prickly, glossy green leaves are a glorious sight, although climate change has led to the traditional red berries appearing in October and being over by Yule. Ivy was sacred to the Greek god Dionysus, who was worshipped with orgiastic rites of excess (the grapevine was sacred to him too). His female followers or Maenads chewed ivy leaves to produce a mildly narcotic effect. It was also sacred to the Egyptian god Osiris, and in Rome to Saturn, so it was used at Saturnalia.

The Christmas tree is a Christian tradition that was first recorded in Germany in the sixteenth century, although it may have its roots in the older Pagan tradition of decorating homes with evergreens. Devout protestant Christians brought trees into their homes and lit them with candles. The custom was believed to have originated with Martin Luther. It was taken by German immigrants to America in the early nineteenth century, and first came to Britain in 1841, thanks to Queen Victoria's husband, Prince Albert, who brought the custom from his native Germany and started the fashion that continues today. Martin Luther and Prince Albert aside, there are good Pagan reasons to honour a fir tree at Yule. In Greece the fir tree was sacred to the moon goddess Artemis, who presided over childbirth, and in the Celtic Tree Alphabet (*see* June) it represents the letter A and its day is the Winter Solstice. It is the tree of the goddess and should be honoured at the Mothernight.

I prefer not to use a commercially grown Christmas tree; the practice of growing a tree just to sacrifice it seems very wasteful. Also, growing them in massive commercial quantities is not good for the environment or wildlife as they acidify the soil. Instead of bringing a tree into the house, I like to go to woodland or a park and conduct a small midwinter ritual with a living fir tree. I honour the tree as Ailm or A, the tree of the Mother who gives birth to the sun, and the tree of Artemis. I give thanks, ask its blessing on the Yule rite and stay for a while to commune with its indwelling spirit.

To decorate the house at Yule, I cut bay, ivy and holly from my garden just before Midwinter. As with my plant allies in summer, I prefer to use the space I have to grow what I need, rather than taking it from the wild. All these plants grow strongly; there is plenty to swap and share with neighbours, and they will soon re-grow in spring. I make garlands and wreaths for the doors and my altar, and decorate the long beam over my fireplace and fill the branches with the kind of decorations that other people use on Christmas trees: suns, moons, stars and birds amongst them. I resist the temptation to cut my evergreens too early. Fresh bay and pine smell wonderful at Yule, but if cut weeks beforehand, in a warm house they will be dry and brittle when Midwinter arrives, so I do this just a few days before Yule. I cut bare stems of twisty red willow and corkscrew hazel (also from the garden) and make a kind of alternative Yule tree and hang it with fly agaric decorations in honour of Odin and the spirits of the forest. I have amassed a fine collection of wooden, glass and fabric agarics over the years and somehow additional ones always seem to arrive as witch gifts at Yule.

The last thing I add is plenty of mistletoe. It usually comes from Somerset, because it does not grow particularly well in Devon. There may be a scientific basis for this, but local superstition says that it is because the people of Devon were rude to the Druids. Whatever the reason, the big masses of mistletoe hanging from trees everywhere in Somerset do seem to peter out around the Devon border.

Mistletoe is, above all others, the plant that symbolises Yule. It is always associated with the ancient Druids, because the description of a Druidic rite of cutting mistletoe from an oak tree with a golden sickle by the Roman writer Pliny the Elder in his *Natural Histories* is one of the few actual descriptions of Druidic ritual practice in Roman times that we have. Mistletoe is held in high regard, not just by those practising Druidry in our own times, but also by witches and those following Celtic and Northern Pagan traditions. It has deep ritual and magical significance, especially at Midwinter, when it is very visible on the bare branches of trees. It is rare to find mistletoe growing on oak trees; amongst its most usual hosts in Britain are apple and hawthorn trees. The sight of ancient apple orchards in Herefordshire and Somerset, with their dwarf, gnarled trees weighed down by huge masses of mistletoe, is unforgettable. In Irish it is called *Drualus* (Druid's herb) and amongst its folk names are All Heal and the Golden Bough. This latter name is easy to understand if you have seen mistletoe at midwinter when the low, slanting sunshine makes its pale green leaves look as if they are made of gold. Astrology attributes mistletoe to the sun.

In the Northern mythos, mistletoe caused the death of Baldur, the shining one or perfect god. His mother, Frigga, made all living things promise not to harm him, but because mistletoe grew neither on earth nor in the sky, she forgot to include it, and through Loki's trickery, Baldur was killed by a mistletoe dart thrown by the blind god Hodur. Its berries are said to be Frigga's tears. On a magical level, mistletoe berries represent the semen of the god; the fertilising principle. The Celts identified it specifically with the semen of Taranis, the god of thunder (who was also closely associated with the oak). It is used in fertility magic, and especially as a charm against male infertility. It has erotic associations too, and this is the origin of the folk custom of kissing under mistletoe.

Mistletoe grows between earth and sky and belongs to neither, and it does not have an annual life cycle like other plants, so it is both inside and outside time, and is a liminal plant of the greatest magical power. Used in magic, it is a gateway to the Otherworld, and a small wand of mistletoe, cut at the winter Solstice, will help the bearer to see into the world of spirit. A pinch of mistletoe is sometimes added to the Yule incense to heighten the magical aspects of the ritual. Mistletoe blends its magical power with that of its host tree, and this explains why mistletoe growing on oak was so special to the druids. Oak is the supreme druid tree, so the powers of mistletoe and oak combined would produce the greatest spiritual and magical effects. The word 'druid' comes from the same root as 'oak' and can be interpreted as meaning 'oak seer'.

A word of warning: mistletoe berries can be toxic if ingested, particularly to cats and dogs.

THE YULE LOG

The Yule log is part of both Northern and Celtic Yule celebrations. The Midwinter fire, unlike those at other seasonal celebrations, is always lit indoors, in the hearth at the centre of the home. It is traditionally a single branch or part of a tree trunk that is large enough to burn throughout the entire Yule season. In the Northern traditions, the Yule Log is made of oak and is usually burned in honour of Odin, although sometimes, as in the North-east of Scotland, in honour of Thor. In the Celtic lands, the Yule log is made of ash. It may be a single bough, but in Devon, Cornwall and some parts of Wales an ash faggot is preferred. This is a bundle of twelve ash logs, one for each month of the year, bound together with ivy and willow. In the Highlands and Western Isles of Scotland the Yule log is sometimes called the Cailleach (*see* November). A fragment of the Yule log should always be saved from the flames at the end of the season and added to the next year's Yule fire. The ash from the Yule log is sprinkled around the outside of the home for blessing and protection at the end of Yule.

There are two kinds of Yule log that can be made for a witch's Yule celebration. If your Yule rite will include an open fire, you can make a faggot to burn. If not, a Yule log can be made to hold the midwinter fire in the form of candles.

A Witch's Yule Faggot

This is my adaptation of the Yule ash faggot that can be burned on a hearth fire, or in a wood-burning stove or fire basket.

You will need

- Four sticks of ash wood, four of oak and four of holly (a stick for each month of the year), each measuring the length of your foot. If you prefer, you can use twelve sticks of ash or oak. Alternatively, if you have studied the Celtic tree alphabet, choose one piece of each of the twelve woods that to you best represent the months of the year. You can use dry, dead wood for this as it will burn easily
- Optional: garden twine
- Scissors
- Three lengths of flexible ivy, long enough to wrap and tie round your bundle of sticks
- Optional: a length each of green, gold and white ribbon, long enough to wrap and tie round your bundle of sticks

Method

Arrange the sticks into a bundle.

Tie the bundle together at each end and in the middle by binding the ivy round the sticks and tying it tightly. If you find this difficult to do, bind and tie the bundle with garden twine first.

If you wish, you can decorate the faggot by tying lengths of green, white and gold ribbon round it.

Burn it on the fire during your Yule ritual.

A Witch's Yule Log

This requires some basic carpentry skills.

You will need

- A small ash or oak log
- A saw and a tool for gouging wood
- Three white candles
- Small sprigs of holly and mistletoe

Method

Using a saw, cut the log in half lengthways. The flat edge created will form the base.

Gouge three equidistant holes in the convex top of the log large enough to hold your candles.

Place the candles in the holes and decorate the log with sprigs of holly and mistletoe. The log can be placed on your altar and used in the Yule ritual.

A word about safety: Ensure your Yule log is stable before lighting the candles. Do not leave the candles to burn down unattended.

MIDWINTER FOLK CUSTOMS

Most Yule or Midwinter folk customs are guising or 'begging' customs in which performers are rewarded with food, drink and sometimes money. Mummers plays enact ritualised mock battles between the light and dark halves of the year in a way that is both comic and rather loving, and take place mostly at Midwinter. The figure representing the light half of the year, often called Saint George, is first killed by his adversary (most usually the Turkish Knight), then revived by a doctor, and then ultimately they do battle again, whereupon George is victorious and the light can return. Mummers may be accompanied by a man in drag, playing a comic old woman, and sometimes by a hobby horse or Mari Llwyd type creature. Mummers plays had been widespread throughout the British Isles and probably originated in medieval times, but had mostly died out by the end of the nineteenth century. The Victorians disapproved of the bawdiness of the custom, and also of the rowdiness and drunken excesses that often accompanied it. The village of Marshfield in Gloucestershire was the first to reinstate its mumming tradition in the 1930s. The Marshfield Paper Boys, dressed in elaborate costumes made of long, hanging strips of paper, perform on Boxing Day (26 December). Mummers plays can now be found during the midwinter period all over England (especially in villages in Sussex and Gloucestershire), Ireland (in Fermanagh and Wexford), Wales and Scotland and are a delight to watch, but Marshfield is still the grandparent of them all and well worth seeing. In Scotland the Yule mummers plays were called Goloshan.

Montol in Penzance is a six-day festival that has reinstated a glorious mix of old and more recent Cornish Midwinter customs. As with the town's summer Golowan festival (*see* June), local Pagans have been involved in creating it, and it includes many elements that witches will recognise and enjoy. The highlight is the procession on 21 December (the feast of Thomas the Apostle) which features guise dancing, guising beasts, a mummers play, a Lord of Misrule, Pen Hood (the Montol Obby Oss) and the old custom of Chalking the Mock, in which a stick figure is drawn on the Yule log or 'mock', which is then burnt on the Montol bonfire. Revellers wear costumes and masks and everyone is welcome. Montol customs are now spreading to other parts of Cornwall.

Hunting the Wren is a folk tradition celebrated on 26 December or Saint Stephen's Day, that was once widespread and that still takes place in parts of Ireland, West Wales, the Isle of Man, and the area of France around Carcassonne, where the Fete du Roi des Oiseaux (Festival of the King of the Birds), was first recorded at Puy-en-Velay in 1524. It seems bizarre to modern eyes, until we remember the wren's place in the mythology of the solar year. In former times, groups of young men would go out and hunt a wren. They would either kill it and mount it on a pole, or imprison it in an ornate 'wren house' decorated with ribbons. They would then parade the wren from house to house, singing special wren hunting songs. As we saw in June, the wren is the bird of the waning half of the year, and at Midwinter the robin takes its place as the year waxes again. The custom has roots in Celtic beliefs and in Ireland is identified with the Druids for whom the wren was said to symbolise wisdom and divinity. In Irish folk magic, wren feathers were used in protection charms. Hunting the Wren, also known as the Cutty Wren, still takes place in Ireland and the Isle of Man, but mercifully, live wrens are no longer killed (wooden wrens or replicas are used). In Ireland on La an Dreoilin (Wren Day), Wren Boys wear straw suits and masks and parade their wren on a pole:

The wren, the wren
The King of all birds

On Stephen's Day
He was caught in the furze.
Though he is little
His honour is great
Rise up kind sir
And give us a treat.

They can be seen at Milltown in County Clare, in Dingle and Listowel in County Kerry, and in Galway and Fermanagh. Wren Day is being reinstated across Ireland and now takes place in Dublin too.

Helg yn Dreain (Hunt the Wren) continues to be an important and flourishing Manx custom; dance is part of the tradition as well as the traditional song, and it can be experienced across the Isle of Man at places including Douglas and Ramsey. In the Welsh mythos Lleu (*see* August and Lammas) is given his name (Lleu Llaw Gyffes/the Fair-Haired One with the Steady Hand) when he shoots a wren between the tendon and the bone of its leg. Hela'r Dryw (Hunting the Wren) took place across Wales and the custom survived in Marloes and neighbouring villages in Pembrokeshire until the early twentieth century. The beautiful wren song 'Please to See the King' comes from Marloes.

Joy, health, love and peace, be all here in this place,
By your leave we will sing concerning our king.[11]

The Pembrokeshire Wren Boys paraded their King in a beribboned wren house and released the bird at the end of the day. A fine example of a Pembrokeshire Wren House can be seen in the Welsh National Folk Museum at Saint Fagans. In England the Cutty Wren tradition has been reinstated by the Old Glory Molly Dancers at Middleton in Suffolk.

WITCH GIFTS

As we have seen, the exchange of gifts at this time of year is both a universal and an ancient custom. However, expensive gifts, waste and excess are at odds with the way I practise witchcraft and do not feature in my Yule celebrations. I want my Yule to be a magical time, and to be sustainable and to honour rather than damage my mother the Earth. True magic cannot be bought, and Yule is the perfect time to reject the consumerist notion that we should constantly buy and consume, and that only spending money gives things value. My coven has a longstanding tradition of making rather than buying Yule gifts for each other. This usually involves the use of found, recycled and inexpensive materials. Often the gifts have magical uses or seasonal meanings, or are small craft projects or edible treats. They could be anything from a lovingly grown and dried bag of lemon verbena or mugwort tea, incense, or a witch stone charm; from candles to chilli pickle or edible golden suns. The possibilities are endless and I never fail to be amazed and delighted at what manifests. Throughout the Witch's Year I have referred to witch gifts, and at Yule the practical magical craft projects you have made as the months have gone by can be given as gifts to family and friends. Witch bottles, pincushions, sloe gin, herb charms or any of the other things you have made with magical intent and love will make thoughtful gifts for the right person. When you gift a spell or a charm, you are not just giving an object, but also making a gift of your own, personal magic that went into making it.

The Yule Ritual

The Yule ritual is celebrated on the Mothernight and is usually held indoors for practical reasons. The altar is decorated with mistletoe and with Midwinter evergreens: holly, ivy, bay and fir or pine. If you have an open fire, burn a Yule log. You can also place the Yule log candle holder on your altar. It should hold three white candles, or you can use gold candles if you prefer. In addition, you will need one small white candle (birthday cake size), and one slightly larger one, sprigs of mistletoe (one for each person present) and water that you collected from a holy well earlier in the year (*see* July) and blessed in the light of the moon. Use frankincense on the incense burner if you can, as it is sacred to the sun.

Preparation

- The colours of Yule are gold (for the returning sun), green (for the evergreens and mistletoe leaves) and white (for frost and snow, and for the mistletoe berries) and you may wish to incorporate these into decorations or altar furnishings. Yule is the last Sabbat and crown of the Witch's Year, so look back over the magical projects you have tried and think about using some of the things you have made in previous months.
- If you made a broomstick, use it to sweep the circle. Add ingredients you have grown and dried to frankincense for the incense burner (I always add a little of my own vervain), and if you made a labyrinth in November, put it on the Yule altar.
- If you have found treasures at the beach or the gods or spirits have provided gifts, have them at the ritual. Try to bring it all together to celebrate everything that has been discovered, made and given throughout the changing seasons and the whole round of the year. If you have made witch gifts to exchange, bring these too.
- The Yule feast should be a joyous celebration. There is no set menu (as with a Christmas meal) so you can serve whatever you like to eat at this time of

year in honour of the returning sun. I like to make spiced cookies with gold and silver icing (for the sun and Holda respectively) and a good drink is the traditional West Country wassail bowl of hot cider with cinnamon, star anise, raisins, pieces of apple and a couple of peppercorns (a non-alcoholic version can be made with apple juice). If you have baking skills, try a plaited circular loaf to symbolise the wheel of the year. Have whatever makes you happiest.

- Yule mirrors Midsummer. If the day is sunny, observe the Solstice sunrise and sunset just as you did at Midsummer and, using your witch's mirror, bathe your body from head to foot in the sunlight. Experiencing the sun at Midwinter can be a powerful and beautiful experience. In northern latitudes, the sun does not rise very high in the sky at this time of year. Its light is a fiery golden-red; it is always low in the sky, and shines direct into the eyes, so that everything seems bathed in a golden haze.
- The ritual I have outlined here honours the Matres, Holda and the Unconquered Sun as a newborn child. You can create a ritual that celebrates Odin if you prefer. The rite should take place after sunset.

The ritual

Begin by lighting the fire, if you have one. Light your three altar candles, honouring the mother goddess at midwinter as the triple goddess; the threefold Matres on the Mothernight. Light the incense and sweep around the circle with the broomstick, banishing all negativity as you go. Then cast the circle in the usual manner.

Stand in the east and ask the powers of air to blow away the cobwebs of the old year and with them old, stale ideas and thoughts. Move to the south, and ask the powers of fire to burn away the dross of the old year. In the west, ask the powers of water to wash away the stresses and worries of the old year, and in the north ask the powers of earth to receive back into the earth whatever the old year has left that needs to decay.

Light the small candle and place it in the centre of the circle. Sit round the candle and watch until it has burned down (with a birthday cake candle this will not take long), meditating as you do so on the year's dying. When the candle has died, light the second, larger candle and place it on the altar. This is the moment of the sun's rebirth. Use the Mithraic salutation, 'Ave Sol Invictus' (Hail the Unconquered Sun) and call on the god as the sun child, the child of promise, the Unconquered Sun and the golden one. Ask the sun to inspire you and create your form of words for this. Conclude the invocation with the words:

The lord of life is born again
Darkness and tears are set aside when the sun shall come up early
The golden one is returned to us
Sorrows be laid, joy to the world.

Then call upon the goddess of midwinter, and honour her as Holda, Lady Holle, Perchta, Grandmother Frost and the Snow Queen (use whichever of these names seem right to you). Find a form of words that sums up her attributes as spinner and weaver, the power and the cold of winter, queen of ice and snow, and leader of the night rides.

Place the mistletoe sprigs and the well water in the centre of the circle. Meditate on the mistletoe, focusing your magical will into it and imbuing it with all the power and strength of the returning sun. Each person present then takes a sprig of mistletoe and sprinkles it with well water, adding the blessing of the Mother to the strength of the sun. The mistletoe will carry the power and blessing of the returning sun and the Mother forward into the coming year. Each person will keep their mistletoe sprig throughout the year, and at the following Yule, the old mistletoe sprigs will be returned and burnt on the Yule fire before the rite is repeated and new ones are given once more.

Holda and the Unconquered Sun are thanked and bade farewell. The three white or gold altar candles are extinguished, but the remaining white candle (lit to mark the return of the sun) is left in a safe place overnight to burn down. The circle is closed in the usual manner. The Yule feast is shared and witch gifts exchanged. The well water should be returned to the earth after the ritual and a little food and drink left outside, as after all Sabbats, as an offering for the Faeries and the spirits of the land.

Yule is done, the sun is reborn, and the Witch's Year is almost over.

A Spell for December: Three Wishes

The final spell of our Witch's Year looks both back over the last year and forwards to the one to come. It should be worked as close to the end of the year as possible. Before you work this spell, think about the witchcraft that you have made this year; all that you have learnt and achieved, and then think about your hopes for the coming New Year.

This spell should be worked at night, after your Yule ritual and between the Winter Solstice and the last day of December. It will be your final magical act of the old year.

You will need

- A piece of paper
- Pen or pencil
- A length of green yarn or thread, measured from the tip of your middle finger to your elbow. Green represents the evergreen holly of midwinter and the old year, and also symbolises renewal and the beginning of new growth
- A small open fire, lit in an outdoor place. I light mine in a fire bowl outside my back door

Method

Thinking about your Witch's Year so far, write three wishes for the New Year on the paper. One of these should be something that you wish to leave behind or get rid of, one should be for something already present in your life and witchcraft that you wish will grow or increase in the coming year, and one should be for something entirely new: a new direction, new magic or new knowledge, perhaps.

Tie three knots in the green thread, one for each wish. Concentrate your magical will and visualise each wish coming true as you tie the knots.

Fold the paper in half, then in half again, and then once more (three folds). Wrap the thread tightly round the paper and secure it with a triple knot, concentrating on your intent throughout.

Light your fire. When it is burning, throw your package of paper and thread onto the fire. Watch the flames and smoke burning your spell away to nothing, carrying it into the night sky and taking your three wishes for the new Witch's Year with it and into the world of spirit. Your spell is done.

A Meditation for December: The House of the Ancestors

It is long ago on the Mothernight, the longest and darkest night of the year. You lie in the dark stone chamber, wrapped in warm animal skins against the cold, and trying with little success to sleep. You remember that you were brought here yesterday just after sunset with two priestesses who helped you climb over the huge stone at the entrance to the great mound, carved with the spiral story of sun and moon, and led you along the stone passage and into the chamber. You remember the white stones of the mound gleaming in the torchlight and then the slow beat of many drums and the flames of the torches fading away behind you as you entered this place, the House of the Ancestors, the place that is both tomb and the womb of new life, and which is only ever entered by the living on this night. This year the Mothernight coincides with the dark of the moon; both moon and sun will be reborn together. The three of you wait, one of you for each phase of the moon: new, full and waning. No one speaks. The deep silence of the mound envelopes you. You know that the ancestors sleep all around you. In three large carved stone basins are fragments of the ashes of those who have recently journeyed on from this life. Something of them sleeps here; a part of their spirit that remains to guide the living, and you sense its peaceful presence with you in the darkness. Although this place is a part of the world of spirit, there is no fear, just the quiet calm of the sleeping ancestors. You know that you and your fellow priestesses hold within you the seeds of all that will be.

Then at last there are sounds outside. The Midwinter dawn is breaking and there is a faint sense of light, nothing more. Then, as you watch, the rising sun across the valley enters the stone passageway through a specially made and carved slit in the stones, carefully aligned over many years of observation to the sunrise on this shortest day. As the sun climbs higher, a thin, rose red line of sunlight creeps down the passageway towards you, coming closer and closer and then suddenly bursts into the chamber where you wait, striking a stone carved with a triple spiral where the ashes of the ancestors lie. The intense light of the rising suns fills the chamber with red and gold and shatters the darkness like fire in your heart.

The ancestors are awakened once more as the year is reborn. You walk slowly down the passageway, bathed in the fiery warmth of the Midwinter sun, and out of the mound, ready to share your dreams and visions. Outside the waiting crowd shouts for joy and a woman holds up a tiny baby. The child of promise is born, the longest night is over, and the sun has returned. The year begins again. Hail the unconquered sun!

So the year turns, the moon and sun dance on together, and it begins again.

Notes

1. Carmichael, Alexander, *Carmina Gadelica – Hymns and Incantations Collected in the Highlands and Islands of Scotland in the Last Century,* 1992, Floris Books, Edinburgh, p81.

2. I have described this festival in detail in my book, *A Sea Witch's Companion*, Robert Hale/The Crowood Press, 2022. An account of the Isidis Navigidium and an encounter with the goddess can be found in *The Golden Ass* by Apuleius, a novel written in the 3rd century CE.

3. Dion Fortune, *The Sea Priestess*.

4. The method of calculating the date of Easter caused controversy in the early Christian church and was a major source of division between the Celtic and Roman churches in Britain. Eventually it was agreed that the date of Easter would be the Sunday following the first full moon after the Spring Equinox, making Easter the only Christian festival that still refers back to the lunar calendar.

5. See Emma Wilby, *The Confessions of Isobel Gowdie*, (Sussex Academic Press, 2010) for a detailed account of Faerie magic in Scotland in the seventeenth century.

6. See Levannah Morgan, *A Sea Witch's Companion* (2022, Robert Hale/Crowood) and Peter Redgrove, *The Sleep of the Great Hypnotist* (1979, Routledge and Kegan Paul) for two contrasting descriptions of the Obby Oss.

7. The story of this cauldron can be found in full in Branwen Daughter of Llyr, the Second Branch of *The Mabinogion*. A good translation is by Sioned Davies (Oxford University Press, 2007).

8. The full story of Blodeuwedd is told in the Fourth Branch of *The Mabinogion*.

9. Robert Graves, *The White Goddess* Faber and Faber, 1961).

10. *The Celtic Tree Oracle* by Liz and Colin Murray is a beautifully-designed set of divination cards based on the tree alphabet and ogham that provides a very good way to learn more about them.

11. The traditional Wren Song from Marloes in Pembrokeshire.

Appendix
Associations for the Months

January

Festivals: New Year (1st), Twelfth Night (6th), Wassailing (various)
Figures: Janus, Mari Llwyd
More than Human: The night sky, robin
Totems and Symbols: Wheel of the Year, circle

February

Festivals: Candlemas (1st), Lupercalia (15th)
Figures: Bride, Juno Februata
More Than Human: Snowdrops, swans
Totems and Symbols: Wolf, white swan, hearth

March

Festivals: Isis Navigidium/Festival of Isis of the Ships (4th), Spring Equinox (21st)
Figures: Andraste, Young Sun God/Horus/Belinus/Mabon/Maponus
More Than Human: Primroses, gorse, hares, catkins, Equinox high tides
Totems and Symbols: Hare, Tinners' Rabbits

April

Festivals: None
Figures: The Others/Faeries/Tylwyth Teg/Aos Sí
More Than Human: Birds, eggs and feathers, hawthorn blossom
Totems and Symbols: Egg, hawthorn

May

Festivals: Beltane/ May Day/ Calan Haf (1st), Obby Oss (1st), Flora Day (8th)
Figures: Maia, Flora, the Green Man, Obby Oss, Jack in the Green
More Than Human: Bluebells, plant allies, spring flowers, trees in new leaf
Totems and Symbols: Maypole, willow

June

Festivals: Midsummer (21st), Golowan/ Feast of John (21st–28th)
Figures: Sun God, Ceridwen, Juno

More Than Human: Bees, roses, Saint John's Wort
Totems and Symbols: Sun, sun wheel, flaming arrow, oak

July

Festivals: None
Figures: Thunder Gods (Zeus/Taranis/Thor, etc.), deities of springs, wells, rivers (Sul, Coventina, Tamara, etc.)
More Than Human: Thunderstorms, the heliacal rising of Sirius, gifts of the sea (shells, pebbles, witch stones, etc.), fossils, snakes/vipers
Totems and Symbols: Thunderbolt, serpent, sea shell (cowrie, conch, scallop)

August

Festivals: Lammas (1st)
Figures: Ceres/Demeter, Ceridwen, Lugh/Lleu, John Barleycorn
More Than Human: Meteors/shooting stars (Perseids), rowan berries, herbs at their peak
Totems and Symbols: Ear of corn, scythe

September

Festivals: Autumn Equinox (21st)
Figures: Arthur of Albion, the Lady of the Lake
More Than Human: Apples, berries (sloes, hawthorns, blackberries, etc.), hazelnuts, salmon leaping, owls at night, Equinox high tides
Totems and Symbols: Apple, salmon, hazel

October

Festivals: Samhain (31st), Calan Gaeaf
Figures: Orion, Hecate, Persephone, the Horned Lord, ancestors
More Than Human: First sight of Orion, spiders' webs, fungi
Totems and Symbols: Orion's belt, spider's web, skull (Mexico)

November

Festivals: None
Figures: The Morrigan, the Cailleach, the Wild Hunt
More Than Human: Corvids
Totems and Symbols: Labyrinth, raven

December

Festivals: Yule/Midwinter/Mothernight (21st), Saturnalia (25th)
Figures: The Unconquered Sun, the Child of Promise, the Great Mother, Holda, the Snow Queen, Odin, Thoth
More Than Human: Wren, mistletoe, evergreens (holly, ivy, bay)
Totems and Symbols: Triple spiral (as at Newgrange), wren

Further Reading

Aldhouse Green, Miranda, *Enchanted Wales – Myth and Magic in Welsh Storytelling* (Calon, 2023)

Apuleius, *The Golden Ass* (Penguin Classics, 1998)

Beth, Rae, *Hedge Witch – A Guide to Solitary Witchcraft* (*Robert* Hale, 1990)

Beth, Rae, *The Green Hedge Witch* (Robert Hale, 2018)

Carmichael, Alexander, *Carmina Gadelica* (Floris Books. 1992)

Davies, Sioned (trans), *The Mabinogion* (Oxford University press, 2007)

Evans, George Ewart, *The Pattern Under the Plough* (Little Toller Books, 2013)

Ganz, Jeffrey (trans), *Early Irish Myths and Sagas* (Penguin, 1981)

Fortune, Dion, *The Sea Priestess* (Aquarian Press, 1989)

Graves, Robert, *The White Goddess* (Faber and Faber, 1961)

Hutton, Ronald, *Queens of the Wild – Pagan Goddesses in Christian Europe – an Investigation* (Yale University Press, 2022)

Hutton, Ronald, *The Witch* (Yale University press, 2017)

Hutton, Ronald, *The Triumph of the Moon – A History of Modern Pagan Witchcraft* (Oxford University Press, 1999)

Jones, Evan John with Valiente, Doreen, *Witchcraft – A Tradition Renewed* (Robert Hale, 1990)

Lenihan, Eddie, *Meeting the Other Crowd; the Fairy Stories of Hidden Ireland* (Gill Books, 2003)

McNeill, F. Marian, *The Silver Bough (Vols 1–4)* (William MacLellan, 1959–1968).

Morgan, Levannah, *The Sea Witch's Companion* (Robert Hale/ Crowood Press, 2022)

Morgan, Levannah, *A Witch's Mirror, revised edition* (The Universe Machine, 2021)

Murray, Liz and Colin, *The Celtic Tree Oracle* (Connections Books, 1998)

Parker, Eleanor, *Winters in the World – A Journey Through the Anglo-Saxon Year* (Reaktion Books, 2022)

Redgrove, Peter, *The Sleep of the Great Hypnotist* (Routledge and Kegan Paul, 1979)

Sikes, Wirt, *British Goblins* (paperback reprint, The Lost Library, undated)

Thomas, W. Jenkyn, *The Welsh Fairy Book* (reprint of original 1907 edition by John Jones Ltd, 1979)

Valiente, Doreen, *Witchcraft for Tomorrow* (Robert Hale, 1978)

Valiente, Doreen, *The Rebirth of Witchcraft* (Robert Hale, 1989)

Westwood, Jennifer, *Albion – A Guide to Legendary Britain*, (Grafton 1985)

Wilby, Emma, *The Visions of Isobel Gowdie – Magic, Witchcraft and Dark Shamanism in Seventeenth-Century Scotland* (Sussex Academic Press, 2010)

Williams, Mark, *The Celtic Myths That Shape The Way We Think* (Thames and Hudson, 2012)

Young, Simon and Houlbrook, Ceri (eds), *Magical Folk – The History of Fairies* (Gibson Square, 2023)

First published in 2025 by Robert Hale, an imprint of
The Crowood Press Ltd
Ramsbury, Marlborough
Wiltshire SN8 2HR

enquiries@crowood.com
www.crowood.com

British Library Cataloguing-in-Publication Data
A catalogue record for this book is available from the British Library.

ISBN 978 0 7198 3167 6

Cover design by Ifan Bates
Illustrations by Nooka Shepherd

Disclaimer
Care needs to be taken in any activity in the countryside, or involving the use of fire. The author and publisher cannot accept any responsibility or liability for any accident or injury caused by following suggestions given in this book.

Typeset by Simon and Sons
Printed and bound in India by Thomson Press India Ltd.

Acknowledgements
I am indebted to Nooka Shepherd for her inspirational illustrations which have captured my vision perfectly. Special thanks go to Elayne Hoskin, Ian Jamison, Aisha Shehu Ansell, Addie Frayne and the late Bryn Jones (goddess rest his lovely spirit) for their companionship and for testing many of the projects in the book; and to Dominic Shepherd, James Riley, Evie Salmon, Tom Chick, Anna Navas, Julian Vayne and Nikki Wyrd for listening to my ideas and critical friendship. Grateful thanks to Rachel Pollack, who sadly passed before the book was completed, for inspiring transatlantic discussions of magic, goddess lore and much besides, and goddess rest her brave spirit. Thanks to Jesse Bransford and Gareth Roberts for walking with me in Ynys Môn, to Ronald Hutton for wise counsel, to Donna Gundry and the library staff at Arts University Plymouth for research support, and to Logan Campbell, tech wizard. My thanks to the team at Crowood, who have been a joy to work with. Most of all, thanks to my constant companion and muse, Duster the cat, for his patience and sitting with me during long hours of writing.